NO FAT CHICKS

How Women Are Brainwashed to Hate Their Bodies and Spend Their Money

October 1996

TERRY POULTON

*For John,
with best wishes.*

KEY PORTER BOOKS

*Cheers,
Terry*

Canadian Cataloguing   in Publication Data

Poulton, Terry
No fat chicks : how women are brainwashed to
hate their bodies and spend their money

ISBN 1-55013-740-9

1. Self-perception in women.   2. Body image.
3. Weight loss.   4. Weight loss preparations industry.   I. Title.

BF697.5.B63P68   1996   155.6′33   C96-930468-4

The publisher gratefully acknowledges the assistance of
the Canada Council and the Ontario Arts Council.

Key Porter Books Limited
70 The Esplanade
Toronto, Ontario
Canada M5E 1R2

Design: Peter Maher
Electronic Formatting: Heidi Palfrey

Printed and bound in Canada

96 97 98 99 6 5 4 3 2 1

For my godchildren, Michael Paauw and Amelia Jackson Purdy, and my nieces and nephew, Elise, Brittany, Emma, and Nathan, with hope that they'll always think for themselves

Contents

Discovering a
Billion-Dollar Brainwash

There's something only Oprah Winfrey and I know from actual experience: Hell is having to show up fat when the whole country knows you're supposed to be thin.

Oprah handled it by wailing to her tear-stained diary about how disgusted she was with herself. I tried something a little goofier during the winter of 1982, while regaining the 65 pounds *Chatelaine* readers had watched me whittle away during my arduous six months of practically camping-out in a gym, living on carrot sticks and little else.

From Truro to Temiskaming to Tofino, my "Chronicles of the Incredible Shrinking Terry" attracted affectionate fan letters and resulted in my photo being plastered on fridge doors and gym walls. After a lifetime as a wallflower, I had become a hero to every woman who longed to be slim.

And then my pet albatross came flapping back to its long-time roost (just as these tenacious birds do to 98 per cent of all dieters). I was a freelance magazine writer in media-savvy Toronto, where all my colleagues knew to the pound what I was supposed to weigh. As I rapidly reinflated, I tried toiling as much as possible by phone and memo, but eventually I had to show up for editorial meetings.

That's when I hatched a gambit worthy of Lucy Ricardo at her ditziest. Instead of wearing a warm winter coat, I flung a big green cape over my pre-diet raincoat. Then, whenever I made an entrance, I dramatically swirled the cape off and remained hidden (I hoped) inside my raincoat. If any of my colleagues caught on, they were kind enough not to squeal.

Today I can finally laugh at that transparent ploy instead of cringing from a sense of failure that's dogged me since childhood. But there was nothing funny about the physical and psychological privations I suffered during my *Chatelaine* series. Or the awful lifelong struggle that preceded it. Or feeling like a fraud, even while taking a very public bow for achieving my goal.

For more than a decade afterwards, I had no idea why I felt so guilty and haunted by what others regarded as an inspirational piece of writing. Now I've finally figured it out: It was because I never *questioned* whether I actually wanted to obliterate a third of my physical self—not when *Chatelaine* asked me to do so, and not for the twenty-five years I dieted so obsessively on my own.

No one questioned it, in fact. It was just a given, a virtual eleventh commandment for women: THOU SHALT NOT BE FAT.

Yet, even while wasting so much time, energy, money, and self-esteem trying to obey, subconsciously I was rebelling. A part of me always knew that people must hold tight to their real identity—whatever it happens to be—and refuse to be squashed to fit any phony, oppressive standard of acceptability. Ignoring this fundamental wisdom by doing my diet series meant betraying myself, and everyone I'd influenced, into blind conformity.

"No one can make you feel inferior without your consent," Eleanor Roosevelt once wrote. Somewhere inside, I knew I'd given my consent to conferring inferior status on not only overweight women, but everyone else who embodies something—anything—our society denigrates.

This realization sank in only after many subsequent spins on the diet carousel, a stomach-stapling operation, and many more years of misery. When I finally understood it, I began achieving what I had really wanted all along: respect, from myself and from others.

For those who don't remember my series, it chronicled what I hoped would be my "diet to end all diets" and was set in motion by *Chatelaine* editors who knew about my Sisyphean, totally typical, lifelong battle with excess weight. Although I was never a compulsive binge eater, I led a sedentary life and ate too many sweet, carbohydrate-laden comfort foods. That, plus decades of yo-yo weight levels, slowed my metabolism and strip-mined my body of fat-burning muscle tissue. Like many of the estimated one-third of North American women who are overweight—and at least 78 per cent who *believe* they're too heavy—I'd been on dozens of diets and had lost and regained hundreds of pounds.

After a lucky start as a precocious, pretty, and beloved child growing up in Alberta, I lost my golden-girl status when I became fat in prepubescence. None of my good qualities seemed to count after that, as praise and friendship were replaced by taunts and ostracism. In photos of me as a teenager, I don't look all that bad, but I *felt* like a monster.

By the time I reached my twenties, bag-of-bones Twiggy had replaced her curvy predecessors as the reigning standard of beauty. I was so desperate to conform to the increasingly narrow parameters of attractiveness that, by my thirties, I had tried even such extreme measures as submitting to noxious daily injections (which compelled me to crave raw meat!) and consuming nothing but liquid protein for five months, *à la* Oprah and with even worse results, as I wound up losing my gall-bladder. Every method worked. But, just like determined homing pigeons, the pounds I lost always found their way back. And through the years, my weight crept up, while my self-respect sank lower and lower.

Enter my editorial chums at *Chatelaine*. They would pick up the tab for sending me to nutritional, fitness, and psychological counselling if I would promise to lose 65 pounds and write about my experiences along the way.

It seemed like every woman's dream. After all, who isn't susceptible to the "if only" syndrome? *If only* I had the money for a personal chef and trainer, plus a free fitness centre in which to go for the burn, we think, *then* I could get in shape and my life would be perfect. Seduced by the opportunity to realize my "if only" dream, I had no idea I was about to enter the toughest and loneliest time of my life, a forced march through my own private boot-camp to meet the scariest deadline of my career.

At first, the pounds came off steadily as I trudged and ached my way along, remaining mostly faithful to my prudent diet and exercise plan. If I just kept on losing a little over 10 pounds a month, I'd have it made. But I fell off the wagon one month while travelling, and hit a plateau during another. Shortly past the halfway point, a fear that was bubbling below consciousness burst into full-blown terror: I still had 40 pounds to lose and only three months until the deadline.

I was in big trouble.

⌐

What no one really understood back then was how implacably the human body is programmed to fight when it perceives famine conditions such as those I had imposed upon myself during and before the *Chatelaine* diet. The less I ate and the more I pushed my body to expend energy, the more stubbornly my metabolism slowed. In other words, it wasn't so much pigging-out as starving that created and sustained my excess body fat. If I were a cavewoman who couldn't find food, this failsafe system would have kept me alive. Instead, with the whole country watching, I was headed for the worst failure of my life.

Defeat or drastic measures were my only options and, characteristically, I chose the latter. First, I pleaded with my editors to extend my deadline by a month, arguing that this would show readers just how tough it is to lose so much weight so quickly, even with professional help. But, locked into irrevocable publishing schedules, they refused. So, to be closer to the fitness centre, which was 20 miles from our home, I walked out on the man I'd been planning to marry, promising to return when I reached my goal. Instead, I ended up losing the love of my life.

Meanwhile, I was alone in a shabby apartment, with nothing but a single chair and a mattress on the floor. In the kitchen, I kept only skim milk and coffee. My nutritionist had forbidden caffeine but, without it, I had no energy at all. To beat the crowd, I hit the gym every morning at about 6:30 and worked out for at least an hour amid disapproving stares from the skinny patrons. Exhausted, red-faced, and breathless, I would then shower, dress, stumble to my car, and race to Toronto to work on writing projects. I had no extra time for family, friends, or anything but the all-consuming need to meet my deadline.

At the end of days during which I often ate as few as half of my prescribed 1,000–1,200 calories, I would zip back to the gym, repeat my morning's workout, and then swim twenty-two laps in the Olympic-size pool. Sometimes sleep brought blessed oblivion afterwards; sometimes I tossed all night, counting, not sheep, but regrets. The following day, and the day after that, I would do it all again.

Then I'd write another segment of my *Chatelaine* series in the sunny style that, in retrospect, sounds like blatant lying. At the time, though, I saw the upbeat, positive tone that satisfied my editors, hid my tattered pride, and conformed with society's agenda as my only option. "Because my diet and exercising have brought such good results," I trilled in a typical prevarication, "my general attitude and self-image have improved tremendously and I'm almost constantly euphoric."

With just a few weeks left before my deadline, another magazine assigned me a feature story on a woman whose lifelong obsession with becoming thin actually killed her. As I listened to the testimony at her inquest and realized that her struggles were only slightly more extreme than mine, I became frightened about the potentially fatal consequences of my regimen. And the suspicion was dawning that, in my hell-bent effort to get slim, I was squandering the gift of just being alive. If I hadn't been so publicly committed to my diet, I would have quit. Instead, I persevered.

And then, in June 1982, there I was, beaming on the cover of *Chatelaine*, 65 pounds lighter and suddenly a media star. As I drifted from microphone to camera to tape recorder, I tried to ignore an inner turmoil stirred by every tactless, backhanded compliment that revealed the contempt in which I had previously been held. Keep smiling, I remember telling myself. You've won. You're finally giving them what they've always demanded. They're finally giving you what you were *really* starving for: not food, but acceptance.

Yet a voice somewhere inside kept shrieking that there was something ugly about all this admiration. Where were these people before I *bought* their approval with hunger pangs, sore muscles, and dread? Why couldn't they see I was the same person I had always been? How dare they force me—and every other woman—in the words of a Leonard Cohen song, *to go begging in beauty's disguise?*

Anger, ambivalence, and disappointment soon drove me back to comfort food, a sedentary life, and the inevitable consequences— regained weight and renewed despair. Even during the next few years, in the glamorous role of TV columnist at the *Toronto Star*, interviewing celebrities and flying to Hollywood and New York, I felt as scorned as ever. Little by little, I withdrew from my family and friends, and fell into the life of a near-hermit. I was on the run, subconsciously trying to escape the feeling that I had made a colossal mistake.

Seven years ago, I left my long-time home in Toronto for Louisville, Kentucky, without really understanding what was compelling me to "run to nowhere," as I put it at the time. Ostensibly, it was to be near my sister and her family and, especially, my two-year-old godson. But that was actually secondary. The truth was I felt like an outcast, so I became one. I'd never married or had children of my own. I'd just put my personal life on hold until I could be thin. Why? Because being overweight meant personifying what society considers the worst disgrace of all for women. And the conflict between feeling "right" about my essential self but being unanimously condemned as "wrong" paralyzed me emotionally.

Then, from out of nowhere, a literary agent tracked me down and urged me to write a book about being fat in a society that demands thin. At first, I refused. That book has already been written, I said, citing such excellent works as Kim Chernin's *The Obsession: Reflections on the Tyranny of Slenderness* and Susie Orbach's *Fat Is a Feminist Issue*. But, as I thought more about it and did some serious research, I found the key that unlocked the psychological prison in which I'd wasted most of my life.

The key is money.

In fact, what I ultimately discovered is that the whole diet phenomenon is *not* about beauty or how much women weigh at all. It's about how much we can be persuaded to spend trying to be thin. The entire process is just a despicable scheme to guarantee annual sales of weight-loss products and services currently estimated at $3 billion in Canada, and more than $40 billion in the United States.

When I really saw the enormity of this deliberate manipulation of perception, emotion, and prejudice, a horrifying word began rocketing around in my mind: "brainwashing." Is the term too strong? I wondered. I raced to double-check it in several dictionaries, and came up with precise corroboration: "Brainwashing: (1) A method for changing attitudes or beliefs, especially through torture, drugs, or psychological techniques. (2) Any method of controlled indoctrination."

Given the magnitude of the mass deception, the name for what I was dealing with was suddenly obvious. It was nothing less than a "billion-dollar brainwash."

Following the Money

Satisfied that I now understood the nature of the beast I was battling, I began my research with two basic questions: Where did the wholly artificial idea that *all* women must be thin come from? and How has the obsessive pursuit of this dubious "ideal" affected, not just large women like me, but everyone else in our society?

Surely, I assumed, ample objective data must exist about something millions of people pursue obsessively nearly every day of their lives. But, time and time again, my search for answers to straightforward questions led me to virtual black holes. Considering that my topic was anything but arcane, it wasn't just maddening to learn how little reportorial, academic, and governmental attention has been paid to it; it was shocking. And what I *did* manage to discover—after not only researching traditional avenues and consulting appropriate authorities, but also soliciting first-person material via (among other methods) queries on the Internet and a classified ad in *USA Today*—is vastly different from what we've all been led to believe.

For starters, waif-like thinness is strictly a twentieth-century concept. Actress Lillian Russell, who was considered the most desirable woman of the 1890s, weighed 200 voluptuous pounds. Paintings of other abundantly endowed beauties still grace gallery walls all over the world, still draw droves of admirers, and still fetch enormous prices. For centuries, in fact, these robust images, with all the flesh and curves that nature designed, have symbolized the essence of "Woman."

Yet, if any of these *femmes idéales* were somehow to step out of her frame and waft from her time to ours, she would find herself, not beloved, but virtually demonized. She would have difficulty obtaining something as ephemeral as a date or as fundamental as a husband. Or a good job. Or equal legal protection. Or first-class health care. Or a good education. Or decent clothing. Or basic human respect.

Today, like the millions of North American women who resemble her, she'd be denounced as a violator of a tyrannical new commandment. A legal and social taboo in any other context, it bellows through all the mass media, from *haute couture* magazines to the crude common denominator of a popular bumper-sticker: NO FAT CHICKS!

True, the "ideal" feminine figure has expanded and contracted, been pushed and pulled, wrapped, strapped, and caged throughout history. Society imperiously demands that women contort their bodies to fit the current fashions. Women sheepishly comply, and everyone praises them for doing so.

And, over and over again, psyches are manipulated by diverse commercial and cultural factions not only to fixate physically on the new image, but also to imbue her with all manner of positive spiritual qualities. Simultaneously, those who least epitomize her are assigned sinister attributes and punished accordingly with measures ranging from derision to exclusion to economic privation.

C'est la vie? Just one of human nature's inevitable games? Absolutely. But, in our day, the game has been fixed.

As profitable as it has always been to wager on the wayward gusts of fashion, there was a fortune waiting for anyone who could know *for certain* which way the next style wind would blow. And then keep it whistling in exactly that way.

But how?

By creating a cash cow, coercing all females into wanting to look just like her, and then selling them the myriad products necessary to recreate the look. That the quest to comply would prove *impossible* for most women guaranteed everlasting profits.

The bovine reference seems ludicrous when applied to a gangly, 91-pound English model named Twiggy. Yet, since her debut in 1967, when she became the darling of the fashion world and the incongruous ideal of nearly everyone else, her image—and that of latter-day clones like Kate Moss—has been milked for billions. During the first Twiggy decade the annual take for the labyrinthine North American anti-fat industry soared to $10 billion, 95 per cent of it from women. And in the following decade, that total *quadrupled*.

Thanks to this "billion-dollar brainwash," our culture's ideas about beauty became more irrational than ever before—so irrational that
• most North Americans alive today have no memory of a time when thinness was *not* a national obsession, and thus have no choice but to regard the artificial as normal;

• the average weight of the models, actresses, and beauty-pageant con-testants we are urged to imitate has plunged to nearly 25 per cent lower than that of the average North American woman;

• nearly 30,000 women stated in the largest such survey to date that they'd rather become thinner than achieve *any* other goal—despite the fact that only 25 per cent were overweight, and another 25 per cent were actually underweight;

• millions of women are so terrified of being fat that they choose to court disaster by smoking, and by abusing laxatives, diuretics, and amphetamines, and thousands eschew birth-control pills for the same reason, resulting in an untold percentage of the millions of babies born to unwed parents;

• formerly fat women say that, rather than regain their weight, they would deliberately choose to be blind, deaf, or have a limb amputated;

• the annual rate of mortality attributable to desperate weight-loss prac-tices, including more than 50,000 surgeries, probably numbers in the thousands, yet goes unnoticed;

• no one has realized that eating disorders have reached epidemic num-bers. In fact, there are *150 times* more women in North America suffer-ing from anorexia and/or bulimia than are living with AIDS;

• 11 per cent of the respondents in a recent survey said that, if genetic predisposition to obesity was identified in their unborn children, they would opt for abortion.

What all this has meant to women like me, who are the antithesis of Twiggy, is the anguish of social marginalization. And our consequent attempts to conform with the narrow new parameters of acceptability have been barbaric.

We have had our jaws wired shut, our stomachs stapled, and yards of our intestines hacked off. We've had chunks of ourselves liposuctioned away. We've had our derrieres injected with HCG (human chorionic gonadotrophin, a noxious concoction containing the urine of pregnant women). And we've existed for months at a time on a gooey "protein-sparing" powder composed, in part, of ground cattle hooves.

We've starved, binged, and vomited. We've jogged and rowed and bench-pressed and stair-stepped ourselves into exhausted stupors. We've ingested appetite suppressants, metabolism accelerators, diuretics, and innumerable other snake-oil placebos.

Some of us have died. Our death certificates probably listed such causes as heart irregularity or exhaustion. But the real cause was not simple misadventure: The victims had so thoroughly internalized society's disgust that their self-loathing proved lethal.

Many of us who survived accepted our punishment as if we really were criminals. We condemned ourselves to a prison of shame and threw away the key, psychologically suspending our lives until the elusive day when we would be validated by thinness.

Ironically, just before Twiggymania began reshaping millions of bodies and torturing millions of psyches, the reigning feminine ideal was epitomized by a buxom, blonde movie star. She had billowy hips, a pillowy belly, and more than a hint of womanly thigh. Her name was Marilyn Monroe and she made Twiggy look like a Popsicle stick. Yet today Marilyn probably couldn't even get an audition.

And in the subsequent three decades, women and girls of all ages, from all strata of society, of *all sizes* have felt compelled to disregard the individuality of our physiques and circumstances, and to squander our self-esteem, relationships, money, time, health, and sometimes even our lives, to duplicate a prized image of emaciation.

No one *really* asks why.

No one asks how modern women, whose eyes were opened to modern female subjugation by the 1963 publication of Betty Friedan's *The Feminine Mystique*, could possibly have knuckled under to a dictum that's as oppressive as Chinese foot-binding and even less achievable.

No one asks why doctors—experts in the physical and the psychological—who know the overwhelming odds against the average woman *ever* sustaining Twiggyesque gauntness, buy into the delusion, are bought off by profiteers, or hop aboard the money wagon themselves.

No one asks why public-health officials turn a blind eye to the lucrative lunacy. Or why otherwise enlightened organizations and employers, after finally recognizing alcoholism and insanity as diseases rather than sins or character flaws, smugly attribute the same kind of blame to the overweight.

Even when belated attention is paid to the eating disorders and emotional problems of thin women, fat women remain beyond the pale. No one called a halt even when potentially eye-opening data began drifting in about the body's set-point mechanism, the adverse metabolic effect of food deprivation, the unalterable *modus operandi* of fat cells, the lethal risks of yo-yo weight levels, genetic destiny, and the 95–98 per cent failure rate of dieting.

Instead, loving parents blithely allow the No Fat Chicks propaganda to simultaneously warp the sexual and romantic appetites of their sons and to savage the psyches of their daughters, who now begin to fret about their weight in kindergarten, and diet from grade school on.

And compassionate people, who abhor every other kind of bigotry, are silently complicit in the prejudice against all females who look more like Lillian and Marilyn than like Twiggy and Kate.

While our loved ones urge us onward, women and girls stampede to enrich the profiteers, who build their empires on the bedrock of instilled shame and choreographed contempt.

When I finally understood how this gigantic scam works, the shame I had felt for a lifetime turned into boiling outrage at the way bogus "beauty" imperatives impoverish individual women's lives and confound our collective progress towards equality. Simultaneously, I learned about cave-age metabolic programming and realized that, all along, it wasn't gluttony that kept me fat, but prolonged dieting. This double epiphany literally liberated me from a lifelong obsession.

It also ignited in me an ambition to incite the biggest jailbreak in history. I now know that no one *has* to wait until losing X pounds before escaping the prison of psychological pain. Anyone can bust out immediately, simply by understanding how the profiteers have brainwashed women to hate our bodies—and everyone else to forget that nature creates people in a rich variety of shapes and sizes. Only when we're free of the supremely stupid and corrupt No Fat Chicks delusion can "overweight" women spurn "inferior" status, and start to feel empowered to do what's best for our bodies and our lives.

Am I promoting unhealthy obesity in this book? On the contrary. I know very well that far too many of us weigh too much for our own good, and nothing in *No Fat Chicks* is meant to deny that reality. But the fact is, the current epidemic of obesity in North America cannot simply be chalked up to gluttony and sloth. Certainly some of us *do* eat too much and exercise too little. But other leading causes of excess weight are our culture's evolution towards sedentary work *and* leisure lifestyles, and the high fat and sugar content in modern convenience foods (which, among other considerations, undid our apron strings and liberated us from long hours in the kitchen).

And, as I explain in the next two chapters, the *major* culprits in many cases—including my own—are the anti-fat profiteers themselves. What makes them culpable? The fact that they've duped us into the incessant dieting that actually creates and sustains obesity by wrecking the metabolism; robbing the bodies of fat-burning muscle tissue; and inducing a physical and psychological need to binge.

But this book is primarily about mending broken hearts and easing troubled minds, not about transforming bodies into marvels of fitness. In fact, my ever-wise mother, Betty Postill, suggested I make it absolutely clear from the outset that it doesn't contain a single diet. She's right. The only reducing advice I want to share is not for your body—because that's entirely your business—but for the heaviness that was deliberately implanted in your heart and soul.

Yet, far from being oblivious to physical health, I have found—to my delight and amazement after a lifetime of fighting my weight every step of the way—that, when my mental attitude was finally healed, my body automatically began sorting itself out. I have dieted for the last time. *And* stopped heeding the voices, inside and outside my head, that tell me to despise myself. Yet my attitude towards what I eat and how I treat my body has been transformed, quite effortlessly, into what it *should* have been during and after my *Chatelaine* weight-loss series. With coercion out of the picture, I now freely choose whether and how I will work out (it varies, depending on my work schedule) and what I eat (mostly vegetables, fruits, and complex carbohydrates, with very little fat, plus occasional sweets, about which I no longer agonize).

And the happy result is that, since my one-woman jailbreak, I've been losing weight *without* dieting. As I write this, the total is probably about 50 pounds. But that's just a guess—I've promised myself *never* to step on a scale again, let alone allow it to measure my self-worth.

When I gaze at my reflection today, whether in a mirror or in other people's eyes, I no longer see the grotesque fun-house distortion that tormented me for so long. Instead, I see what I always wanted to be: not a raving beauty, just a contented, self-respecting, *normal* person. I'm not slender, but neither is the average North American woman, especially in middle age. Nor am I "proud to be fat," as some advocates for the admirable size-acceptance movement declare.

I am just me. And it's finally enough.

No Fat Chicks necessarily begins by tracing a dark, depressing, and infuriating story. But even a game as astronomically profitable as the "billion-dollar brainwash" can't last forever. In fact, "time" is already beginning to be called by the most powerful team on the field—those wizards of fundamental change, the Baby Boomers—in ways I never believed I'd live to see.

Just as they rewrote other rules they considered unjust, many are now realizing that the odious weight-based scam that surrounds us must be exposed and resisted. Demographically, most of the Boomers are thickening as fast as they're ageing. And their priorities have shifted away from frivolous youthful pursuits, such as unrealistic thinness, and towards maturity, practicality, and true physical and psychological health. The result is logical: The almightiest dollars of all are slowly starting to reverse the artificially induced, three-decade pandemic of delusion.

So the words of the prophets "written on the subway walls" (to borrow from Simon & Garfunkel) are changing from "Thou Shalt Squash Thyself" to "Thou Shalt Get Real." And the most prescient lifestyle profiteers, from advertisers to manufacturers, have begun to trumpet the desirability of everything from loose-fitting jeans to putting the fat back into premium ice cream.

At last, medical reports about the realities of the body's weight imperatives are being heeded. Finally, anti-discrimination organizations such as MediaWatch, the National Organization for Women, the American Civil Liberties Union, and the Equal Employment Opportunity Commission are recognizing the inequities affecting society's last scapegoat.

Artists and cultural commentators are starting to explore a theme that's rife with dramatic possibilities. Crusade-loving politicians are recognizing, if not their public responsibility, at least the opportunity to mount a fresh white horse.

And the activism of size-acceptance organizations such as the National Association for the Advancement of Fat Acceptance (NAAFA) is finally beginning to attract a glimmer of respectful media attention. Their collective voice is still as audible as that of a gnat trying to out-shout a baboon, but someday their putative clout is bound to result in a widespread wake-up call.

Best of all, some of the primary weight-loss moguls are being forced into some serious reducing of their own. A few have even been prodded in a saner direction by federal trade regulators and public-health officials. Yet, true to form, the chief response of these money-hungry predators was to launch "Operation Waif" (actually, "Twiggy Revisited") to try to get their skinny ducks back in a row. When that didn't work, they simply switched gears and barraged women with identical editorial and advertising messages equating fitness with power—even though it's obvious that all they're *really* touting is just more unrealistic, profit-producing narcissism.

I wrote this book to keep them from getting away with it any longer. And to signal the beginning of the end of the detestable No Fat Chicks era; to help consign that period to the oblivion it deserves as just another blip on history's time line; to provide a step-by-step exposé of how the *de facto* conspiracy to get rich by stigmatizing large women—and traumatizing the rest of the female population—came about; and to name names, and point an accusing finger directly at those who peddle shame by the pound and prejudice by the dollar.

Above all, I want to inform, dignify, encourage, and empower my fellow Fat Chicks by placing the blame where it belongs—not on the victims, but on those who deliberately victimize us and, in the process, barbarize our society into legitimizing cruelty. *No Fat Chicks* aims to provide large women with the factual and psychological means to end the merciless litany of prejudice, exploitation, and discrimination that dogs our days and poisons our lives. But I also want to help smaller women—and especially young girls—to see the "billion-dollar brain-wash" for the trap it is and to liberate themselves from its coercive power.

Marching gratefully along the trail blazed by such cultural heroes as Betty Friedan (*The Feminine Mystique*), Naomi Wolf (*The Beauty Myth*), Susan Faludi (*Backlash: The Undeclared War against American Women*), and Susie Orbach (*Fat Is a Feminist Issue*), I am hoping that *No Fat Chicks* will place one more scattered piece into the giant jigsaw puzzle that's gradually revealing the truth about women's lives.

CHAPTER ONE

Juliette

Of all the people I've written about, the only one who haunts me is a woman I never met. Her name was Juliette Christie, and she'd been dead for six months by the time I began investigating how her lifelong obsession with losing weight killed her.

It was the autumn of 1981, and I was teetering at the halfway point in my own "diet to end all diets." Coast to coast, I was being cheered on by thousands of women who read my magazine diary, identified with my struggle, and believed in its goal as unquestioningly as I did. But the pounds weren't coming off fast enough to hit my deadline, and I had begun to think I was headed for disaster. Then the phone rang and the editor of *Toronto Life* magazine asked me to write an article about Juliette's death.

I knew I shouldn't do it, because my diet series in *Chatelaine* was taking every ounce of time, energy, and courage I could scrape together. But I said yes anyway, telling myself it was because this was a plum assignment that could boost my writing career. And that I was bound to do a good job because I could bring a great deal of expertise to the story. But that wasn't the reason.

The truth was so brutal I've never admitted it until now. What motivated me to tackle Juliette's story was the same compulsion that drove me to a circus side-show when I was a teenager. I thought I should *force* myself to stare at the Fat Lady. I thought looking at her as if she was a mirror reflecting my own disgusting image was the punishment I deserved for being overweight. I hoped this do-it-yourself shock therapy might jolt me into finally getting rid of my excess pounds. And, most of all, I prayed that performing this degrading penance would buy me redemption for the sin I had evidently committed.

There were just the two of us in the musty tent. The Fat Lady sat on a platform about six feet from the makeshift fence that separated us. She glanced at me for a brief moment with no change in expression, no flicker of the filial recognition I'd been expecting. Then she silently dismissed me and gazed impassively towards something I couldn't see.

My pathetic little pilgrimage didn't work. When I looked at the Fat Lady, I couldn't see myself after all. In fact, I couldn't see anyone inside that massive barrel of flesh. She wouldn't let me—any more than Juliette would, years later. She was dead. Maybe the Fat Lady was too. Maybe I'd be joining them soon, at the rate I was going.

At least that's how I felt as I sat through a coroner's inquest, exhausted, heart-broken, hungry, and frightened by the familiarity of what I was hearing. But these feelings would soon be compounded by dismay at an outcome that failed to draw the obvious conclusion: society's hatred can be lethal.

None of the testimony about her was very personal. But somehow I gathered that Juliette wasn't much of a reader, and probably never knew the legend of Sisyphus. Yet for much of her miserably conflicted life, she was trapped in just such a classic struggle. Fat was her rock—100 pounds too much of it by the end—and the mountain was her own obstinate body. No matter how hard she tried, how stoically she denied her appetite, or even how successful she was—more than once accomplishing heroic losses of over 50 pounds—her burden always came rolling back. And along with it, the anguish of belonging to the one group it's still all right to mock, despise, and discriminate against.

As clear a symbol as the skull-and-crossbones on a bottle of poison, Juliette collapsed and died on the doorstep of a weight-loss centre. Flat on her back in a pool of vomit as an exhausted heart surrendered on her behalf, she became another of the untold, unmourned casualties of a deadly scourge it would take me fifteen more years to recognize as the "billion-dollar brainwash."

For all the good it did her, the day she died, four days short of her fifty-seventh birthday, Juliette had a family who loved her, and she was under the care of a fully qualified physician and a reputable pharmacist. But she was en route to yet another appointment with yet another anti-fat profiteer. It happened to be a branch of the (now defunct) Weight Loss Clinics of America. But it could have been any of the temples of corporeal salvation that have mushroomed in the three decades since our society was conned into fixating on the image of a scrawny teenage model.

It seems dreadfully significant, however, that the clinic's headquarters were located in a narcissistic community like Marina Del Rey, California. Halfway between the frenzy of LAX and the phony paradise of Venice, it was about 3,000 miles away from the lobby where Juliette died. Yet its stock-in-trade was powerful enough to leap the geographic and socio-economic gulf that, logically, should have prevented the emotional enslavement of a middle-aged Canadian matron.

But logic played as minor a role in this story as it does in the ongoing ordeals of millions of other women who try so hard to achieve the impossible. And Juliette's obsession with conforming to her culture's artificially manipulated aesthetic standards made her just as vulnerable as the Haitian refugees who were then in the headlines for risking everything aboard another type of manifestly dubious vessel. Their bodies were washing ashore in Florida at about the same time Juliette's inquest concluded in Toronto.

By then I knew a lot about how she died. But exactly what kept her trapped in jeopardy at that late a stage of life still eluded me. "The biggest question," I wrote, "[must] remain unanswered:

> How could she have reached ostensible maturity, successfully raised a
> loving daughter, lived to enjoy two grandchildren, maintained a
> reportedly happy relationship with her husband and a job she loved,
> and *still* be controlled by a compulsion that most women in her posi-
> tion would, surely to God, have felt fulfilled enough to abandon
> decades earlier?

It Must Be Worth It

The beginning of the end for Juliette was her decision—after a lifetime of dieting—to put herself in the hands of the nice nurses who staffed the Weight Loss Clinic in northwest Toronto. She weighed 251 pounds, which she told them she knew was at least 100 pounds too much for her 5' 5" frame. But, as a beginning, her short-term goal was to knock off 50 pounds in time for a family reunion in Quebec City on her birthday, which was just four months away. Would this be possible?

No problem, the nurses assured her. Yet achieving such a large loss so rapidly would require a whopping deficit of nearly 1,500 calories every single day—by someone who was nearly sixty years old, had a dismal track-record, was known to crave sweets, and whose only physical exercise consisted of a gentle aquabic routine once in a blue moon. Mind you, she did exert herself prodigiously on the job as a Red Cross homemaker, tending to the personal and practical needs of the elderly and chronically ill, and frequently going beyond the call of duty by scrubbing their walls and floors.

Her salary for this was barely above minimum wage, and her seventy-four-year-old husband brought in only a military veteran's pension. Yet Juliette somehow came up with the Weight Loss Clinic fee of $626.40. Later on, when her daughter became alarmed enough about her condition to urge her to give up the diet, Juliette said (in her native French so her husband wouldn't understand), "Are you kidding? Your dad would kill me if I spent all that money and didn't lose the weight."

This was far from the truth. It showed, rather, that the clinic's steep fees were more of an inducement than a repellant for Juliette, who seemed to be one of the many people who are predisposed to the notion that if something costs an outrageous amount of money, it *must* be worth it. Which explains why the majority of the anti-fat scammers' most blatantly exploitative articles and advertisements appear in the media vehicles pitched to people with the least education and sophistication. (See any issue of any supermarket tabloid for obvious examples.)

Granted, the Weight Loss Clinic's staff didn't just grab Juliette's cheque with no questions asked. They took her blood pressure, just as they would do every week until she died, and found it acceptable. Later, when questioned at the inquest as to whether they always used a large-size blood-pressure cuff on her fat upper arm, they insisted they had. But a medical expert testified that the final few readings before Juliette's death were so rock-bottom they could have been produced "only by a healthy teenager." Yet the nice nurses had seen no cause for doubt.

Nor, at the outset, had they been concerned about Juliette's negative medical history, which included gall-bladder disease, hypertension, recurring gout, shortness of breath, and low blood pressure. Or the daily diuretics she said she was taking for her gout, even though these are known to rob the body of vital elements such as potassium. None of these factors discouraged the nurses from putting Juliette on the clinic's second-most rigorous program—a scant 800 calories a day.

What they didn't know about—Juliette was so desperate to lose weight that she lied—were the many other medications she was taking, which caused the crown attorney to characterize her later as "a walking drugstore." Hidden at the back of her breadbox, and discovered by her daughter after Juliette's death, were appetite suppressants, antidepressants, Tylenol, 282s, tetracycline, and antihistamines.

Almost all had been prescribed by her regular physician and provided by a neighbourhood pharmacist who knew Juliette well enough to say during the inquest that he "just knew something like this was going to happen sooner or later."

The Weight Loss Clinic had no physician on staff or on call—just the endorsement of psychologist Joyce Brothers, whose smiling image was then appearing in numerous print and TV ads. Usually, she was photographed reading a letter which was ostensibly from yet another satisfied customer. "Dear Dr. Brothers, I can't tell you what it means to be able to wear short white shorts in public. . . ."

No one knew if Juliette was attracted to the Weight Loss Clinic by one of these ads. But when her physician—who happened to be a fairly recent immigrant from Guyana and apparently didn't know Dr. Brothers from Dr. Seuss—took the stand, she was asked whether she had believed the clinic's medical supervision was sufficiently safe to allow her patient to follow the strict regimen. "Well, yes," she said. "It's in all the advertisements. It's Dr. Joyce Brothers."

So Juliette's doctor confidently okayed the clinic diet in writing. Nowhere on the printed consent form was there a query about proscribed medications. There were, however, two other crucial questions: (1) Were any modifications to the program necessary? In her reply, the doctor made no mention of the pharmaceutical cornucopia she was prescribing, noting only that her patient was allergic to penicillin. (2) Did the doctor wish to receive regular reports on her patient's progress and physical condition? This one went unanswered.

Accordingly, the clinic didn't inform Juliette's physician that she was having a tough time. She lost only 2 pounds in the first six weeks. But then she went into a yo-yo pattern, with sudden drops of 6 or 7 pounds, followed by mysterious gains of roughly the same amounts. During this time, her oblivious doctor renewed her prescriptions time and time again, despite being told by the pharmacist that Juliette was depleting some of them too quickly.

Three weeks into her diet, although Juliette's blood pressure was purportedly normal, her uric acid was sky high. The doctor sent her to a specialist for tests but inexplicably didn't receive the results for nineteen days. She was concerned enough about the report to arrange a repeat test, yet raised no objection to it being scheduled a good six weeks after the original alarming reading. The results of this one reached the doctor's office while she was on vacation. And after she returned, she didn't get around to reading them for about two more weeks. Then, she testified, she tried without success to reach her patient by phone.

Just a few days later, Juliette would be dead.

What had the specialist's report said? That the patient's condition was not being helped, but actually exacerbated, by every medication her doctor kept represcribing. And that she should be taken off them immediately.

Meanwhile, Juliette's weight kept fluctuating. Her ankles were swollen and her face was gaunt and sagging. She was so weak she couldn't leave the hotel room on a family visit to the Quebec Winter Carnival. She fainted three nights before her death, but didn't tell anyone except her mild-mannered husband, who obeyed her request to keep quiet about it. She was, however, so dizzy she made a rare complaint on one of her last visits to the clinic. So the nurses, who were still recording reasonable blood-pressure readings, allowed her the minuscule modification of adding a quarter-teaspoon of salt to her diet to slow down fluid loss.

But it was too little and too late. On her way home from work one day that spring, just four months after starting what she had ironically vowed would be her last diet, Juliette stopped off at the Weight Loss Clinic. She walked across the lobby, crumpled to the floor, and died.

Nobody to Blame

The autopsy failed to reveal a specific cause of death, but two expert inquest witnesses testified that it was almost certainly arrhythmia (irregular heartbeats). This dangerous condition is well known to be brought on by the loss of potassium associated with diuretics, and it has also been linked with the other medications Juliette had been taking for years.

When all the testimony was complete, the coroner sent the jury off to deliberate, reminding them that their duty was not to ascribe blame to anyone but, rather, to come up with recommendations for preventing similar calamities in future. Two hours later, they came back with about a dozen eminently sensible suggestions. Then the inquest was over.

But not for me. I kept thinking that *somebody* must be to blame. The doctor, for her bumbling incompetence. The pharmacist, for not finding a way to override the doctor's okay on overlapping prescriptions. The Weight Loss Clinic, for taking such a big chunk of Juliette's money and then not only failing to help her lose weight, but letting her wither in front of their eyes.

But what about Juliette? Was she actually responsible for killing herself? Could she possibly have been courting disaster subconsciously, or even deliberately, as a form of punishing herself—just as I had by visiting the circus Fat Lady? Could her reckless behaviour really have sprung from simple ignorance of pharmaceutical dangers? Or was this to have been the ultimate atonement for the "sin" a lifetime of hearing anti-fat propaganda had convinced her she'd committed?

She certainly hadn't said anything of the kind, judging by what I heard at the inquest. But there had been a lot of testimony suggesting that she rarely spoke about her physical problems at all, and I knew this was a trait she shared with many obese people. We have the feeling that we aren't *entitled* to complain. Actually, we are loath to speak of our bodies at all, hoping that, if we don't, we may escape the disgust that accompanies the inevitable attribution of gluttony.

Juliette left no conclusive evidence to prove this. But logic and a little informed intuition convinced me that what she did during the last few weeks of her life was panic about her fast-approaching deadline. Her yo-yo weight levels *had* to have been caused by bingeing—probably in a desperate grab for energy to get through the day—followed by doubling, or possibly even trebling, her diuretics so water loss would make her feel that she was succeeding. If my theory is correct, the wonder is that she survived as long as she did.

Juliette never made it to her deadline, but mine was getting closer and closer. In a fog of outrage, exhaustion, and dread, I wrote her story. My editors liked it, but they requested a rewrite. They told me to conceal the fact that my own life was wracked by the same obsession that killed Juliette. After raising a feeble objection, I ended up agreeing that doing so would enhance the appearance of pristine journalistic objectivity.

But I knew even then that my capitulation was really caused by my feeling mortified. I had forced myself to "bleed onto the page" only because it was impossible to interview Juliette, and her family could tell me little because they never understood what drove her to a lifetime of dieting. But I was positive I knew that what put her in mortal danger was the agony of obsessively pursuing a goal you never manage to reach. And I had said so in the only way I could.

Yet when talented wordsmiths didn't consider my own ordeal appropriate to the story, I thought I must be the one who wasn't seeing straight. Years later, though, I stopped doubting my own judgement when I realized that my editors had simply been embarrassed by my candour. And that what really prompted the bowdlerization was squeamishness about my admitting to being one of society's untouchables. "Obese" just wasn't a dignified status for smart people like us.

Even so, I was initially quite proud of what was published. I enjoyed a fair amount of praise, and people said it was a powerful piece. None of us realized that I had missed the most important element of all. Yes, I captured the *how* in exhaustive detail. But I never even speculated as to *why* Juliette was so driven, for so long, to become thin. The closest I came was a paragraph that was never published:

> I know, as she knew, the demons that drive a young girl, a teenager
> and a young adult to deny herself a moment's peace about her appearance (which she's been brainwashed into interpreting as her worth).
> But Juliette had a couple of decades on me, as well as an adoring

husband and loving offspring. It terrifies me to contemplate her example: another twenty years of anguish and then, finally, failure to conquer either the flesh or the obsession.

Fifteen of the twenty years that separated Juliette and me have now passed. As it turned out, I learned no more from her than I did from looking at the Fat Lady. I had written in horrified tones about Juliette's self-imposed privations, but continued inflicting them (all but the drugs) on myself. I had condemned weight-loss surgery as "brutal enough to make a medieval torturer cringe," but had my stomach stapled just three years later. And then, when nothing worked and I remained fat no matter what I did, I spent the next decade slowly sinking into isolation and hopelessness, and ultimately escaping to the bitter haven of anonymity.

Then, literally when I least expected it, my redemption found me. I began doing research for this book and discovered what was missing from the story about the woman who dropped dead at the weight-loss centre. The inquest jury hadn't been allowed to assign blame, and the closest I'd come was to implicitly fault Juliette herself for being fatally obsessed. Then I unconsciously imitated her example for a decade and a half, remaining mired in the same obsession, assuming I had only myself to blame.

But I couldn't have been more wrong. Nor could Juliette. The truth is we were exactly like hopeless laboratory rats. There was no way out of the maze we'd been duped and coerced into entering. We were *supposed* to fail, and then to keep on failing. That's how the "billion-dollar brainwash" works. It's the only way millions of people can be robbed of billions of dollars, year after futile year. Juliette just did it all a little too well.

Secret Casualties of a Secret War

I have retold Juliette Christie's sad story here because she epitomizes the hundreds—possibly even thousands—of other women throughout North America who are virtually *murdered* by anti-fat forces every year. A wild exaggeration? I'm afraid not. When you add in those who die from weight-loss surgery, plus those whose lives are sacrificed to anorexia and bulimia, plus the many who perish because they try to control their weight by smoking, we may be talking about tens of thousands.

But guess what? Nobody's keeping score. We never hear the names of the casualties in what amounts to a secret war. We aren't even told that they die, let alone why. And if we do happen to find out, blame is never assigned to anything but, at most, foolish, inexplicable vanity. Why in the *world* do women do these things to themselves? Tsk, tsk. What a shame.

Obliviousness and flat-out indifference, even on the part of national authorities whose duty is to safeguard public health, made trying to ferret out the mortality rate attributable to weight-loss efforts the most frustrating part of the research for this book. Ultimately *failing* to dredge up irrefutable proof about the grisly toll the "billion-dollar brainwash" is exacting has been a bitter disappointment for me.

I began my research confidently enough with the standard writer's technique of checking periodical indices and electronic databanks to see what facts other journalists had come up with, and especially for clues about relevant authorities to interview. But none of the many "keywords" and topic combinations I tried paid off. There was *nothing* to be found about deaths resulting from drastic diets, fasts, bariatric surgery, contributing chemical abuse (such as Juliette's), or even eating disorders.

So I moved on to major newspapers. *Nothing*—except multiple articles about the risks of obesity, sprinkled with many sky-is-falling quotes from profitmongers themselves, whose endorsement of various reducing schemes should have been considered conflicts of interests instead of being obediently reported as genuine news.

I saved what I thought would be a research treasure trove for last: the health databanks. Surely abundant attention *must* have been paid to the fatal consequences connected with practices that millions of people have engaged in on a daily basis for decades. But I was astounded to be proven wrong.

So I decided to play the only trump card I had. I punched into the library computer the one victim's name I knew for sure: singer Karen Carpenter, the most famous casualty to date of the weight-obsession epidemic. People all over the world knew her music and were stunned when she died of anorexia in 1983 at the age of thirty-two. Her tragedy prompted the hundreds of news stories it deserved, and shocked the public into focusing on a disease few had previously known about. But—just a decade after her death—she has practically become a missing person. There are hardly any references to her in the databanks for the 1990s.

Discovering this sinister blank was so upsetting that I began to wonder if fatalities had somehow been deliberately "disappeared." But even I don't really think that's it. I came up with a more plausible theory after striking out—despite thorough checking with the American and Canadian medical associations, the National Institutes of Health, the Centers for Disease Control, the National Center for Health Statistics, the American College of Surgery, the American Society of Bariatric Physicians, the American Society of Bariatric Surgery, the National Library of Medicine, and the American Hospital Association, among other organizations.

I believe the failure to even count how many people are being sacrificed in the name of thinness is systemic—merely one more cruel, disrespectful disservice done to those whose legitimate membership in the human race was all but cancelled by a *de facto* cabal of anti-fat profiteers.

There's a major story to be told here, with the possibility of uncovering thousands of secret deaths, plus massive custodial oversight, and possibly even pay-offs somewhere along the line. This makes the situation juicy enough to tempt a tabloid. But it will surely take a skilled investigative journalist from the mainstream media to penetrate the dead end that defeated me—namely, that mortality statistics of all kinds are tabulated and analysed according to data collected from death certificates. And there is no such cause-of-death category as "excessive reducing," let alone "Waif Syndrome"—the appropriate name if a sorely needed new category of such fatalities *is* ever instituted.

Death and Silence

"Hush money" is another crucial reason why weight-loss-related deaths aren't hitting the headlines, according to researchers at the National Institutes of Health's Obesity Research Center in New York. After reviewing private records regarding a number of unresolved lawsuits, they reported in a recent issue of the *Healthy Weight Journal*—which, to my knowledge, is the only publication even trying to keep track of the mortality rate in this context—that "Sudden Death Syndrome," as well as other weight-loss-related fatalities, are common. But when survivors sue for wrongful death, defendants generally try to settle out of court, on condition that the plaintiffs keep their mouths shut forever.

According to a variety of medical professionals who contribute to the journal, the typical patient who ultimately dies from attempting to lose weight is a woman whose basic health is good. Mortalities most commonly occur during total fasting; while on severely restricted regimens (usually below 600 calories); during weight-loss surgery; or during the refeeding periods that routinely follow fasting and surgery.

The most likely causes of her death will be arrhythmia; electrolyte abnormalities; nutritional inadequacy, including a lack of minerals such as potassium, magnesium, and copper; and grossly reduced heart weight. Pre- and post-operative stress belong on this list as well, according to Dr. Janis Fisler, of UCLA's cardiology division. Her conclusion, arrived at after investigating dieting deaths for the past decade, is based in part on the fact that bariatric-surgery patients often suffer such acute anxiety that even something as innocuous as a loud noise can provoke fatal arrhythmia.

Although no one in the medical community is likely to conclude that obesity is *good* for a person's health, many practitioners are reportedly coming to the conclusion that drastic weight-loss methods can often be even more dangerous. "One of the fundamental tenets of the weight-loss industry is if you get people to eat less, they'll lose weight . . . and be better off," epidemiologist Steven N. Blair reported to a 1994 American Heart Association meeting. But, he added, "there is no evidence to support either [contention]."

Blair backed up what's considered to be a controversial statement by citing the results of a study (inexplicably limited to males, despite the fact that at least 90 per cent of dieters are female). It determined that, among chronic dieters, as compared with subjects who weren't in the habit of dieting, heart disease was more than twice as prevalent, hypertension was 15 per cent more common, and diabetes occurred five times more often.

The other facts I *was* able to glean are equally shocking:
• Liquid-protein diets (such as Oprah and I endured) have been blamed for at least fifty-eight deaths since their introduction in the 1970s. Yet they're still in use, and recently became available without doctors' prescriptions.

• Liposuction was invented in France and quickly resulted in the deaths of nine women. Yet, soon afterwards, the procedure was approved for use in North America. During its first six years here, according to a U.S. congressional subcommittee, there were at least twenty deaths. Authorities evidently suspect that liposuction is currently producing *many* more deaths. But, again, money buys silence.

A Hundred and Fifty Times as Many Victims as AIDS

Despite being disappointed by the dearth of references to Karen Carpenter's death, I had no trouble getting reliable statistics on the incidence of anorexia and bulimia. They're even grimmer than I had guessed.

In Canada, the National Eating Disorder Information Centre confirmed that more than 300,000 Canadian women and girls are afflicted, which represents at least 7 per cent of the female population. And the mortality rate is considered to be at least 15 per cent.

The total number of American females with eating disorders has now topped 11 million, according to the National Association of Anorexia Nervosa and Associated Disorders, and the mortality rate is thought to be similar to that seen in Canada.

No prominent Canadian woman has yet died because of an eating disorder. But the senseless demise in 1993 of a twenty-two-year-old Torontonian named Sheena Carpenter, whom anorexia—provoked by being turned down by a modelling agency because her face was "too fat"— had whittled down to just 50 pounds, is currently prompting some overdue soul-searching. This is thanks, in part, to the fact that her mother works for a newspaper—the *Toronto Sun*—and is determined to have something worthwhile result from her daughter's example. Hence, plans are now in the works for Sheena's Place, which will be Canada's first transition hospice to help recovering anorexics' re-entry into normal living.

Athletes—such as gymnast Christy Henrich, who died of anorexia in 1994, weighing 47 pounds—are particularly vulnerable to eating disorders. So are actresses. Among those whose eating disorders have become public knowledge are Jane Fonda, Sally Field, Lynn Redgrave, Sandra Dee, Ally Sheedy, and Tracey Gold. Stolen medical records (which were later officially confirmed) revealed that even Princess Diana has struggled with bulimia.

Even when they don't die, at least 80 per cent of both anorexics and bulimics suffer multiple relapses before being cured. Bulimia is considered far less reversible than anorexia, and has been known to persist for decades, just as it did in Fonda's case. While we were watching her smiling through her movies, she was forcing herself to throw up as many as twenty times a day.

What frequently starts out as a quick crash diet to lose a modest amount of weight—say, just enough to look like a favourite fashion model—often spirals out of control. And eating disorders can be accompanied by so many side-effects that their victims often become physically and psychologically incapacitated. These include hypothermia, dehydration, electrolyte imbalance, abnormal heart rhythm, kidney failure, hiatal hernia, tooth erosion (from frequent exposure to stomach acid), esophageal damage, infertility, and osteoporosis.

To put all this in some sort of perspective—but without meaning to minimize the catastrophe of HIV/AIDS—there are *150 times* more women on this continent who suffer from eating disorders as there are female AIDS patients. But no coloured ribbons are worn to call attention to, or express compassion for, those who have been felled by the edict that all women must be thin.

Our Sisters' Keepers

No one was able to talk Juliette Christie out of a lifetime of dieting. Her husband testified at her inquest that he'd often tried to reassure her that he "liked her just as she was." And her daughter said she'd tried many times to help Juliette accept the fact that "some people are just meant to be big." But neither their patient persuasion nor their abiding love was powerful enough to undo the psychological damage done by the "billion-dollar brainwash." In the end, even the people who loved Juliette best were unable to save her life.

But at least they tried. Many of us can't summon up the right words, or the courage to say them, when people we care about seem to be drifting into danger because of their obsession with being thin. I must count myself among this group of chicken-hearts.

One of my dearest friends, whose adult weight stabilized at an average level for many years (after some juvenile chubbiness), suddenly began losing weight a few years ago. Discreet queries elicited only the information that she had discovered fitness training. When I saw her again recently after an interval of three years, her body had dwindled down to what seemed like shocking thinness. Yet I somehow couldn't find the words to ask her point-blank how it happened. In every other way, she was the same wise, intensely funny, hyper-aware woman I'd known for more than fifteen years. We spent only a few hours together during a reunion, so I found it easy to rationalize not bringing the subject up. But even though we're separated again, I certainly know her phone number and address, and could tell her about my concern. So why haven't I?

The closest I can come to answering is to remind myself that I've always had a hands-off policy, unless someone specifically asks for advice. My own body has been criticized so cruelly throughout my life that I'm reluctant to venture even a gentle cavil about someone else's. Feeble excuses? Absolutely. But they're all I've got. So I'm hoping that my beloved friend will recognize herself when she reads this and volunteer answers to the questions I've been too cowardly to ask. And that this failure to act, on the part of someone who knows all too well what's at stake, will serve as a galvanizing influence on others whose silence may be imperiling their loved ones.

Bottom Line

Thanks to three decades of incessant, inescapable indoctrination by the multifaceted factions I call the "billion-dollar brainwash," millions of Canadians and Americans deprive and exhaust themselves every day of the year, trying to become thinner. At least 90 per cent are women whose lives are, at best, restricted and, at worst, poisoned by the implacable pressure to do so. In my view, this should automatically make the obsession with weight loss, and the dangerous behaviour it encourages, *the* top priority with medical and public-health officials, the news media, and, especially, women's organizations and publications.

But—as demonstrated by my fruitless search for even something as fundamental as the total number of people who die every year just from trying to lose weight—apparently no one in a position of authority sees the situation in this light. A highly placed associate of the Centers for Disease Control told me, off the record, that he seriously doubted *anyone* would be able to track the mortality rate. Did that concern him? I asked. "Not particularly," he replied, in a matter-of-fact tone.

I was so flummoxed that anyone dedicated to controlling major diseases would express such indifference—when the annual death toll may well be in the thousands—that I didn't know what to say. So I just thanked him for his time and hung up the phone.

Then I went for a long walk amidst tumbling autumn leaves. Their cascading colours reminded me of the same season back in 1981, when I was trying so desperately to make a third of my body vanish. And when I was so afraid that I, too, would become one of the casualties no one wants to talk about.

I thought some more about Juliette. I never got to meet her, yet I feel as though I did. It's probably because I *am* her in so many ways. We struggled with an identical obsession for an identical length of time. We were both dupes of the same despicable profiteers. And both of us starved, physically and psychologically, for years and years, subsisting on little more than hope and magazine dreams.

The only essential difference between Juliette and me is that she can never awaken from the brainwashing. She died. But I lived, after all. And I finally learned that, while some things are worth dying for, beauty— especially the phony, tawdry, supremely superficial version of it women and girls have been force-fed for decades—is not one of them.

CHAPTER TWO

Better Dead Than Fed

We *think* we think for ourselves. Our eyes are wide open, and we make all our own choices, right? Sorry. If this were true, we wouldn't believe the most preposterous fairy-tale ever concocted: that to be fat is to be like Cinderella's stepsisters—ugly, lazy, mean, and stupid—and to be thin is to live happily ever after.

And the kicker is the notion that what bamboozled us into this mass delusion just sort of happened, or that women created it themselves, probably out of our insecurity about storming male bastions. Right. Just as the Davy Crockett coonskin-cap craze of the 1950s "just happened" and had nothing to do with the marketing genius of Walt Disney!

Here's what really occurred. It's the history we must learn from if we're ever to stop repeating it.

New York, March 20, 1967—The awkward, near-skeletal, English teenager who jets in on TWA flight 703 looks nothing like the cash cow she is destined to become. Nor do her elfin face and urchin figure (91 pounds on a 5' 7" frame) identify her as a Trojan horse whose secret mission is to entrap the female population of North America for the next three decades.

Reporters loitering at a newsstand wait impatiently for the press conference to welcome Lesley Hornby, the gawky, seventeen-year-old fashion model who swept to the top of the heap in Swinging London the previous year, despite being so scrawny she was nicknamed Sticks, OxFam, and, ultimately, Twiggy.

Flipping through magazines to pass the time, the journalists find nothing surprising in the photo spreads of popular beauties. Grown-ups are still in style, and even those who sport the flamboyant new "mod gear" don't look much different from many of the women who amble through the airport. More photogenic, perhaps; but roughly the same age and size as the kind of real-life ladies who've been considered attractive for as long as anyone can remember.

As a bright orange coat and two coltish, mini-skirted legs hove into view, the world wobbles imperceptibly and starts spinning in a sinister new direction.

In a wacky, six-week whirlwind after Twiggy's arrival at Kennedy Airport, the diminutive cockney "bird" metamorphosed into a mammoth, a completely unprecedented marketing phenomenon. Her image was plastered everywhere. Her photo sessions caused near-riots all over Manhattan. Modelling agencies trampled one another to sign her up. Hairstylists duplicated her cropped locks as fast as their scissors could snip. Mannequins matching her 31-22-32 silhouette suddenly appeared in Fifth Avenue windows, hastily clad in the Twiggy Enterprises line of clothing, which was being imported from London at the rate of $500,000 worth per week.

Before she winged back across the Atlantic, Twiggy was the object of a genuine media frenzy from which not even the stodgy *New York Times* could remain aloof, even though it described her as "just like your next door neighbor, if he happens to be a skinny 12-year-old boy." Scribes from *Life*, *Look*, *Mademoiselle*, *The Saturday Evening Post*, *The New Yorker*, *McCall's*, and *Ladies' Home Journal* followed her everywhere. A huge press contingent turned out just to watch her get her famous hair trimmed. *Women's Wear Daily*, even while denouncing Twiggy in a front-page editorial as just "a massive publicity stunt," nevertheless splurged with a sixteen-page feature on her.

The rest of the fashion press positively swooned. At the head of the pack was quirky Diana Vreeland, *Vogue* editor and long-time *doyenne* of *haute couture*, who gushed that Twiggy was "charming . . . disarming [and] delicious," and booked her for four cover shoots with *crème de la crème* photographer Richard Avedon. Privately, though, Vreeland opined in a memo that "Twiggy is dreadfully swaybacked . . . [and should be told] to pull in her behind [so we'll] have a glorious girl and not an ill fed adolescent."

Why the commotion? Timing. There were then more than 30 million teenage girls in North America eager to spend their allowances on anything that differentiated them from their mothers. With rock and roll foment-ing rebellion, Baby Boomers of both sexes were overthrowing parental dominion. And even though the famous "pig in a python" metaphor had yet to be coined to symbolize the sociological clout of these youngsters, what was obvious was that their spending power amounted to a gold rush for marketers.

Even so, few pundits recognized the revolutionary redefinition of beauty Twiggy represented, nor that, in terms of marketing, she was treading where no mere model had ever gone before. One exception was *Newsweek*, which splashed her on its cover and dubbed her "the first child star in the history of high fashion." While other reporters cracked jokes, *Newsweek*'s anonymous feature writer cut right to the big question: "Whether the Twiggy look will now sweep across the U.S., emaciating American teen-agers as it goes. . . ."

It was the right query, but it underestimated the geography. Girls *all over the world* began shortening their skirts, lengthening their eyelashes, and cutting back on calories—although not to any alarming degree, because youth was still on their side. But Twiggy's older fashion col-leagues hit the panic button. "It was a nightmare, trying to keep up," model Gillian Bobroff recalls in Michael Gross's *Model: The Ugly Business of Beautiful Women.* "I . . . started killing myself . . . I never ate." Statuesque Wilhelmina, a top international model of the day, put herself on what she called the "hummingbird diet," eating only twice a week, with cigarettes and black coffee sustaining her between Sundays, when she had a small steak, and Wednesdays, when she ate "a little bowl of soup . . . or a little piece of cheese on a cracker . . . so I wouldn't get too sick. . . ."

Other fashion models, indeed all women whose beauty was their professional stock-in-trade, soon felt pressured into adopting similarly stringent regimens, often augmented by diet pills and bulimic behav-iour. Two of the most prominent were actresses Jane Fonda—who has admitted suffering a twenty-year eating disorder while trying "to get closer to the bone"—and Sally Field, who developed bulimia in response to feeling "immensely unattractive [because] everybody . . . was Twiggy, except me."

But what's most significant here is that, even in ordinary walks of life, it was only a matter of time before the girls who had found it fairly easy to look like Twiggy grew up to be women whose bodies had other plans—but whose minds, by then, had been infiltrated by the message of the anti-fat profiteers: that all women have an *obligation* to be slim.

If you like historical "if only's," here's a lulu: One year after Twiggy's sensational North American debut, something happened in Atlantic City that might have averted, or at least mitigated, the pandemic of physical and spiritual starvation she launched—if the media that covered it hadn't got away with one of the most blatant whoppers ever told.

We all know that the bizarre practice of bra-burning began at the 1968 Miss America pageant, right? Wrong. The *real* scoop is that a plucky troupe of pioneering feminists, seeking a way to spotlight their aspirations, staged a demonstration to protest the beauty contest. To explicitly signal their rejection of the phony, constricting trappings of "the feminine mystique," they tossed make-up, hair curlers, steno pads, copies of *Playboy*, high heels, girdles, and bras into what they dubbed a "freedom trash can." They also crowned a sheep as the new Miss America. The demonstration was certainly radical for its time, but the symbolism—and the press releases and media interviews—weren't exactly indecipherable.

Yet how was the protest reported? In a way that not only diminished that specific event, but almost fatally trivialized the women's movement itself. What was set afire that day? *Nothing*. But that didn't stop journalists from calling the event a "bra-burning"* and saddling feminists with an enduring legacy of ridicule and misunderstanding.

If only the demonstrators' wake-up call *had* reached and influenced massive numbers of women in 1968, *and* been followed by responsible coverage of the issues and inequities at the core of the women's liberation movement, our phenomenal subsequent progress might have included the one crucial victory that still eludes us—namely, the enhancement of women's self-respect enough that we understand how bogus, self-defeating, and socially regressive the "beauty" imperative really is.

Instead, for nearly a decade, all that the majority of women ever saw or heard were sarcastic, irresponsibly distorted portrayals of "libbers" as hairy-legged, combat-booted, man-hating crazies whose goals couldn't

---

*A sloppy parallel to males burning their draft cards to protest the Vietnam War.

possibly have anything to do with the real lives of women and families.

But the dishonest coverage of the Miss America protest was scarcely the first time women have been lied to or about, with devastating results. Let's backtrack to a time when—unbelievable as it seems in our looks-above-all era—there was no such thing as a tyrannical ideal that all women were pressured to imitate.

The Evolution of the Incredible Shrinking Woman

Standardized clothing sizes didn't even exist until about 130 years ago. Before then, garments were fitted to individual bodies, *not* the other way around. Fashion had none of the dictatorial power it has today; it was merely a whimsical indulgence of the well-to-do, who were consequently the only folks with strong ideas about how people "should" look.

For most of recorded history, the only way of documenting the faddish evolution of desirable female forms was through statues and paintings. The oldest known example is a tiny clay figure called the *Woman from Willendorf*, which dates back some 30,000 years. By modern standards, this Earth Mother is a portly conglomeration of rounded masses adding up to perhaps 250 pounds. The increasingly sophisticated statues that turned up later gave us the "classic" notion of feminine beauty that more or less persists today. But would it surprise you to learn that the measurements of the revered *Venus de Milo* were 43-31-40?

After Venus's ample "buns of marble," there were many more changes to come before anyone dreamed up today's preposterous "buns of steel." Rosy, rounded buttocks were all the rage in one era, and sloping shoulders in another, while breasts were raised, lowered, and sometimes flattened to accentuate enormous bellies or hips. Meanwhile, waists wandered in and out, desirable body weights bobbed up and down, and many other permutations came and went. The front-runners in this historical parade were the "Rubenesque" damsels whose abundance promised fertility.

But here's the point: The shifts in female body shapes were not real, but merely artists' interpretations. And since mass communication was non-existent, and art and fashion were almost exclusively the property of the rich, so few people *saw* these images that their power to dictate arbitrary standards of beauty was negligible.

Then came the Industrial Revolution. Mass-manufacturing required a mass market and, when the process was eventually extended to encompass clothing, a new chapter in the story of women's bodies began to be written. By the mid-nineteenth century, technological breakthroughs were revving up the production of textiles and some finished garments for both sexes. But it wasn't until the invention of dressmakers' patterns, by Ellen Butterick in 1863, that the need for standard sizes arose. Even then, it was easy enough for a skilled seamstress to yo-yo her seams in or out, according to the client's proportions, which she did (presumably in diplomatic silence) if she wished to be rehired.

At about the same time, an Englishman named Charles Frederick Worth sailed for Paris, where he came up with a prototype for the salons that gradually nudged dressmaking out of cottages and into shops. This commercialization of the process eroded the concept of catering to just one customer's figure at a time. A marketing as well as a design genius, Worth was ahead of his time in many ways and, with another innovation—employing live mannequins to enticingly parade his gowns through the salon—he bequeathed to the general public the concept of the "ideal" figure.

Tastes changed radically thereafter, with colossal crinolines giving way to bodacious bustles, only to be succeeded by the S-shaped curves of the Gibson Girl. But, as in earlier times, these shifts in the way women *seemed* to be built were accomplished, not by demanding the actual transmutation of bodies, but by altering the designs of clothing as well as the undergarments that coaxed flesh into whatever shape was currently in style. As cruelly uncomfortable as these corsets and other gadgets undoubtedly were, what was on the way was worse—and it would still be tormenting women more than a century later.

But live mannequins didn't capture the public's attention very quickly (as hard as this is to believe in the age of the "supermodel"). In fact, looking as much as possible like a marketer's arbitrary ideal wasn't really a consideration for quite some time. However, when the apparel industry began to be dominated by pre-sized, ready-to-wear clothing shortly before the turn of the century, the die was permanently cast. From then on, the wearer would be required to fit the garment instead of vice versa.

The Rise of Women's Magazines

Another decisive event in this abbreviated time line was the advent of a means of communication by which women could be taught what was expected of them, beauty-wise (and, later on, in many other ways). This virtual operator's manual was the same thing it is today—the women's magazine.

The first two of these secular bibles were piloted by Sarah Josepha Hale. The year was 1828, the venue was Boston, and the publications were, first, *Ladies Magazine* and, then, *Godey's Lady's Book.* Savvy Sarah told readers early on, in an obvious bid to forestall charges of uppity-ness, that "husbands may rest assured that nothing found in these pages shall cause [their wives] to . . . encroach upon prerogatives of men."

What did get encroached upon in short order were the dimensions of feminine desirability. Thanks to the sheer novelty of *Godey's Lady's Book*, thin was in for the first time. While Europeans looked on in amazement, "the American craze," which lasted only from about 1830 to 1850, prompted such rampant dieting that reformer Harriet Beecher Stowe complained: "Our willowy girls are afraid of nothing so much as growing stout . . . [and] when we see a woman made as a woman ought to be, she strikes us as a monster."

Sound familiar? There was even a prescient omen of our current epi-demic of eating disorders in an article written by J.-A. Brillat-Savarin in the year *Godey's Lady's Book* was founded. He told of a young friend named Louise who, after being teased about her size, put herself on a diet con-sisting of one glass of vinegar per day. Two months later, she was dead.

All in all, the *raison d'être* of the earliest women's magazines was identical with that of today's. As *Ms.* founding editor Gloria Steinem reports in a riveting exposé titled *Sex, Lies, & Advertising*, the publica-tions existed, then as now, "to create a desire for products, instruct in the use of products, and make products a crucial part of gaining social approval. . . ."

The first of these products was, of course, ladies' clothing, which could now be viewed simultaneously by thousands of far-flung readers. What had been missing for centuries—a way to deliver visual images to masses of potential consumers—had finally arrived. Yet, with photo-graphic reproduction still a few decades in the future, the latest fashions had to be sketched by artists, and their renderings of female figures were too idealized and exaggerated to be taken seriously as edicts on how readers should really look.

The coming of the camera would change all that. Now, as historian Anne Hollander writes in *Seeing through Clothes*: "Perfect feminine beauty no longer formed a still image, ideally wrought by a Leonardo da Vinci. . . . It had become transmuted into a photograph, a single instant that represented a sequence of instants. . . . For this kind of mobile beauty, thinness was a necessary condition."

With the mistaken conviction that cameras cannot lie, it was clear sailing for what came to be called "the tyranny of fashion." Now, as Caroline Routh expresses it in *In Style: 100 Years of Canadian Women's Fashion*: "[Women] found it necessary to remodel their body shape in favour of the prevailing silhouette. . . ."

Magazines and Marketers Tie the Knot

Poised on the threshold was another kind of tyranny that would be inimical to women's ability to feel at peace with their bodies—advertising. Even without running ads, the earliest women's magazines had effectively touted wares that complemented their genteel messages about the proper way to conduct one's life. But it wasn't long before nascent marketers spied the potential of women's magazines and came a'courting. When the union between product and vehicle was consummated, as Steinem put it, "for the first time, readers could purchase what a magazine had encouraged them to want."

In Canada, the dozen or so women's journals that began publishing in the 1880s were soon peppered with advertisements, many of which focused on fanciful bodily ills—which snake-oil producers were only too eager to cure. Given the immense popularity of such generously endowed women as Lillian Russell, and the long-standing association of fatness with both physical and financial prosperity, it was no wonder that the "heartbreak of corpulence" would not become an editorial and advertising staple until after the First World War.

Instead, publications all over the continent were apt to target the opposite condition. Chubbiness was considered so desirable that even the beloved actress Sarah Bernhardt was frequently mocked for being too skinny, and caricatured with her head atop such narrow, cylindrical objects as broomsticks, canes, and snakes. Meanwhile, anti-slenderness ads, such as one placed in *Woman's Home Companion* in 1908 by a company called Nature's Rival, became common. "Does your form lack normal development?" queried the ad. No problem: "You can display a perfect figure, showing the natural, well-rounded bust form of a beautifully developed woman by using . . . an air form corset waist inflated to any desired size. . . ."

But both fashion and advertising did an abrupt about-face as the Roaring Twenties approached, and a number of postwar factors led to the debut of a newfangled, hair-bobbed, beanpole-shaped woman called a "flapper." Seemingly overnight, the elaborate coiffures and lush but trussed-up physiques of the Victorian and Edwardian eras came to symbolize a past that had enslaved women for too long. "The hoop-skirt, the small waist . . . the artificial helplessness, the wretched discomfort . . . [were] are all emblazoned in sartorial terms," fumed an equal-rights tract dated 1920.

Now looking as "narrow as an arrow," to quote some memorable ad copy, was what it took to signal both attractiveness and women's newly won autonomy. Off went long, cumbersome hair. Up went draggy skirts. Out went Mama's mores. Yet, while the "jazz babies" congratulated themselves for escaping corsets and stays, they overlooked a fundamental contradiction: Achieving the androgynous new contours by binding themselves fore and (if necessary) aft, as well as eating far less than in the past, wasn't exactly a radical improvement.

Why didn't flappers realize this? Chiefly because of the heady feeling of victory that came with winning the right to vote in federal elections for the first time in history. But also, to a great extent, because the popular-culture vehicles of the day co-opted and trivialized the women's own emancipation rhetoric, just as their heirs would do during the second feminist wave of the 1970s. Even the term "flapper"—connoting the pointless flapping-about of a beheaded chicken—was dismissive, as "libber" would be later on.

It may sound overly simplistic to say women were hoodwinked into believing that societal permission to reveal their legs, doff their old-fashioned underwear, and adopt boyish silhouettes equalled all the freedom they needed. But the red herring of superficial cultural concessions worked well enough in both eras to stall political momentum. Consequently, as Anne Hollander noted, "the rapidity with which the new, linear form replaced the more curvaceous one [was] startling." In fact, the flapper craze spread faster than any trend had before, or would again until Twiggy came along.

The accelerant was the newest means of mass influence: the movies, especially those featuring whippet-thin stars like Clara Bow and Mary Pickford. As Jeanine Basinger, author of *A Woman's View: How Hollywood Spoke to Women, 1930–1960*, describes this effect: "Women measure themselves by the cultural norms that are presented to them. What is a woman? How is she supposed to look and act? Movies . . . provided models to answer these questions, and women . . . gobbled them up."

Even more influentially, women's magazines began preaching a stern and—except for the Depression and the war years—*unrelenting* No Fat Chicks sermon that continues to this day. *Vogue,* for example, scolded in 1918 that "there is one crime against the modern ethics of beauty which is unpardonable; far better it is to commit any number of petty crimes than to be guilty of growing fat."

That same year, *Diet and Health with a Key to the Calories* became the first North American best-seller in the weight-loss arena. In it, Los Angeles physician Lulu Hunt Peters advised women who were noticeably wider than arrows that they were "viewed with distrust, suspicion, and even aversion."

What was a woman to do if she was guilty of the new crime of corpulence? Why, just flip the pages of her favourite magazine until she found an article or an ad promoting the very latest in reducing schemes, potions, gimmicks, gadgets, and gizmos. Her only problem would be choosing between "quasi-scientific diet programs [including] lemon juice, milk and bananas, special breads and seaweed; patent medicines or 'fat reducers' advertised as Citrophan, Figureoids, Berledets, Allan's Antifat, Rengo, Kellogg's Obesity Food, and Marmola [plus] treatments with special baths, pastes, and thinning salts," according to Joan Jacobs Brumberg's *Fasting Girls: The Emergence of Anorexia Nervosa as a Modern Disease.*

If none of that worked, women took other forms of drastic action, and in such large numbers that, by 1926, Brumberg says, medical and public-health authorities had become alarmed enough to convene an Adult Weight Conference. One of the speakers reported a practice that is only too well known seventy years later: "Many of our flappers have mastered the art of eating their cake and yet not having it, inducing regurgitation, after a plentiful meal, either by drugs or mechanical means." And if bulimia didn't do the trick, there was one more dangerous option, also still practised in the 1990s: smoking. "To keep a slender figure . . . Reach for a Lucky instead of a sweet," advised a 1928 ad for Lucky Strikes cigarettes.

Whichever weight-loss scheme she tried, the modern miss could check her progress by hopping onto one of the new home scales (a million of which were sold by the Detecto company in 1925 alone). And if her new regimen should create an unhealthy pallor, well, it was no longer considered scandalous to wear make-up, and buckets of it were now pouring onto the market. In fact, everything a modern woman could possibly want was ostensibly hers for the buying. "We grew up founding our dreams on the infinite promise of American advertising," mused Zelda Fitzgerald, who epitomized the "smart young things" of the Jazz Age. "I still believe that one can learn to play the piano by mail and that mud will give you a perfect complexion."

Flappers like Zelda were heartily encouraged to assume that they had come a long way. But, in terms of inescapable beauty imperatives, they were actually as reined in by the marketers as were their predecessors, and their descendants three-quarters of a century later. Meanwhile, the true emancipation sought by the original suffragists remained out of reach.

With supreme irony suggesting that misogynist gods were playing a cosmic trick on women, both national female suffrage and the trend-setting Miss America beauty pageant turned up in the same year—1920. But it wasn't a celestial prank; it was actually one of the recurring checks and balances that have so far prevented women from attaining equality as human beings.

The fact is, only *after* they won the vote was there any impetus for women to eschew the physical abundance that had been favoured since the beginning of time and shrink down to the diminutive dimensions of powerless adolescents. Yet, the significance of this virtual checkmate had been anticipated by visionary suffragist Lucy Stone way back in 1855: "It is very little to me to have the right to vote, to my own property, etcetera, if I may not keep my body, and its uses, in my absolute right."

Women's bodies and dreams were still up for grabs after the vote was won, as far as marketers were concerned. As long as they kept bombarding consumers with the message that the true New Woman had to be thin, anti-fat profiteers of all stripes could continue making a buck. And advertisers had become a lot more adept at the "art" of spinning such schemes than they were in, say, 1899, when the cleverest concept the National Biscuit Company's agency could come up with was a lame and unsubtle rechristening of the product as "Uneeda Biscuit."

The Great Depression of the 1930s put a crimp in everyone's plans, to put it blandly, and temporarily halted the mania to become skinny. It wasn't simply that spending power plunged; for the majority of women, the necessity of scrambling to get by left little time for preoccupation with artificial beauty standards. And it's easy to stay slender when you can't always afford enough to eat. Perhaps that explains why, judging by the *Reader's Guide to Periodical Literature*, there were seldom more than one or two magazine articles on the topic of slimness published per year during this period.*

Women's weight pretty much took care of itself during the Second World War as well, with the rationing of such fattening foods as meat, sugar, and butter, and, for many, physical labour in the war industries. Other jobs vacated by men for the duration also sorely needed to be filled and, accordingly, women were admonished by a raft of magazine articles to break out of domestic confinement. Some of the most adamant of these were "Women Must Work, Not Only Weep" (*Social Welfare*, 1939), "The Hand That Rocks the Axis" (*Collier's*, 1942), "Key to Victory: Women in War Industries" (*Woman's Home Companion*, 1942), "Mrs. Homekeeper, Here's a War Job Only You Can Do" (*Canadian Home Journal*, 1942), and "Women in Slacks Speed Plane Production" (*Reader's Digest*, 1942).

---

*Even so, the canniest profiteers went right on developing diet pills such as amphetamines and testing other drugs, including digitalis and various sedatives, for use as weight-loss aids.

But as armistice approached, bringing with it the need to open up jobs for returning men, magazines began shoving women in the opposite direction. The social and psychological pressure for Rosie the Riveter to swap her dungarees for frilly dresses, and to otherwise "refeminize" herself, was swift and relentless. Certainly, much of this came from a genuine desire to restore family life. But the obligation for women to abruptly surrender the independence that had come with holding down jobs and managing on their own was rigidly reinforced by an onslaught of articles, short stories, and poems such as those in the January 1945 issue of *Ladies' Home Journal.*

Up front was the deceptively titled "The New Woman in the New America" by renowned columnist Dorothy Thompson. "The fact that in this war America has emerged as the premier world power," she wrote, "does not affect the cooking of breakfast, the dressing of children, the getting them off to school, and all the other routines of the domestic lives which are our [women's] normal sphere."

Feature stories in this issue included "Diary of Domesticity," "A Mother-and-Daughter Room," "The Plus in Your Wardrobe," and "Where the Heart Is." The half-dozen fiction pieces focused on romance, and had such titles as "You'll Marry Me at Noon." Among the poems were "My Bride Forever," "Loving a Little Boy," and "None But the Lonely," the last a wing-clipping little tract which began: "None but the lonely hearted find / The road that leads to the highest place."

The "get thee homeward" theme was reinforced by many of the accompanying advertisements, especially those featuring teary-eyed women embracing returning soldiers and sailors. These ads included those for Trushay lotion (headlined "Part of your love story"), Community Silverplate ("Back home forever"), and Pond's creme ("It's easy to see why her tall blond Navy fiance adores Patricia!"). In an ad for Lux soap headlined "I hurt Bob's pride by my dishpan hands," a chagrined woman extends her hand to an older man, who looks at it disapprovingly, while hubby, Bob, wearing an army uniform, stands between them, scowling. Scott tissue's slogan was "He needs you more than ever in a war-changed world." And, tellingly, a packaged regimen called DuBarry Success Course featured a woman boasting "I lost 77 pounds in 6 months!"

Typically themed articles in other periodicals during this period included "Little Woman, What Now?" (*Maclean's*, 1944), "Has Your Husband Come Home to the Right Woman?" (*Ladies' Home Journal*, 1945), "Should Women Return to the Home?" (*National Home*, 1945), "How Good a Mother Are You?" (*Hygeia*, 1945), "No Women Being Hired" (*Canadian Forum*, 1946), "Have Babies While You're Young" (*Parents*, 1946), "The Best Place in the World" (*House Beautiful*, 1947), "Femininity Begins at Home" (*Ladies' Home Journal*, 1947), "Women Must Choose Privileges or Rights" (*Saturday Night*, 1947), "The Art of Staying at Home" (*Reader's Digest*, 1948), and "How to Get Whistled At" (*Collier's*, 1948).

Only a decade and a half earlier, the new possibilities epitomized by winning the vote had inspired numerous articles and short stories that "mirrored the yearning for identity and the sense of possibility that existed for women then," to quote what Betty Friedan would later write in *The Feminine Mystique*. This was startlingly evident even in material about traditional subjects such as "The New Era in Housework," published in the June 1929 issue of *Ladies' Home Journal*, which began: "There are at least six reasons why we have got this much nearer the workless home of the millennium. First, nowadays the female half of the race is taken as seriously—almost—as the male half, and a good many first-rate brains are working on the problem."

Articles extolling loftier endeavours included "Women's Air Derby" (*Literary Digest*, 1929), "Opening the Pulpit to Women" (*Literary Digest*, 1929), "Women Winners of Foreign Trade" (*Business Week*, 1929), "How to Make Money in Wall Street" (*Woman's Home Companion*, 1930), "Our Glorious Sports Girls" (*Ladies' Home Journal*, 1930), "Power: United Forces of Women Can Provide Leadership" (*Ladies' Home Journal*, 1932), "She Got the Order: Only Saleswoman of Steel in the World" (*Collier's*, 1932), "I Can Count on Myself: Reflections of a Woman of 50" (*Scribner's*, 1933), "Women Intensify Their Flight to Peace" (*Literary Digest*, 1933), "Women's Orchestra Makes Its Debut" (*Commonweal*, 1935), "Brought Up to Do Something" (*Ladies' Home Journal*, 1935), "Women Microbe Hunters" (*Independent Woman*, 1936), and "What Ho! Able-Bodied Seawomen" (*Christian Science Monitor*, 1936).

In Canadian periodicals, there were equally strong articles about—to name just a few professions—female aviators (*Chatelaine*, 1931 and

1937), gold prospectors (*Canadian Home Journal*, 1930), judges (*Chatelaine*, 1929 and 1935), newspaper publishers (*Canadian Home Journal*, 1925), and even advertisers (*Canadian Home Journal*, 1927).

After the end of the Second World War, however, the same magazines were, as Friedan phrased it, "crammed full of food, clothing, cosmetics, furniture, and the physical bodies of young women [with no trace of] the world of thought and ideas [or] the life of the mind and spirit." Now a cacophony of voices lectured women on how they should take care of their husbands, children, and homes, and what they should look like while doing so. In the January 1950 issue of *McCall's*, for example, the features included "You Too Can Make a Perfect Souffle," "New Gas Ranges Fill the Bill," "Seven Steps to a Youthful Look," "Brush a Glow into Your Skin," and "The Last Word in Coat Dresses." Eleanor Roosevelt's popular "My Day" column, which had addressed more ambitious queries not so long ago, now answered questions about turkey stuffing and meddling mothers-in-law.

In Canada, such home-grown magazines as *Chatelaine*, *Canadian Home Journal*, *Mayfair*, and *Canadian Queen* added their voices to the carping chorus of such border-spanning biggies as *Vogue*, *McCall's*, *Harper's Bazaar*, and *Vanity Fair*.

And the celluloid dream machine kept pace, quickly replacing such inspirational pre-war movies as *Hail the Woman* (1921), *Christopher Strong* (1933), *Design for Living* (1933), *Imitation of Life* (1934), *A Woman Rebels* (1936), *Dark Victory* (1939), and *Gone With the Wind* (1939), and motivational war-era movies like *Mrs. Miniver* (1942), *So Proudly We Hail* (1943), and *Tender Comrade* (1943), with such inanities as *The Bachelor and the Bobby-Soxer* (1947), *The Egg and I* (1947), *It Had to Be You* (1947), and *June Bride* (1948).

The Propaganda Machine Begins Going for the Burn

All in all, by the time the troops had marched home and women had been herded back to the kitchen, the real battles in what would eventually become the "billion-dollar brainwash" had begun in earnest, and articles about the necessity of being slim were becoming inescapable.

A golden opportunity for the anti-fat brigades to pounce presented itself in 1947, when Parisian designer Christian Dior decreed the "New

Look." After two decades of relatively comfortable fashions, waists and midriffs were suddenly expected to squeeze into the tiny circumferences that best complemented Dior's voluminous new skirts. This was an especially tricky task for millions of mothers who'd grown a mite pudgy while giving birth to the first wave of Baby Boomers, and there was open rebellion for a short while (as we shall see in Chapter 9).

But women didn't really stand a chance of heading off an avalanche of admonitions to literally belittle themselves. Between 1949 and 1955, there were no fewer than sixty-five articles on slimming in major magazines, including "What Do They Say about You?" (*Woman's Home Companion*, 1949), "Thin Rats Bury the Fat Rats" (*Harper's*, 1949), "No Fads for Fatso" (*Newsweek*, 1950), "Hypnosis for Hips" (*American*, 1951), "Lucy Learns to Be Pretty" (*Woman's Home Companion*, 1951), "Talk Your Fat Away" (*Coronet*, 1951), "Hollywood's Favorite Sweat Shop" (*Collier's*, 1952), "How the Stars Stick to Their Diets" (*Woman's Home Companion*, 1952), "I Want to Have Babies and My Figure Too!" (*Ladies' Home Journal*, 1953), "Overweight, Our Biggest Health Menace" (*McCall's*, 1954), "Why Do People Eat Too Much?" (*Mademoiselle*, 1954), and "I Was a Hopeless Fatty, Now I'm a Model" (*Ladies' Home Journal*, 1955).

By 1948, the anti-fat profiteers had enlarged their target prey to include young girls. "Nobody Loves a Fat Girl," admonished a contemporary Ry-Krisp ad that appeared in many publications. And a typical short story in *Seventeen* magazine, entitled "The Fattest Girl in the Class," followed the Cinderella-style formula that would thereafter be a staple of both fiction and non-fiction: girl gets fat, girl is ostracized, girl goes on diet, girl finds happiness. Other obvious examples of this phenomenon included "No Fatties in the Family" and "Don't Let Your Child Be a Fatty!" (both in *Ladies' Home Journal*, 1953).

Was it mere coincidence that all such women's magazines were then sailing on a bountiful sea of ads for the new consumer goods flooding into stores, including diet and beauty products? Not a chance, according to Earl Shorris, author of *A Nation of Salesmen: The Tyranny of the Market and the Subversion of Culture*. He argues that, by using teams of researchers, demographers, statisticians, psychologists, writers, editors, producers, and actors, marketing had become a science "that could determine the desires of the buyer . . . [and reach] into the process of imagination to the very soul. . . ."*

And when the omnipotent new medium of television was added to the mix of "persuaders" who set their sights squarely on female consumers, Shorris says it was strictly no contest. The consumerism-equals-happiness formula was drilled into viewers by the powerful sponsors of such early shows as *People Are Funny*, *I Remember Mama*, *The Arthur Godfrey Show*, *As the World Turns*, and *My Little Margie*. Result: "Before television, tastes changed slowly, but once life could itself be mediated every morning, noon, and night . . .," says Shorris, "[marketing] had become one of the forces that determined the world."

The stifling effect of all this less-than-gentle persuasion on a captive audience of homebound women was not recognized until *The Feminine Mystique* made its explosive debut in 1963. But economist John Kenneth Galbraith has characterized the insidiousness of such pressure: "Behavior that is essential for economic reasons is transformed into a social virtue."

Some of the *quid pro quos* were amazingly blatant. Preceding a March 1953 article in *Ladies' Home Journal* titled "I Was Too Fat to Have a Baby," for example, were no fewer than seven large ads related to the desirability of either looking slim or actually losing weight. These included one for Metropolitan Life Insurance that stated: "Overweight is our country's Number One health problem today"; another for Starlac non-fat dry milk; and four ads, each a half-page or larger, for girdles with such evocative names as "Curvallure," "Secret Panel," "Profile," and the "Playtex Streamliner." This last ad featured actress Zsa Zsa Gabor posing in a strapless evening gown beside the words: "Hollywood stars and famous designers call Playtex *the* perfect girdle."

Just two pages after the feature article about the woman whose doctor allegedly told her that obesity prevented fertility was a big advertisement for Florida grapefruit that began: "Don't give an inch to your waistline." Four pages later, there was another diet story titled "How Florence Delfino Lost 25 Pounds as Millions Saw Her Do It on Television." Complete with "before" and "after" photos, this article was

---

*Incidentally, the market-research industry itself would grow to be a $2.5-billion-per-annum business by 1994.

actually an "advertorial" for Knox Gelatine's "Eat-and-Reduce Plan," which promised that you could "Eat your fill and lose 2 to 5 pounds a week." Turn two more pages and there's a picture of a woman in high heels and a revealing shortie robe peering down at a scale and touting the advisability of "Start[ing] each day the Health-O-Meter way!"

This ad-heavy issue was typical of the women's magazines during these years, most of which ran stories nearly every month similar to the following, which appeared in *Ladies' Home Journal*: "I Lost Weight and Am Just Beginning to Live" (1952), "The Diet That Launched a New Life" (1953), and "A Size 18 in Red" (1952). This last one included a diet plan specially designed for "wistful Wilma," who was pictured gazing longingly at a bright red dress in size 12 even though she admitted that, unless she lost weight, her choices would be limited to "the size 18 racks of slenderizing blacks or subdued colors . . . to hide her superfluous padding."

By the end of the 1950s, the titles grew racier, and included: "From Hippo to Slimmo" (*Ladies' Home Journal*, 1957) and "From Fatso to Cool Cat" (*Parents*, 1958). "Reducing at $500 a Week" (*Reader's Digest*, 1958) was evidence of the growing popularity of expensive weight-loss spas.

And, trumpeted the accompanying ads, galloping to the rescue of anyone who couldn't accomplish the feat on her own was a zealous cavalry brandishing an ever-expanding arsenal of weapons specifically designed for attacking avoirdupois. But, "as in all wars," said a *Newsweek* article on the phenomenon, "it is the arms makers who are growing fat. . . . [B]y promising to melt and float the fat right out of your body— absolutely no dieting required—several hundred firms each year float $100 million out of the pockets of some 5 million Americans determined to be thinner." Echoed *Reader's Digest* in 1959: "They Take Your Money, You Keep Your Weight." In fact, so many of the new weight-loss products belonged in the snake-oil category that the U.S. federal government appointed a congressional subcommittee to look into fraudulent reducing aids.

Why So Vulnerable?

If you're wondering how this lunacy could possibly have enticed so many millions of otherwise sensible people (an estimated 80–90 per cent of whom were women), you're ready for another "if only." And it's a biggie.

Overall, as I noted at the beginning of this chapter, grown-ups were still in style and in charge. So even if girls didn't want to look like their *own* mothers, they were still just as eager as their predecessors to grow up and enjoy the status of mature women.

Enter Twiggy, who symbolized the factors that stopped that aspiration cold, and pared the former variety of beauty standards down to a single icon for the first time in history. Her arrival was actually part of a mosaic of events, rightly dubbed a "youthquake," that happened when nearly 80 million North American Baby Boomers hit their twenties. It should have been as predictable as it was inevitable that this demographic 500-pound gorilla would soon be getting whatever it wanted. But, as you'll remember if you're in the vanguard of the boom, kids weren't yet taken seriously. You simply didn't count until you were an adult.

What helped overturn this verity fits the "if only" category. Who were the influential cultural arbiters up to this time? Before and during the Second World War, many were feisty women who were part of the first generation of females ever not only to vote, but also to build professional careers. They were bold, visionary, and passionate about the potential of their gender. And they filled their magazines, movies, novels, and plays with messages that inspired women to be all that they could be.

But by now, these trail-blazers had died, reached retirement age, or been finessed out the door to make way for men. And because of the paroxysms of the Depression and the Second World War, they never got a chance to pass the torch of independence on to younger women, who consequently remained oblivious to the struggle for female equality. So the media vehicles pitched at women limited their agendas to the pure domesticity that best served marketers. The initial result of the pioneers' disappearance was, as Friedan expressed it, that "the feminine mystique began to spread through the land, grafted onto old prejudices and comfortable conventions which so easily give the past a stranglehold on the future."

But it's the long-term effect that's crucial in the No Fat Chicks context. These perceptive, mature, *self-respecting* women, who had always fought for female equality, were simply not around to help mediate the havoc the youthquake was about to wreak, leaven the strictly male way of seeing things, or pass on to a new generation of women the principles of independence that had been struggled for for so long and won so recently.

If only the legacy of their perspective hadn't been dumped and forgotten like last year's skirt length, the march towards equality would, almost certainly, have continued, instead of languishing as little more than a faint memory until the late 1960s. And many aspects of modern life might be much healthier today. Near the top of a tantalizing list of might-have-beens is the probability that the "billion-dollar brainwash" could have been headed off, or, at the very least, alleviated by sheer common sense.

Friedan had amply substantiated the disappearance of material about the achievements and aspirations of women, and other important general topics, by analysing the July 1960 issue of *McCall's*. With a circulation of more than 5 million in Canada and the United States, this magazine was a giant voice, speaking at a terrifically interesting time in history. Yet a male editor told her: "You just can't write about ideas or broad issues of the day for women. . . . They aren't interested in politics, unless it's related to an immediate need in the home, like the price of coffee."

Consequently, that issue of *McCall's*, like its contemporary rivals, consisted of articles that, as Friedan expressed it, confined "woman's world . . . to her own body and beauty, the charming of men, the bearing of babies, and the physical care and serving of husband, children, and home."

Smack dab in the middle of the magazine was a glamorous four-page spread titled "Reduce the Way the Models Do." The article, which was highlighted on the magazine's cover, included a 1,200-calorie diet for "when, horror of horrors, a size 9 becomes a little snug. . . ." And, sure enough, nearby was a half-page ad for a new liquid saccharine product called Sucaryl: "No thanks! No calories!" declares a slender woman in a striped bathing suit as she pours Sucaryl into a glass of iced tea.

Canadian magazines of this period were no less explicit about the primacy of domestic roles for women. Striking examples include dozens of features on food, fashion, beauty regimens, home decor, marital relationships, and the complicated factors involved in raising children. Accompanying these were a host of related advertisements, a sprinkling of which featured newly invented weight-loss products.

The anything-but-coincidental juxtaposition of ads and articles conveying *identical* messages illustrates the state of the union between magazines and marketers by the early 1960s. To extend the connubial metaphor, there had been a complete reversal in who courted whom. Competition among women's magazines for revenue-producing ads had become so fierce that five such publications had already perished and several others were teetering on the brink. Thus, thanks to the law of supply and demand, the role of the marketer had changed from ardent suitor to domineering partner.

Actually, this was getting to be old news, even though the pretense of an impenetrable wall between the editorial and ad-sales departments persists today. The elaborately concealed truth is that the wall began crumbling as far back as 1899, when *Ladies' Home Journal* was brutally taught a prophetic lesson. After rejecting ads for dubious patent medicines, the magazine was hit with a boycott by all its other advertisers.

It wasn't long afterward that the advertising tail began wagging the editorial dog—a fact that's obvious just from the placement of big glossy ads on the right-hand pages of magazines and the relegation of editorial text to the more awkward left-hand pages, forcing frustrated readers to flip back and forth in pursuit of the articles for which they buy publications in the first place.

But this inconvenience is insignificant compared with the dire effects marketers have had on the volume and content of that wandering text. During the three decades since the 1960 issue of *McCall's* in which the Sucaryl ad was "editorially complemented" by a feature on dieting, advertising in women's magazines has reached such a saturation level that the average ratio is now 70 per cent advertising to 30 per cent editorial text. In the February 1994 *McCall's*, the content of only 49 out of a total of 184 pages was not ads or complementary copy.

What effect did this have on consumers along the way? Says *Village Voice* columnist Leslie Savan, one of only a handful of journalists whose full-time job is ad-watching, it was Pavlovian-style conditioning to get us to "pulse to the . . . one–two beat that moves most ads: problem/solution, old/new, Brand X/hero brand, desire/gratification." Watching and reading ads, she asserts in an intriguing book titled *The Sponsored Life*, gives us our "notions of what's desirable behavior, our lust for novelty, even our visions of the perfect love affair . . . [and] cultural forms that don't fit these patterns tend to fade away. . . ."

Après Twiggy—The Deluge

By the time Twiggy arrived in New York in 1967, the No Fat Chicks messages had been drummed in so thoroughly that dieting was already becoming a big business. Weight Watchers had enrolled nearly 500,000 members in its twenty-three franchises and spawned several imitators, all of which employed the peer-pressure techniques developed by company founder Jean Nidetch.

Within a year after Twiggy's debut, the editorial and advertising cheering sections at women's magazines had shifted into high gear, and added exercising to their lists of must-do's. They were also pushing the concepts that being slim was a discipline women owed themselves, and that this was the only route to good health. *Mademoiselle*, for example, editorially lectured its readers in no uncertain terms: "Creampuffs, there's no escape. Whip yourself into super shape and stay that way." *Chatelaine* even sold its own diet plan.

Unsurprisingly, advertisers were kicking in some pretty big bucks by now. A saccharine company launched its "$500,000 SweetaStakes" with a full-page ad in *Ladies' Home Journal* and several other women's magazines in 1968. It featured rear views of four bikini-clad young women splashing into the surf atop a slogan that read: "If only we could send all you Sweeta Girls to Hawaii!" This ad appeared simultaneously with many others for such new diet products as Carnation's Slender shake and chewy, chalky (as I recall) Ayds pseudo-candies, which sponsored full-page advertorials with such headlines as "Inside I was Crying Until I Lost 105 Pounds." Even such older products as laxatives, fruit, and margarine got in on the act by positioning themselves as diet aids. A Fleischmann's ad showing a pyjama-clad family doing sit-ups, for instance, appeared in a magazine near a cover story titled "How I Lost 80 Pounds in 19 Weeks by a Governor's Wife."

Two years after Twiggy's big PR bash, Weight Watchers' gross revenues had leapt to $5.5 million. And this was only a fraction of what *Business Week* estimated as the $200-million annual "waistline industry," which, the magazine stated, "was not only better than any previous year, but about $50 million over expectations." Included in the total were $50 million spent on exercise machines and gadgets and "multi-millions [more] on diet foods, diet advice, slimming sessions at expensive spas and at thousands of health clubs."

What was motivating so many people to spend so much money? More than any other single factor: the addition of morality to the weight-loss imperative. Being slim was no longer just the best way to be attractive, or even healthy. Now it had become the same kind of fire-and-brimstone character issue that sexuality had been in Victorian times. Any woman who "let herself go" was now regarded as a sinner, and therefore a fair target for disgust, ridicule, and ostracism.

That the simple desire for thinness had been transformed into a full-blown and far-reaching obsession by 1969 was evident in contemporary surveys among high-school students indicating that the number of girls who considered themselves too fat had risen, in just three years, from 50 per cent to 80 per cent.

Before long, grade-school children would be expressing fears of becoming fat, and attempting to limit their food intake. This was scarcely surprising, considering that, among other brainwashing factors, they were specifically targeted by ads such as a TV spot for Fibre Trim. Two girls, who looked to be about seven or eight years old, spoke in French (with subtitles) about how slender one of their mothers was. "Aren't you jealous?" asked one. "Not as long as she tells me her secrets," replied the other.

Later, studies on even younger children would reveal that anti-fat prejudice was affecting kindergarteners, who preferred dolls with such physical deformities as missing limbs and disfigured skin to those that were oversized. Why? Because, the children said, the chubby dolls were "ugly," "lazy," and "ate too much."

The psychological effects of this prejudice on overweight youngsters grew cruel enough to contribute to widespread depression and a teen suicide rate that has quadrupled in North America in the past three decades. Bitter evidence of this was provided when a fifteen-year-old Florida boy named Brian Head brought a gun to school in 1994 after being taunted for years about being overweight. "I can't take it anymore," he said, and then shot himself to death in his classroom.

By 1970, an estimated 70 per cent of American families were eating "low-cal" products. And serious money was also being spent at the doctor's office. In addition to handing out diet sheets and dashing off gimmicky best-sellers, physicians were by now prescribing some *10 billion* amphetamines. Soon, thousands of them would add weight-loss surgery to their range of services. For the sake of fairness, it should be noted that what led many medical professionals to ride the weight-loss rollercoaster were reports from insurance companies that repeatedly ratcheted supposedly desirable weight levels downward.

Skip ahead two more years, to 1972, and it was almost impossible for anti-fat profiteers *not* to make a bundle. Weight Watchers had spread to forty-nine American states, plus Canada, England, Australia, West Germany, the Philippines, and Israel; signed up more than 3 million people (a number that would triple in the next five years); and added a cookbook, a monthly magazine, and its own line of frozen dinners, soft drinks, and skimmed milk.

Among those who tried more drastic measures, the first generation of liquid-protein diets had resulted in at least three deaths. Temporarily banned in the United States in 1977, so-called protein-sparing fasts would make a big comeback after TV talk-show host Oprah Winfrey later used one to lose 67 pounds (which rapidly found their way back during the following year).

With the 1981 publication of her *Workout Book*, Jane Fonda began creating a one-woman fitness empire that would soon extend to videotaped exercise lessons and many other products. Fonda also inspired a parade of other celebrities, who followed her lead with a stream of their own diet and fitness products. (By 1994, the total amount spent on exercise videos in North America would exceed $285 million.)

In 1981, as well, *Business Week* estimated that "the diet-food business . . . represents . . . the fastest-growing segment of the food industry [with] 6.6% of all U.S. food sales [for a total of] $450 million . . . excluding diet soft drinks, which bring in an additional $400 million." Those figures, the magazine added, "may double, or even triple, within the next five years. . . ."

What was even more significant in the No Fat Chicks context was that giant conglomerate companies, including Nestlé, Stouffer, and H.J. Heinz (which bought Weight Watchers in 1980), had jumped into the diet industry and were by then "mounting intensive ad campaigns [to] garner shares of the lucrative market," according to *Business Week.*

By 1982, during the time I was struggling with my *Chatelaine* weight-loss series, the number of listings in the *Reader's Guide to Periodical Literature* regarding what, by now, was referred to as "dietmania" covered more than three pages and numbered more than 250 articles, mostly in women's magazines.

Later in the decade, liposuction would be imported from France, despite having caused the deaths of nine women. During its first six years here, at least twenty deaths were reported. Yet these casualties received so little publicity—in women's magazines or elsewhere—that the procedure became the most frequently performed cosmetic surgery in history.

A ghastly counterpoint, although the cause-and-effect connection garnered little attention, was a growing number of articles about eating disorders. The first mentions of anorexia nervosa were, in the United States, a single entry in *Science Digest* in 1970 and, in Canada, a 1976 article in *Maclean's*. Over the next two decades, particularly in response to the 1983 death from anorexia of singer Karen Carpenter, coverage of eating disorders leapt to dozens of articles every year. Yet most lacked perspective and continuity, and as a result were too haphazard to sound enough alarm bells about an epidemic that would ultimately claim more than 11 million women and girls.

Strong-Arming the Little Ladies

Sey Chessler, who was editor-in-chief of *Redbook* from the 1960s to the 1980s, calls the relationship between marketers and publishers "a holdup." "Advertisers want to know two things," he told Gloria Steinem for her *Sex, Lies & Advertising* exposé: "What are you going to charge me? What else are you going to do for me?" Chessler added that he thought "advertisers do this to women's magazines especially, because of the general disrespect they have for women."

Steinem is one of only a few other editors to go public about the "What else?" pressures that are routinely exerted by marketers. She cited some especially revealing examples from the years before *Ms.* finally booted advertisers out the door in 1990 and began subsisting solely on subscription and newsstand revenue. Clairol, for example, cancelled its contract in retaliation for a brief news item in *Ms.* about the carcinogenic potential of hair dyes. And even when this was widely reported elsewhere and resulted in Clairol changing its formula, the company refused to ever again advertise in *Ms.* Later, Revlon stomped off in anger over a story on events in the Soviet Union because the women featured on the cover weren't wearing make-up.

But nothing contributed more directly to the No Fat Chicks credo than the terms of *Ms.*'s contract with Maidenform lingerie, which presumably still apply to other magazines (I was unable to elicit confirmation or denial of this). "The very nature of the product [appeals] to the positive emotions of the reader/consumer," stated a standard ad contract. "Therefore, it is imperative that all editorial adjacencies reflect that same positive tone." What kind of articles did Maidenform explicitly exclude?—"... illness, disillusionment, [and] *large size fashion* ..." (emphasis added).

An eye-popping article in the *Columbia Journalism Review* in 1990 not only amplified Chessler's and Steinem's contentions, but reported that newspapers, too, are now succumbing to similar squeeze plays. Even the once-sacrosanct *New York Times* now runs "fluff" pieces about such exploitative beauty preparations as firming creams, complete with references to advertisers' products. These sorts of features, and especially those fairy-tales for grown-ups—the "makeovers" that have become a perennial in women's magazines—represent a "value-added" bonanza for marketers, all of whom are credited in the editorial text free of charge.

The *CJR* piece also spotlighted other methods by which marketers have helped create a hideously distorted and limited cultural climate for women of all sizes. Because so many new magazines are flooding the market (580 in 1989 alone), the fight for pieces of the advertising pie became so ferocious that it led to a "revolution in marketing ... [aimed at] specific groups of people with spending money." The result, says *CJR* writer Michael Hoyt, is that, "many magazines are hatched more as marketing concepts than as editorial ideas. ..."

To see for yourself what Hoyt means, just check any newsstand for such obvious examples as *Fit, Self, Shape* and *New Body*, plus such Frankensteinian slap-togethers as *Vie.* The July 1995 issue of this last publication sported Jane Fonda on the cover above the headline "Celebrity Diet Issue," and inside what its publisher described as "the health club industry's cutting-edge source for information and news" were ninety-six ad-packed pages that repeatedly touted fitness clubs and activities the magazine itself co-sponsored, plus a cover line and no fewer than eleven big ads for its own powdered diet supplement.

As for the daily press, when the *Wall Street Journal*'s G. Pascal Zachary investigated the increasingly incestuous relationship with marketers, he concluded that, "with newspapers facing tough times financially, [we] see an increase in [their] tendency . . . to cater to advertisers or pull their punches when it comes to criticizing advertisers in print."

Lest readers conclude that only the print media are dirty-dancing with advertisers, the *Journal*'s Joanne Lipman reported that NBC TV recently reversed the cart-and-horse formula that always prevailed in planning television shows and, instead, "solicited advertisers first—and promised to feature them in [a] program" that would be created later and custom-tailored to their wishes.

In addition, many movies are now similarly influenced by marketers, who contribute hugely to their budgets not just in return for on-screen "product placements," but also for having their say about what movies get made and which actors are cast. (McDonald's, for example, whose fatty foods virtually *manufacture* future customers for the anti-fat conglomerate, gave the producers of *Santa Claus—The Movie* $1 million, in part to fund the construction of a set resembling a glorified McDonald's restaurant, and spent $18 million more on advertising and cross-promotions.)

Just a Fairy-Tale

The reason I've gone on at such length about the way marketers got their stranglehold on the mass media is to document the reality behind one of the most dangerous myths in our culture. We believe that those in the mass-communications business—upon whom we are obliged to depend for news and information, and from whom we absorb ideas that help shape our lives—enjoy free speech. We are wrong. And it's costing us, big time.

The problem isn't just the deluge of diet-till-you-drop propaganda. It's also that economic self-interest excludes all contrarian balances to this point of view, while simultaneously limiting the space for coverage of other vital subjects. Put another way, as David Croteau and William Hoynes contend in *By Invitation Only: How the Media Limit Political*

Debate: "The media may not directly influence what the public thinks, but it can have a profound effect on what the public thinks *about*" (emphasis added). And, adds journalist Mort Rosenblum in *Who Stole the News?*, to enhance profits, news organizations "favor impact over information and neglect . . . subtle but vital undercurrents . . . [that] like . . . deadly virus[es] gradually spread into a worldwide pandemic."

There could be no better example of this than the scant attention paid to the epidemic of potentially lethal eating disorders that authorities now say affects more than 11 million women and girls in North America. This is *150 times* as many females as are currently estimated by the Centers for Disease Control to be infected with AIDS.

Certainly there was a spate of scare stories about anorexia after Karen Carpenter died. But where is coverage of the fact that bulimia is now so prevalent among female college students (estimated at between 20 and 50 per cent) that many dormitories have designated "vomiting bathrooms"?

And why wasn't writer Tina Gaudoin publicly rebuked for her irresponsible answer to charges that women's magazines exacerbate eating disorders by exclusively featuring super-thin and super-young models? "People were dieting long before newsstands were invented," she wrote in the July 1993 issue of *Harper's Bazaar*. Insisting that the skinniest models "eat like horses" and that "thin is their natural body type," Gaudoin added, in a facetious tone, that "the Greeks binged and purged, as did the Egyptians."

Quisling-style equivocations like this should alert us to the fact that freedom of the press has become just another of the fairy-tales we're encouraged to believe. Yet another is that advertisements are, at worst, merely petty annoyances that are no more life-threatening than gnats buzzing in our ears. But in terms of venerable fables, advertising is actually more akin to the king in the Rumpelstiltskin story, everlastingly holding consumers hostage so we can produce gold.

Or, phrased less fancifully by the authors of *By Invitation Only*: "Major advertisers, not individual readers or viewers, are the primary 'customers' for mass media organizations, who essentially 'sell' the audience to advertisers." *Ladies' Home Journal* provided dramatic proof of this contention when it placed the following ad in *Advertising Age* magazine:

Hey Coke, want 17 1/2 million very interested women to think Diet? Better than one out of three Ladies' Home Journal readers buy and drink diet soft drinks. . . . And, we give you all these trim, fit readers at the lowest, most efficient [cost]. . . . We give you a very healthy environment for your ads, too. With editorial that feeds the appetite for information . . . [and] with lively articles about staying in shape. . . .

What makes the whole situation even more insidious, charges investigative journalist Eric Clarke in a scorching book aptly titled *The Want Makers*, is that "the more we are bombarded by advertising, the less we notice, and yet, almost certainly, the more we are affected."

Ironically, just three years after Twiggy's Manhattan triumph, she retired from modelling, saying she was sick of being "a thing, not a person." Her farewell statement might also have served as a fitting *finis* to the mania for extreme thinness she initiated, especially since she proceeded to gain 20 pounds so she could become a credible actress.

But no one paid attention, and the fashion revolution Twiggy inspired rolled on without her. The swinging "unisex" styles kept zinging across the ocean from London's Carnaby Street to boutiques that sprouted up like psychedelic mushrooms from Halifax to Vancouver. As youthful egalitarianism quickly supplanted high society's traditional influence on culture, mini-skirts climbed higher and higher, bodices grew tighter and barer, bras were discarded, and girdles were out of the question. Soon there was nowhere to hide any body that was chunkier than those of the bony young "birds" who populated the coffee-houses and discothèques, as well as magazines, movies, and television.

If all this had been just a madcap fling for youngsters who were trying out their newly acquired wings, no permanent damage would have been done, and relative cultural sanity would have prevailed as usual. But the stylish image the youngest, slimmest women achieved so effortlessly was no longer just one of *many* available choices, depending on one's age, size, and circumstances.

This variety had always pertained in the past, as evidenced (for example) by the simultaneous screen popularity—just before the youthquake of the late 1960s—of *zaftig* movie stars like Marilyn

Monroe, Elizabeth Taylor, and Sophia Loren; ethereal Audrey Hepburn; petite teenager Sandra Dee; and bony spinster types portrayed by Katharine Hepburn and Thelma Ritter. Concurrently, other prominent women were as variously sized as U.S. first ladies Mamie Eisenhower (stout) and Jacqueline Kennedy (svelte) and, in Canada, two wildly disparate prime ministers' wives: Marion Pearson (plump) and Margaret Trudeau (flower-child slender).

But *after* Twiggy, the standard of beauty crystallized into a single dominant body image mandated by those who, knowingly or unwittingly, were doing the bidding of marketers. So, even when hot pants, hip huggers, and go-go boots disappeared into history, just one body style remained entrenched as the only acceptable one to have.

The unprecedented power of this mandate is evident from the fact that every woman who aspired to stay in fashion had to obey the onerous new imperative. Standards became so extreme that the Duchess of Windsor's thirty-year-old aphorism—"A woman can never be too thin (or too rich)"—was taken literally for the first time. Even Jacqueline Kennedy, who *had* looked as narrow as an arrow throughout the Camelot years, now went on a diet to achieve the "right" look.

Meanwhile, those who couldn't clone the new image began what would become thirty years of alienation, marginalization, and exploitation. The devastating effects of this phenomenon on Fat Chicks like me, and the emotional distress that escalated into an epidemic of eating disorders among smaller women, are detailed throughout this book. For now, let's see how an already dire situation was exacerbated when women's bodies were taken hostage by what Susan Faludi rightly dubbed the "backlash" against women's equality.

A Pig in a Poke

As the 1960s ended, feminists began achieving a modicum of credibility, despite stubbornly reactionary media obfuscation of their mission. Principles and aspirations that had been virtually forgotten in the half-century since women won the vote began drifting back into national consciousness on both sides of the border. Early consequences of this reawakening included, in Canada, the impetus for the Royal Commission on the Status of Women (1967), and, in the United States, the Women's Strike for Equality on the fiftieth anniversary of American female suffrage (August 26, 1970). The parallels between the 1920s and the 1970s were unmistakable, and extended well beyond the pro-youth transformation of music, movies, and other forms of popular culture—and the illusory fashion "liberation," once again represented by shorter skirts, scantier undergarments, and boyishly thin physiques.

What's far more significant is that the same Big Lie was trotted out by the powers-that-be in each era—namely, that society's blessing on these superficial changes somehow added up to the very freedom and empowerment women were demanding. This was howlingly untrue, as many cultural commentators, including Faludi, have pointed out. In *Backlash: The Undeclared War against American Women*, she writes that "the feminist entreaty to follow one's own instincts became a merchandising appeal to obey the call of the market—an appeal that diluted and degraded women's quest for true self-determination."

Historian Roberta Pollack Seid translates the situation into the No Fat Chicks context in a powerful book titled *Never Too Thin: Why Women Are at War with Their Bodies*: "Ironically, as the role of women was redefined, theoretically empowering them, these very freedoms trammeled them even more with one enduring traditional pressure—the pressure to be thin."

The result? A cunning and hugely profitable smokescreen stalled the crucial advances women were on the verge of achieving in the 1970s, exactly as its predecessor had done in the 1920s.

Zoom with me now back to some smoky boardroom in an advertising agency on, say, Bay Street or maybe Madison Avenue, circa 1968. The fellas slumped around a long shiny table seem a little dejected. That's odd. Just yesterday, they'd been jubilantly slapping each other's backs as they pored over the latest stats from the demographics department.

Yum yum! Eighty million Baby Boomers busting loose, feeling their oats, making their own money, just ripe for the plucking. And half of them are women—who'll buy anything that promises to make them beautiful. Here comes my cottage in Muskoka. Hell, make it Palm Beach!

But the topic on today's agenda is bumming everybody out. Seems there are these broads writing books and making speeches and stomping around capital cities saying the end is nigh for every scheme and dream that worked so well in the past. This so-called New Woman is rising out of the rubble and rip-offs that lured her mother and grandmother into pursuing happiness by shopping their fool heads off. But the new chick says she's got no use for such gewgaws and fripperies. She's set her sights on—get this, Fred— saving the world. What the hell are we gonna do?

Fred takes a long pull on his $5 stogie, swings his Guccis up on the table, and chuckles. Sit down, shut up, and stop getting your knickers in a twist, pal. The way out of this one is strictly a no-brainer. It worked before and it'll work again. Can't miss. All we gotta do is give her what she wants.

Say what!!??

Ever heard of a little thing called a pig in a poke? That's when you say you're giving some stupid schnook what he asks for but you keep it wrapped up in what Southerners call a poke sack. Trust me, you tell him. You asked for a pig and that's what's you're getting. It's a wonderful pig. Probably the best in the world. You're lucky to get it. Off goes the schnook, happy as a clam. And by the time he finds out that what he really bought is a worthless alley cat, it's too late.

You say these broads want liberation? Well, we'll give it to 'em. Morning, noon, and night. They're demanding freedom and power? No problem. All we gotta do is keep coming up with the best damn poke sacks there's ever been.

Break out the brandy, boys, and let's get to it. The world is still our oyster.

Seen in retrospect, the marketing campaigns that responded most directly to what was then called "women's lib" were blatantly transparent. The most obnoxious example was, of course, "You've come a long way, baby," the ubiquitous slogan for Virginia Slims cigarettes.* But many similar ads, such as the grinning, pant-suited blonde striding aggressively on behalf of Charlie perfume, echoed the same strategy of appearing to salute women's new power while simultaneously implying that the truly savvy Ms. could score even bigger by buying their products. And the Canadian federal government's unpopular and glaringly half-hearted "Why Not?" ad campaign (as in: Why not let women enter this or that

---

*Virginia *Slims*. Get it? This name proved so successful that the company later upped the ante by bringing out Virginia SuperSlims. Slogan: "More than just a sleek shape."

profession?) publicizing the U.N.'s International Women's Year in 1975 was an even more feeble attempt at piggybacking.

Except for this new "libber" twist, though, there wasn't anything novel about conning women into painting, powdering, perfuming, or clothing themselves. What apparently came into sharper focus among market researchers at this time—judging from the tenor of the contemporary articles and ads—was that the *real* gold to be mined was the body itself.

Not only was there a finite limit to how many new lipsticks, hair dyes, or dresses a woman was likely to buy in an average day, but a sharp downturn in both women's apparel sales and magazine subscriptions at this time evidently set off an alarm. It must have seemed just possible that the pesky feminists would rouse their sisters from their Rip Van Winkle snooze and foment widespread rejection of advertising's fundamental message—that women are not good enough as nature makes them.

But if the conviction could be implanted deeply enough, and reinforced strongly enough, that slender bodies actually *symbolize* the attaining of revolutionary goals, there'd be no end to the products that could be dreamed up and sold. Bodies as skinny as Twiggy's are not easy to attain or sustain. So if you're not born that way, you'll need a lot of "help." (Right, Fred?)

With that epiphany, the brainwashers kicked into overdrive. "Corporations saw . . . that there was gold in them thar thighs," writes media professor and critic Susan J. Douglas in *Where the Girls Are: Growing Up Female with the Mass Media.* It is arguably the best of a slew of recent blow-the-lid-off books by a new generation of reform-minded women who are picking up where those 1920s pioneers were forced to leave off. In it, Douglas argues that the mass media and the marketers who fund them did indeed co-opt the tenets of the women's liberation movement—and then sold them back to us in a variety of artful disguises, as well as in such blatant rip-offs as that employed by Weight Watchers to introduce a new low-calorie bread: In a TV commercial and print ads, a trio of slim young women danced and sang ecstatically about the "taste of freedom."

As time wore on, more and more marketers of more and more weight-loss products wised up to the "libber" strategy. The resulting ad campaigns ranged from pitches as obvious as Weight Watchers' to the far more subtle approach employed by pedlars of exercise equipment. These slick geniuses succeeded in almost subliminally equating physical fitness with political and economic power—even though what they *really* sell amounts to little more than personal narcissism.

Editorially complementing this type of advertising were scads of articles purportedly celebrating women's new clout. Seen through 1990s eyes, though, many of these were clumsily patronizing, and others were downright demeaning. The latter category included, in 1970 and 1971 alone, such outrageously sexist titles as "Women's Lib, the Tooth Fairy and Other Myths" (*Ladies' Home Journal*), "Pronoun Envy" (*Newsweek*), "Hey, Lady, What Are You Doing Here?" (*McCall's*), "Bride of Frankenstein" (in *Mademoiselle*'s "Man Talk" column), and "It's Really the Men Who Need Liberating" (*Life*).

In Canada, the "clumsy" category was defined by a piece by Hartley Steward in *Toronto Life* in 1970 titled "Learning to Live with Women's Lib." Noting that the average male reacted to feminism "much as an Arab prince would respond to a sit-down strike in his harem," Steward went on to warn men that "you'll probably notice a sort of creeping feminism . . . [in] a whole range of choices hitherto considered the male prerogative. . . ."

Even worse was "Watching All the Liberated Girls Go By" (*Chatelaine*, 1971), in which psychiatrist John Rich began: "All mass movements have a lunatic fringe, but women's lib seems to have a lunatic centre," and then repeatedly used the term "Libchicks." And the *Vancouver Sun* characterized the Royal Commission on the Status of Women as "a wailing wall for every scatterbrain, malcontent and pope in skirts."

Marketers were generally much savvier than that. And their most ingenious light bulb blinked on when they apparently realized that the way to guarantee profits forevermore was to cast the standard of bodily perfection at lower and lower weights, until the "ideal" actually became unattainable for about 95 per cent of female body types—but was ostensibly possible for those who purchased the right products.

There were even bonuses for those who swiped liberation's rhetoric: A woman didn't necessarily have to think of herself as a feminist to be hooked. If what she wanted was control of her professional career, this was soon so inextricably linked with controlling her size that salaries and opportunities for heavy women plummeted (as we shall see in Chapter

6), so she probably had to diet. If she wanted to look good to men, other women, or just to herself, as "good" was defined by the mass media, the standard was now so thin that she probably had to diet. If she wanted to fit into the most stylish clothing, which was rapidly being downsized (as discussed in Chapter 9), she probably had to diet. Even if all she wanted was to feel good about herself as an intelligent, responsible person who was maximizing her potential, she probably had to diet.

Achieving Orwellian Saturation

As with other propaganda campaigns throughout history, it wasn't long before what started out as an artificial, self-serving premise worked its way into the popular culture as accepted wisdom. A given. Just the way things are. Anything else becomes, at best, passé and, at worst, anathema.

Thus we ended up surrounded by inescapable reinforcement for the proposition that all women must be thin. It flickers before our eyes every waking moment in the estimated 1,500 images seen daily by North Americans in print ads, TV programs and commercials, posters, store windows, billboards, movies, sports, magazine features, books, greeting cards, cartoons, and even gag items.

Editors and writers developed amnesia about all but one body type. Casting directors narrowed their choices for plays, movies, and TV down to skinny and young. Comedians, both professional and amateur, easily grasped that, even amid growing "political correctness" regarding other minorities, it was still okay to make fun of fat people. Talk shows, if they addressed any facet of obesity at all, usually tried to outdo the competition by creating a circus freak-show atmosphere. And somebody somewhere let out a guffaw, slapped his knee, and came up with the moronic bumper-sticker that gave this book its name: NO FAT CHICKS!

As the iconographic power of slimness grew, even the venerable Coca-Cola bottle was streamlined to eradicate its classic hourglass shape. Later, the lady in the flowing robes who had graced every Columbia Pictures movie for seventy years would be whittled down. Later still, the Saks Fifth Avenue store mannequins that had been cast to resemble actress Grace Kelly's size 8 were replaced by size 6 clones of "superwaif" model Kate Moss.

In the magazines and on the fashion runways, the twirling girls grew thinner and younger by the year. In the movies, the actresses looked skinnier and skinnier. Watching television, we were trained by clever dialogue and canned laugh-tracks to disregard the evidence before our eyes and accept that, in *The Mary Tyler Moore Show*, for example, the Rhoda character was too fat, while the Mary character, played by an actress whose diabetes kept her gaunt, was ideal—which, by then, was synonymous with normal.

As time went by, the beauty images women were trying so hard to imitate drifted even farther from reality. The weight of actresses, models, beauty-pageant contestants, and even *Playboy* pin-ups plunged from a reasonable 8 per cent below that of the average North American woman in the 1950s to 23 per cent lower by 1988 and has continued dropping ever since.

Meanwhile, real women were getting plumper with every technological advance that made physical labour obsolete, and with every new fat-laden prepared food that came on the market. By the early 1990s, the average weight and height of North American women was about 140 pounds and 5' 4". But the brand of beauty they were being urged to attain was epitomized by Kate Moss, who weighs in at a wispy 105 pounds. Although, at 5' 7", Moss is only a few inches taller than the average woman, most of the other "supermodels"—who, by now, had achieved such primacy over actresses and other types of beauty icons that they've spawned their own magazine*—stand 5' 10" or taller. The futility of trying to eradicate this wide a gulf should have been obvious. Yet, by the early 1990s, millions of women were obsessively attempting to do just that.

All of which meant that, as one leading physiological authority expressed it, "We now have cultural norms that are way out of sync with our biological heritage."

As if all this weren't enough to put "the feminine esthetic at odds with femaleness in its natural state," as Susan Brownmiller phrases it in *Femininity* (another good contribution to setting the record straight), the beauty icons were becoming more and more bogus. Many, if not most, models were undergoing cosmetic surgery, usually to enlarge their breasts—thus manufacturing an anomalous body type virtually

---

*Elle Top Model, published in twenty-three countries.

unknown in nature: buxom, but as skinny and narrow-hipped as a boy.

And the photographs that inundated the visual landscape were also being "perfected" by increasingly sophisticated technology, which evolved from camera air-brushing to digital computer techniques. So, to quote a recent *New York Times* article, women now aspire "not to look like the great beauties of the generation but like an invented, manipulated, unattainable idea of beauty, a product of camera, darkroom, and computer technique."

This practice reached a peak of outrageousness (one hopes!) with the September 1994 cover of *Mirabella* magazine. The slender, unclad lass whom the editors touted as "personifying today's all-American beauty" wasn't even human. She was a "cyber chick" entirely concocted by a computer.

For real women, as we will see in the next chapter, the increasingly frantic dieting turned out to be the equivalent of a forced march in the wrong direction. Food-deprived bodies fought back, exactly as they were programmed to do during cave-age famines, with the result that millions of women got fatter and fatter just by trying to get thinner and thinner. Like cars stuck in mud, the more we accelerate our efforts, the more hopelessly we are trapped.

Recently, a bold new brand of poke sacks was launched. Dieting is *out*, rejoiced a choir of familiar voices; "fitness" is what the truly modern, truly intelligent woman owes herself. It's a fine concept. Too bad fitness is just a euphemism for thinness. Too bad that yowling from the depths of this chic new poke is the same scrawny critter that's been trapped there for three decades, repeating the same old tune: "Buy, buy, buy!"

Bottom Line

Put plainly, what I call the "billion-dollar brainwash" was created by deliberately teaching women of all sizes to hate our bodies. And three Big Lies underpin the entire process: (1) that fatness is the worst cultural catastrophe possible for women; (2) that obesity *must* be voluntary because slenderness is available to all who pursue it with sufficient diligence and money; and (3) that the sole cause of all excess weight is therefore despicable self-indulgence.

   Brainwashing the entire population to accept these lies unquestioningly paves the way for stigmatizing Fat Chicks—and guarantees that
women *of all sizes* will frantically spend money on products that promise
escape from that punishment. As the definition of the "ideal body" was
set thinner and thinner, it literally became the impossible dream for the
vast majority of women.

   But am I saying the "billion-dollar brainwash" is really a conspiracy?
Yes. Absolutely. The same kind of *de facto*, unorganized, ethereal conspiracy that kept women from voting for so long and prevents us from
achieving economic and political equality today. Can I prove it? Nope.
All I can do is piece together the facts that are known, some for quite a
while now, until the irrefutably horrifying puzzle portrait is revealed.

CHAPTER THREE

Misery Loves Companies

Never in the history of the whole hapless world has there been a hoax as lucrative as the "billion-dollar brainwash." It is the closest thing to alchemy ever discovered—with a formula that turns fat into gold, and prejudice into profit. For marketers of a crammed cornucopia of weight-loss products, services, books, and clubs, it's like manufacturing your own customers. Better: It's like having them manufacture themselves and march to your door like a legion of zombies.

As historian Carter G. Woodson once wrote about African Americans: "When you control a man's thinking, you do not have to worry about his actions. You do not have to tell him not to stand here or go yonder. He will find his 'proper place' and stay in it."

Nothing could exemplify this dynamic better than a pair of appalling attitudinal surveys: one done in 1984 by *Glamour* magazine, in which a huge majority of the 33,000 female respondents declared that they would rather lose 10 to 15 pounds than achieve any other goal in life, despite the fact that only 25 per cent were overweight and another 25 per cent were underweight; and another poll, reported in *Newsweek* in 1990, in which 11 per cent of the surveyed couples stated that, if informed in advance about a foetus's predisposition to obesity, they would opt to abort it.

Consequently, just fourteen years after Twiggy's debut, the annual take by the multifaceted weight-loss industry had burgeoned to an estimated $10 billion. That preposterous total would quadruple during the following decade and a half. All in all, as of this writing, the latest figure being cited by a credible source (the *New York Times*) as the total annual spending in North America on weight-loss products and services is more than $40 billion.

And the true genius of this cavalcade of chicanery is that it prospers despite achieving the exact opposite of what it promises. No one even makes the connection between the deliberately induced delirium and the fact that, during the three decades since Operation Twiggy hit the Atlantic beachhead in 1967, most of us have become, not thinner, but fatter.

So, by the desperate, gullible millions, we continue to scrape up every dollar we can spare and trudge off to spend it on an array of snake-oil products and services that are almost as idiotic as the mythical fat-eating tapeworms women used to wish for, or the absurdities Dave Barry dreamed up for one of his best humour columns ever. My favourite among his imaginary devices: the "incredible Squee-Zer-Ciser with the revolutionary new Iso-Flex Modular Torsion Units, which look to the untrained eye like rubber bands."

Am I exaggerating? You decide, after checking out the following outrageous examples of the innumerable diets, gimmicks, books, and club techniques that began trickling onto the scene in the late 1950s, revved up to warp speed a decade later, and roll on inexorably today like a monstrous avalanche.

The first pebbles to roll down a molehill that became a mountain of mendacity were laughable. These included such gadgets and gizmos as a "magic couch" called the "Slendro Massager Table," on which clients at some 100 branches were gently jiggled during the mid-1950s for $2 per session. Then there were Slim-Skins—rubber blow-up trousers attached to a vacuum cleaner so women could, according to an ad, "lose seven times faster." If that wasn't rapid enough, you could try mummy-like body wraps soaked in an astringent that caused dehydration; or a rolling pin with suction cups; or a waist-constricting, heat-exhaustion–producing Astro-Trimmer sauna belt. All these products were, of course, "guaranteed" to make enormous amounts of flab disappear in incredibly short periods of time.

Later on, there were earrings to be massaged to thwart hunger pangs, but they usually produced only nausea; an electric "eating fork" with built-in red and green lights to tell you when to eat and when to stop; and a battery-operated device that yelled at you whenever you opened your refrigerator: "Are you eating again? Shame on you! No wonder you look the way you do." Later still, talking scales voiced similar insults, and subliminal-suggestion tapes played soothing music while, underneath, a faintly audible (and wholly false) message was nattered: "The fat is melting away."

Another range of choices—pills and potions—really took off after the introduction, in 1960, of a powdered mix called Metrecal (an abbreviation for "metered calories"). Just add water, stir, and consume instead of food. A few years later, there was liquid protein, a powder ostensibly consisting of just enough essential minerals to keep the body from looting lean muscle tissue. Four million people ended up trying it, according to Newsweek, despite the fifty-eight related fatalities investigated by the U.S. Centers for Disease Control. Liquid protein's death-defying appeal was enhanced by the marketing flair of Dr. Robert Linn, who, in The Last Chance Diet, claimed that his own brand, Prolinn, had "the full pink tint of a Beaujolais. . . ." And Prolinn was labelled with an ingenious "cover-your-assets" statement that soon became the anthem of the entire weight-loss industry: "The program cannot fail. Only you can fail."

If liquid protein didn't appeal, you could try human chorionic gonadotropin (HCG), composed in part of the urine of pregnant women, administered by expensive daily injections in the gluteus maximus, and supposed to dissolve fat. Did it work? Sure, as long as you ate only the accompanying daily 500 calories prescribed by doctors, who sometimes augmented HCG with amphetamines and/or diuretics to ensure convincing losses.

Yet another option for desperate dieters was delving into the many books that began jockeying for position in the health and self-help sections of bookstores. Actually, a few—such as Pray Your Weight Away, and Help Lord—The Devil Wants Me Fat!—even muscled their way onto the religion shelves. For those who stopped short of seeking divine intervention, there were tomes such as Eat Fat and Grow Slim, which was so ineffective that it quickly flopped. Yet, in 1961, an identical concept was published by Dr. Herman Taller as Calories Don't Count. Some 2 million copies were snapped up, even after the good doctor was convicted of conspiracy and mail fraud for touting and prescribing the (equally useless) safflower capsules he himself helped manufacture. Taller got away with a suspended sentence, a $7,000 fine, and a stern "tut tut."

Dr. Atkins' Diet Revolution, published in 1972, trumpeted the sensational claim that the more fat one ate, the better. This preposterous notion so angered the American Medical Association that Atkins was called before a congressional committee in 1979. But, since his books continued to sell in the millions, he continued to laugh his way to the bank and write more best-sellers.

By 1983, there were 360 diet books in print. One of the most extreme of the gotta-have-a-gimmick biggies was *The Beverly Hills Diet*, in which author Judy Mazel recommended six weeks of eating practically nothing but fruit. Anticipating (correctly) that this would produce serious diarrhoea, she wrote: "The more time you spend on the toilet, the better. On watermelon days especially, you can expect to urinate a lot. That's the idea."

If that wasn't horrid enough, you could try *Fasting as a Way of Life*, in which Dr. Allan Cott addressed the obvious problem of starvation by callously claiming that "any so-called hunger 'pangs' are simply normal gastric contractions or stomach spasms. They represent the sensation of hunger rather than true hunger."

By 1995, there were more than 700 weight-loss-related titles listed in *Books in Print*. These included *The Complete Scarsdale Medical Diet*, *Beyond Pritikin*, *Dr. Atkins' Diet Revolution*, *Fit for Life*, *Medical Makeover*, *The Fat to Muscle Diet*, *The Diet-Type Weight-Loss Diet*, *Thin So Fast*, *Eat to Succeed*, *The 35 Plus Diet*, *The 120-Year Diet*, *The Two-Day Diet*, *The Hilton Head Metabolic Diet*, *The Beverly Hills Diet*, *The I Love New York Diet*, *The Bloomingdale's Eat Healthy Diet*, *The Rice Diet Report*, and *The Macrobiotic Diet*.

For those who preferred less solitary pursuits than reading, there were soon thousands of coast-to-coast fitness centres. So many, in fact, that, by 1992, annual revenues were estimated at $8 billion in the United States and more than $321 million in Canada. If fitness were, indeed, the real stock-in-trade of these enterprises, their gargantuan profits might be justifiable. But truth would prevail only if they changed their names to "thinning centres." Of course, this prospect is as unlikely as the possibility that they'll begin revealing their duplicitous techniques—which include persuading desperate people to sign contracts for expensive promises that cannot possibly come true; routinely selling far more memberships than their spaces can accommodate (deliberately depending on high attrition rates by discouraged members); and contributing to the dangerous myth that we cannot be fit unless we incessantly "go for the burn" with complicated, exhausting workout routines that few of us can actually perform without the "professional" help available only at their establishments. The implication that there's no use in the rest of us even trying is unforgivable.

(By the way, if you ask a Fat Chick what it's like to don a leotard and stroll into the average fitness centre, she'll probably say she can't remember, because it's been so long since she ventured into the Land of the Snobbish, Sneering, Neon-Thonged Skeletons. Don't believe her. The crushing embarrassment of being the fattest, most blatantly stared-at and laughed-about person in the room never goes away. What actually disappears, in this order, are a Fat Chick's money, her confidence, and, finally, herself—never to return to the killing-field.)

But the senior partners among the anti-fat profiteers were definitely the weight-loss clubs. Among the first in North America was TOPS (Take Off Pounds Sensibly). There was a small membership fee, but nothing to buy—only a swell chance to damage your self-esteem forever, because the club's *modus operandi* was based on shame.

Like those of its many successors—most notably Weight Watchers—TOPS sessions generally began with communal weigh-ins, before which most women jettisoned every scrap of clothing and jewellery possible, right down to their wedding rings, to reduce the scale readings. This was followed by Alcoholics Anonymous-style confessions, with each member guiltily citing dietary transgressions, or triumphantly recounting her successful abstention. The group would then boo or applaud, accordingly, after which a (formerly fat) counsellor would praise the losers and probe the rationalizations of the gainers. A typical exchange (quoted in a contemporary publication) went as follows:

COUNSELLOR: Why did you gain?
MEMBER: It was my birthday.
COUNSELLOR: So what did you give yourself—a pot of fat?

In the early years, TOPS sessions were even crueller than that. Members who hadn't lost weight during the previous week were required to wear pig bibs, deposit fines in a piggy bank, and sing "the pig song," which went: "We are plump little pigs/Who eat too much/Fat, fat, fat/Fat and forlorn."

For those who gained, rather than lost, it was even worse. They were tried in a "court of weights and measures," and placed in the running to be crowned "Queen Pig."

Still Strictly Caveat Emptor

If you're thinking we're too sophisticated to fall for this kind of senseless bunkum today, think again. Among the hottest current front runners are a Japanese-manufactured seaweed soap that claims to lather fat away; any number of "organic" creams that supposedly make unsightly cellulite vanish; and dozens of dubious products available in, not only pharmacies and supermarkets, but gas stations. These sport such aggressive names and slogans as Thera-Thin ("Neutralizes All the Calories in the Food You Eat!"), and Maxi-Slim ("The Ultimate Weapon Against Fat"), and are frequently packaged with testimonials from doctors. And, stacked in bookstores from coast to coast right now are such transparently dubious best-sellers as *The Angels' Little Diet Book* (in which the author insists that heavenly helpers enabled her to lose 150 pounds), *Good-Bye Diet Demon, Lose Weight Religiously, 32 Days to a 32-Inch Waist, Sun Signs Dieting, Gone With the Fat,* and *The Love Hunger Weight-Loss Workbook.*

But by far the most pervasive, and persuasive, of the would-be latter-day miracle workers are commercial diet programs such as Jenny Craig, Weight Watchers, Nutri/System, Diet Center, and Physicians Weight Loss Centers—all of which are excoriated by the authors of a powerful exposé called *Feeding on Dreams: Why America's Diet Industry Doesn't Work.* What these "unqualified, unregulated, and unlikely to change" companies really sell, say authors Diane Epstein and Kathleen Thompson, are hope and instant gratification—"no work, no muss, no fuss. Just walk through our doors . . . and we'll turn your world right side up and put a smile on your face."

How do the programs lure so many millions of customers despite their, by now, well-publicized failure rates of 95 to 98 per cent? Epstein knows all too well. She worked for twenty years at weight-loss companies she now declines to name, for fear of being sued. The trickery begins, she says, with advertisements heralding low, no-strings-attached, introductory offers. Especially ubiquitous after New Year's to capitalize on post-holiday guilt,* these are usually just classic "bait-and-switch" techniques designed to lure customers into showing up, ostensibly for individualized free consultations—but actually to be bombarded with high-pressure sales pitches. Epstein says that any counsellor caught deviating from her company's telephone script by quoting the real fees is automatically fired.

So what *are* the actual costs, what do they buy, and what happens when an unsuspecting woman walks in the door? It varies, but not by much. To begin with, there will almost certainly be a warm welcome from attractive, slender, female "counsellors." These women may or may not be wearing crisp white lab coats that suggest medical qualifications few of them actually possess. They will undoubtedly weigh the customer and measure her pertinent girth—although the resulting numbers may be artificially increased by a deliberately loose measuring tape, and/or the secret depressing of the scale by a sly finger. In any case, the numeric results will be dutifully recorded in a "personalized" chart. The friendly staffers may or may not take the customer's blood pressure and ask for details about her health history. All smiles and solicitousness, they will wax poetic about their dedication to providing their clients with supportive counsel, nutritional education, and behaviour-modification techniques.

This is window-dressing. The real function of these "counsellors" is to reel in the fish their companies' ads hook. To that end, they will probe their customer's motivation for wanting to lose weight. Is "that special man" less attentive these days? Are the kids reluctant to bring friends home? Is a deserved promotion proving elusive? Has appearing in a swimsuit become embarrassing? Not to worry. That's exactly what the counsellors are there to help with.

---

*In January 1994, for example, there was a "$50 million spending spree" on TV, print, and radio advertising for weight-loss products, according to *Marketing* magazine. This was, of course, complemented by a flood of editorial stories about how to lose the pounds supposedly packed on during holiday feasting.

Oh, no it isn't. Their real function is to "upsell" so effectively that what starts out as a "limited time offer" freebie, or possibly a $19.95 special, or perhaps a dollar-a-pound deal, metamorphoses into a commitment of hundreds, and even thousands, of dollars.

How? In most cases, the introductory fee will cover only the first four weeks. Remaining in the program longer may cost as much as $80 a week, although this total is frequently veiled by incremental packages, billed seductively as "super-savers," or some such. How many weeks will you be advised to sign up for? That depends on how many pounds there are between you and your "goal weight." Who sets this? Not the customer, but the counsellor, whose trusty computer has been programmed to recommend Twiggyesque weight levels.

The basic process is illustrated by an astounding, but typical, example cited in *Feeding on Dreams*. A woman walks into a diet centre with the notion of paying $19.95 to lose 10 pounds. No, no, insists the computer; you should really lose 20 pounds, at the eminently safe rate of 2 pounds per week. Now, says the counsellor, we'll need your cheque for the registration fee (which ranges from $52 to $79, depending on location), and, after that, the weekly fee ($37 to $53). And, since retaining weight loss is such a chore, we strongly recommend that you enroll in our maintenance program, which lasts a whole year and costs only $110. Plus, you can't go wrong with one of our motivational tapes, audio or video, for only about $90.

All of which adds up to a total tab of between $642 and $829, right? Not after another quick upsell, it doesn't. The dieter's got to eat something for those ten weeks, but counting calories and grams is so tedious and confusing. Far better to buy the company's very own packaged foods and drinks. What's the tab? About $70 to $80 per week, which brings the total up to between $1,342 and $1,629—a far cry from $19.95. And what will these big bucks buy? Usually just a hasty weekly weigh-in, a few (scripted) minutes of a counsellor's time, and yet another shopping session for packaged foods.

Is anyone ever turned away because she's not heavy enough? Most diet centres say yes, but admit that they keep no records to back up the contention. Which is why an enterprising television reporter, who weighs only 109 pounds, recently hid a camera under her size-XS sweatshirt and ventured into a Jenny Craig outlet. Would they help her achieve an ideal figure? asked Karen McCairley, of Toronto's Global TV news team. Absolutely, she was told. And all it will take is a registration fee of $170, and a six-month stint at $100 per week, including meals.

But let's say you're too savvy to get sucked into this expensive quicksand. You've decided to stick with good old feet-on-the-ground Weight Watchers. No phony lab coats, no quickie medical exams, and membership fees of only a reasonable $12 a week. Time was, your logic would have been impeccable. But, after the humongous H.J. Heinz Company bought Weight Watchers in 1980, the top brass suddenly saw that membership fees were nothing but small potatoes (pun intended). Since then, the once-humble support group has been transformed into a virtual supermarket of more than 250 food products bearing the WW label. From breakfast, to lunch, to dinner, with snacks galore in between, there are multiple choices of foods and drinks. They're now available in food stores, corner convenience marts, and even at Weight Watchers' own retail shops, which recently began appearing in cities all over the continent.

What's a typical tab these days? Repeating the example of a woman who sets out to lose 20 pounds in ten weeks, we would begin with a registration fee of approximately $39, followed by $12 per week for the remaining nine weeks. Meals, on WW's popular Personal Cuisine plan, will run about $70 per week for the first three weeks. That goes down to about $50 per week for the final seven weeks, because members are advised to begin resuming "normal" eating for two meals a day. Total: $707. Mind you, that's if she doesn't snap up any of the cute items on display at the WW shops and in advertisements in its monthly magazine, which range from gourmet coffee to tote bags, T-shirts, barbells, and cookbooks.

Is my use of the term "chicanery" at the outset of this chapter starting to seem more charitable than churlish? How about if I toss in a scandal that recently made headlines after governmental weights-and-measures inspectors raided a popular chain of reducing centres in England, where the scales had been rigged to fool customers into believing they're losing weight?

Or the fact that a company doesn't even *have* to run a club, or operate a centre, to get in on the action? If the "billion-dollar-brainwash" hadn't turned millions of us into desperate fools, would a company like Nestlé think it was worthwhile to launch a single new meal-replacement beverage—Ultra Slim-Fast—with a $77.6 million advertising splurge? Would Weight Watchers follow suit with an annual ad budget of $40 million, or Jenny Craig top even that with an annual $50 million binge, if they *weren't* convinced we're now so crazed we'll buy anything that promises weight loss—and spend any amount on it? "What have you got to lose?" Jenny Craig asks in most of its sales pitches, and in the title of one the founder's best-selling books. To which, I believe, we should all be replying: What indeed?

Jenny probably won't answer the question. But, incredible as it seems, a group of scientists did so fifty-two years ago—when, to their surprise, they learned exactly what's at stake for people who embark on deprivation diets.

To understand the basis for their conclusions, let's trek back to pre-history, when cave dwellers existed in feast-or-famine conditions. One week, they'd be gorging on woolly mammoth (or whatever), and the next, they'd be starving. The bodies of those who survived became very efficient at storing and retaining fuel—in the form of fat—to tide them over until their next feast.

Many millennia later, thanks to the legacy of natural selection, we're still programmed for survival in exactly the same way. Which means that, whenever we drastically limit our food intake, the technique that worked so well during cave-age famines locks in and holds on tight to the very fat we're trying to get rid of. How? By first using the other available elements of water and muscle. And only when those are drastically depleted does the body dip into its warehouse of fat for fuel. Then it cleverly slows down the metabolic rate at which activity burns off the remaining fat.

As if this fail-safe mechanism weren't enough to scuttle even the most determined reducing effort, what happens when we *stop* dieting is even worse. As we resume normal eating, the body, strip-mined by now of the lean muscle tissue that would have helped burn the increased food intake—if it hadn't been jettisoned to keep us alive—stays on "famine alert" by keeping our metabolic rate so sluggish that exercise and other activities burn off fewer calories than if we weighed the identical amount but had never dieted. As proven by several studies, most notably that done at Rockefeller University, each time we repeat the process, we incrementally boost our "set-point" (which is the biologically determined natural weight level our bodies strive to maintain). So, no matter how low our post-diet weight, even moderate eating packs the original pounds back on, plus more to boot, because the body is trying—even harder than before—to store up fuel.

Multiply all this by the number of times a woman has dieted, and you'll see what I've dubbed the "Cro-Magnon Catch-22" to the max. It's called the "yo-yo" syndrome, but that's not really accurate because a yo-yo stays the same size during its travels. But a body that endures repeated deprivations gets bigger, and more metabolically inert, with every bounce. Yet the sad irony is that most people, including Fat Chicks ourselves, *think* we stay heavy because we aren't trying hard enough.

This reality is, of course, the exact opposite of what we have been conditioned to believe. To counteract this smokescreen of misinformation, we have only to consider a ground-breaking scientific experiment that should convince even the stubbornest naysayer that the body's imperatives are implacable, and that food deprivation has such a powerful effect on the mind and body that depression and bingeing are the inevitable consequences.

It began three months before I was born and I can't help thinking that my life, and those of millions of others, might have been completely different if its findings had been embraced by the medical community. In November 1944, thirty-six conscientious objectors to the Second World War volunteered for a project at the University of Minnesota which remains the most comprehensive examination of semi-starvation ever undertaken. All the participants were healthy young men of average height and weight, and they were reportedly enthusiastic about the exercise, whose purpose was to learn how best to restore the health of people who were starving in the war zones.

For the first three months, the volunteers ate well-balanced meals, totalling 3,500 calories per day, and everything was peachy. Then their rations, although still sufficiently nutritious, were cut in half for three months. All hell broke loose. The formerly cheerful men became irritable, lethargic, apathetic, food-obsessed, and so argumentative that their regular group meetings had to be cancelled. Two of the volunteers had emotional breakdowns and had to leave the project, while a third chopped off the tip of his finger so he would be allowed to drop out. Even though the men were not starving, according to medical criteria, they were obsessed with food and barely functional. As Dr. William Bennett and co-writer Joel Gurin describe the situation in *The Dieter's Dilemma*: "The only clear fact was that prolonged deprivation of food was sufficient to produce extreme misery."

The final segment of the experiment was to have been a three-month period during which normal eating would be gradually reintroduced. But it didn't work out that way. Bennett and Gurin quote the original report: "The urgent desire for dietary freedom expressed by the men was extreme; postponement for [even] another week could have produced severe emotional crises and possibly open rebellion."

This despite the fact that the volunteers' daily intake was by then 4,000 calories—500 more than they had started with! And the men were still ravenous when they got together for a farewell banquet four months after the program ended. "The overriding sense of hunger these men felt was not appeased even by a large daily excess of food," say Bennett and Gurin. "Thus, even though their bodies were taking in considerable food energy, the profound psychological alteration that semi-starvation had produced remained with them."

Keeping this fascinating tale in mind, ask yourself how many diets you've ever been on that allowed you to eat *as many* calories—i.e., 1,750—as these guys nearly went bonkers on. In fact, how many of us eat that much even when we're *not* dieting? Fifty years later, this kind of deprivation is just considered normal for women.

Actually, for many dieters, it's even worse. As Naomi Wolf reminds us in *The Beauty Myth*, "At Treblinka [concentration camp], 900 calories was scientifically determined to be the minimum necessary to sustain human functioning." Yet some of the most popular diets of our time allow little more than *half* that amount.

When I fasted for five excruciating months, consuming only water and a liquid protein called Optifast, my daily intake was a scant 600 calories. Did I flip out? Not quite. I banished every food from my kitchen except mustard. And late at night, when I couldn't sleep because of hunger pangs, I found it comforting to dip my finger in the mustard and slowly lick it off. Pathetic, yes. But at least I didn't chop my finger off, like that poor conscientious objector, who was taking in nearly three times as many calories as I was and wasn't holding down a full-time job, let alone suffering psychological stress from a lifetime of feeling ashamed.

It has taken nearly half a century for medical scientists to begin catching up with their collegial ancestors. In fact, only in the past few years have researchers managed to shelve the automatic assumption that all obesity is caused by the sins of gluttony and sloth. Their subsequent discoveries—particularly the isolation of the "ob" gene that apparently regulates fatness in the human body—are extremely promising. Similarly, the recently announced theory that fitness can result from, not mandatory hours of exhausting daily workouts, but as little as thirty minutes per day of such sensible, practical exercise methods as walking, is a tremendous boon.

Needless to say, however, the anti-fat profiteers are not taking all this lying down. Their mega-fortune is threatened as never before by the prospect that the conundrum of obesity may soon be solved. Their collective back is not to the wall yet, but it's abundantly evident that they are fighting hard to preserve the status quo.

So, for the foreseeable future, our perspective on the "billion-dollar brainwash" must continue to be guided by this nutshell analogy: Suppose that 95 per cent of all the computers on the market either didn't work from the get-go or crashed later on. Whom would we blame? The designers of the computers? The manufacturers? The retailers who sold them? The advertisers who touted them as magical marvels? The repair technicians who, when asked for help, just shrugged their shoulders? How about the sales people—in the stores and in the mass media— whose persuasive powers clinched the deals by convincing everyone that life without computers wasn't worth living?

Answer: None of the above, because denouncing any of these factions could lead to financial disaster. The only way to protect profits is to blame the poor schnooks who bought the computers.

So we tell everyone it's the schnooks' fault the computers don't work.

And that, truth be told, they're really just a bunch of hopeless whiners anyway. Then we repeat, repeat, repeat this message until everybody believes it without question, laughs out loud at the schnooks, and takes every opportunity to accuse them of screwing up their own computers because they're lazy, stupid, and shiftless. Then we pass the belief on to children as accepted wisdom.

Result? Crazed by guilt and bewilderment, and desperately seeking a way to escape all the punishment, the schnooks have only one option: Buy another computer. And when that one doesn't work, buy another. And then another . . .

Substitute weight-loss schemes for computers, Fat Chicks for shnooks, doctors for technicians, and anti-fat profiteers for sales people, and you'll see the whole mendacious mess for what it is: a colossal con game.

CHAPTER FOUR

Prescription for Profit

In *Sleeper*, Woody Allen's quirky comedy about a man who's thawed out after two hundred years of cryogenic sleep, a couple of chain-smoking physicians chat about how amazingly misguided their professional ancestors were. In the twentieth century, says one, doctors actually thought steak, ice cream, and smoking were *bad* for people. The second quack shakes her head in amazement and takes another puff.

I wish I had something equally droll to say about the medical community's philosophical see-sawing on the subject of obesity. But there's nothing amusing about the fact that those whose sworn duty is to protect our health have mostly snoozed, squabbled, or profiteered during the past three decades, allowing the "billion-dollar brainwash" to flourish unimpeded.

Those *most* culpable in the creation of prejudice-for-profit are, of course, the actual pedlars of weight-loss products, and the advertisers and media vehicles that help them vilify Fat Chicks and traumatize all other females. That said, there's still plenty of blame left over for those inside and outside the health field, who either stand silently by or enthusiastically hop aboard the money wagon. The worst of these "unindicted co-conspirators" are in the medical profession.

Why haven't physicians seen through the No Fat Chicks charade and called a halt, especially after several major authorities officially declared that obesity is not a moral failing, but a disease? Because "fat people are waddling reminders of the failure of medicine to come to a safe, workable program for long-term weight reduction, just as poor people and homeless people are stark reminders of the failure of the economic system," charges author Hillel Schwartz's in *Never Satisfied: A Cultural History of Diets, Fantasies and Fat*, adding the scathing comment that, "like politicians, physicians blame the victims."

For the record, let me make clear, in no uncertain terms, that excess weight can be a health hazard for many individuals, especially those who are extremely heavy. Nothing in this book is meant to contradict that reality. The topic addressed here is *not* the legitimate physical consequences of obesity, but the false claims and psychological coercion used by profiteers to dupe virtually the entire population of North America.

Yet, in terms of the "big picture," national obesity-related health-care costs are estimated at a whopping $70 billion in the United States alone, which makes this the second-worst risk category (after smoking). I have no way of knowing how this figure was arrived at, or how accurate it is. And, unfortunately, I was unable to unearth an equivalent estimate applicable to the Canadian scene.

But there's *no* question that it's a stinging indictment of fat people, right? Not necessarily. Before blindly accepting this assumption, we must consider three crucial factors.

One: That the lion's share of the blame for creating this situation belongs, as we saw in previous chapters, far less to individual self-indulgence than to the propaganda machine that incessantly baits an array of traps to ensure that millions of people get fat and stay that way.

Two: Simple knee-jerk reasoning, as Marcia Millman expresses it in *Such a Pretty Face: Being Fat in America*, fails to take into account the fact that "fat people are blamed for problems and expenses [that are actually] created by the structure of our medical care system and its profit orientation. Blame for the failure of the health system is shifted to individuals who are actually more its victims than its perpetrators."

Three: The source for the sky-high estimate of weight-related health-care costs is former U.S. surgeon general C. Everett Koop. While I have no evidence suggesting that he is anything but sincere in his desire for a healthier country, the fact is that the organization Dr. Koop now fronts—called Shape Up America—is largely funded by Weight Watchers, which, in turn, is owned by the H.J. Heinz food conglomerate. And it was this giant company that recently chose Koop as the recipient of the $250,000 Heinz Award for his work on behalf of enhancing public health.*

In addition, the late 1994 news conference during which Koop announced the formation of Shape Up America, and denounced the gluttony and laziness that he cited as the causes for rampant obesity, was called mere days after widespread headlines about the discovery of the "ob gene." Again, as a layperson, I have no way of evaluating the data concerning this purported breakthrough. But I certainly *can* infer, from excitement within the scientific community, that the identification of a gene that causes excess weight levels may eventually lead to the elimination of fatness altogether. By logical extension, this will one day mean the loss of the $40 billion-plus annual fortune raked in by anti-fat profiteers!

To be completely explicit here, what I'm saying is that we've got to ask ourselves a cogent question: If we owned the largest weight-loss organization in the world—Weight Watchers—but our membership was dropping 15–25 per cent in the United States, and 32–40 per cent in Ontario alone, since 1989, wouldn't we have a vital stake in convincing everyone that obesity is their worst enemy? In addition, it seems worth mentioning that Koop's personal foundation has a hefty financial interest in selling newsletters and other material regarding the urgent necessity for nearly everyone to lose weight.

Yet, even more to the point, the startling truth the anti-fat profiteers don't want us to know is that "fat" and "fit" are *not* mutually exclusive terms. Extra weight is actually beneficial in various medical circumstances. And ample evidence supporting this heretical point of view is now turning up in study after study, as will see in a moment.

But even if being overweight *were* unequivocally unhealthy—to both individuals and the national economy—it's no contradiction to say that doctors should have done something to mitigate the forced march in the wrong direction dictated by the "billion-dollar brainwash." The medical profession has been on the front lines of the phenomenon. Doctors and other professionals have seen their patients'

Rump Parliament, a feisty size-acceptance publication described in Chapter 10, made its opinion crystal clear by publishing a cartoon depicting Koop as a hand puppet operated by the diet industry. Lecturing from the podium, he declares, "Let me assure millions of fat Americans … we're only doing this for your own good."

obsession and misery at first hand, and they possess the professional expertise to judge what is happening.

Or, rather, what *isn't* happening.

Instead of becoming permanently thinner by dieting, millions of women are steadily growing fatter, and suffering physically and emotionally along the way. Other patients stay slim only because they develop anorexia or bulimia, or deliberately court disaster by smoking to curb their appetites, or popping excessive amounts of amphetamines, diuretics, and laxatives. And countless other women have succumbed to hopelessness, as well as hostility from their doctors, by ceasing to seek medical treatment at all.

Why haven't doctors noticed all this? Or interpreted it correctly? Or evidently even cared? There are only a few possible reasons and, I'm sorry to say, they all have ugly names. Let's start with *prejudice*.

Ask any Fat Chick what it's like to go to the doctor and you'll get an earful about the antipathy, mistrust, indifference, and downright contempt with which we're often treated. And this is in addition to the dismal situation that all female patients find themselves in, according to the 1993 Commonwealth Fund study, which found that one out of every four women is "talked down to" by doctors, while one out of five is told that her problems are "all in her head." Another study, at the University of Rochester, concluded that the average length of time patients (of both sexes) are allowed to speak before being interrupted by their physicians is a scant eighteen seconds.

But it's even worse for Fat Chicks. Some physicians refuse to treat us at all until we lose weight. Others grow angry when we fail to achieve or sustain weight loss. Some don't bother with such elementary tasks as using large-size blood-pressure cuffs to obtain accurate readings on fat arms. And no matter what ailment we have, medical personnel often either imply that it's related to our obesity, or ignore our actual complaints and address themselves solely to our weight. This is roughly akin to taking your car into the shop because of a faulty carburetor but being told there's no use even discussing your problem until you get a new paint job.

I can personally attest to most of these discriminatory practices. For example, when I consulted a doctor about my broken ankle a few years ago, he told me to walk the length of a corridor. I assumed he was assessing the impairment of my gait—but, when I turned around, I saw that he was blatantly looking me up and down. "Have you ever thought about getting your stomach stapled?" he asked. Then, when he *finally* got around to discussing my ankle, he implied that the accident that caused it probably happened because of my excess weight—a ludicrous notion, as he'd have realized if he'd actually listened to my explanation.

Gynaecologists are among the worst offenders of all, according to a recent report to the U.S. Medical and Health Research Association. Examples included a traumatized woman who was brought to a hospital by police after being raped and was then harangued about her weight by the doctor examining her for legal evidence; and another patient who, while seeking a birth-control prescription, was asked who could possibly be interested in having sex with her, except maybe whale-hunting Captain Ahab. I will never forget my own humiliation when a gynaecologist roughly prodded my stomach and complained about having to examine me "through all this upholstery."

What can *possibly* account for such a massive dereliction of duty on the part of people who sincerely devote themselves to the caring profession? It's the "Lose 50 Pounds and Call Me in the Morning" syndrome, says biomedical researcher Paul Ernsberger, author of "Rethinking Obesity: An Alternative View of Its Health Implications," a special issue of the *Journal of Obesity and Weight Regulation.* In it, he cites studies revealing that "one third of family practice doctors admit to feelings of discomfort, distaste or hostility when treating obese patients." This contention is amplified by the results of a national survey published in the *Journal of Family Practitioners,* which indicated that a majority of the respondent doctors consider obese patients to be "weak-willed," "ugly," and "awkward."

These points echoed in a forceful speech by Dr. William Bennett, co-author of *The Dieter's Dilemma.* "Unlike most 'sick' people, who get some benefit from the presumption of innocence that goes with having a disease, fat people have been subjected to a guilt trip . . . [for being] 'bad' patients," he said, adding that "this state of affairs has disastrous consequences for [their] health care. . . . Examinations may be done carelessly with the excuse that 'the fat gets in the way.' Symptoms may not be pursued and treatments may be half-heartedly offered with the thought, often unspoken, 'If he doesn't care about his health, why should I?'"

Unfortunately, Dr. Bennett's speech, which was given at a National Association for the Advancement of Fat Acceptance (NAAFA) convention way back in 1982, seems to have fallen on deaf collegial ears.

The second ugly term that must be applied to many physicians is *ignorance*, which causes them to fail their overweight patients in at least half a dozen ways:

First, they simply accept the premise that thinness is desirable for everyone, regardless of age or circumstances, and continue ordering their patients to diet—despite overwhelming evidence indicating that all diets have a 95–98 per cent failure rate and are therefore useless at best, and dangerously counter-productive at worst. And anyone who's been handed yet another badly photocopied sheet of yet another "one-diet-fits-all" scheme has seen this type of ignorance and indifference at first hand. Also, repeatedly receiving handfuls of the "freebie" diet pills that the most recent pharmaceutical smoothie dropped off at your doctor's office—followed by expensive prescriptions for that exact brand of pills—is equally disillusioning. Other physicians even exacerbate their patients' problems by restricting dietary carbohydrates so severely that muscle tissue and water are lost, but no body fat. And, of course, many of the more enterprising doctors have dreamed up their own diet "philosophies" and gone on to fortune and fame with best-sellers extolling such absurd propositions as inducing weight loss by eating all the carbohydrate-laden meat, cream, and cheese you can swallow (Dr. Robert Atkins), or consuming nothing but "protein-sparing" powder the doctor himself concocts, manufactures, and markets (Dr. Robert Linn).

Second, many physicians overlook the distinct possibility that their patients' conditions (such as elevated blood pressure, high cholesterol, heart and gall-bladder maladies, and major depression) are caused, not by obesity, but by drastic and repeated weight-loss efforts, and/or stress provoked by being the object of rampant societal prejudice. Yet proof of these possibilities began to be compiled and published in medical literature as long ago as 1983, when University of Toronto researchers Janet Polivy and C. Peter Herman published *Breaking the Diet Habit: The Natural Weight Alternative*. Their findings were corroborated in later studies by Harvard Medical School and the Michigan Department of Public Health.

Third, many doctors either remain oblivious to, or quarrel among themselves about, such critical research breakthroughs as the discovery of fat cells; the set-point theory; the relatively benign effect of excess weight on "pear-shaped" women (whose hips and legs are heavy), as opposed to those who are "apple-shaped" (with excess fat concentrated higher up); the "Cro-Magnon Catch-22," which I described in Chapter 3; and the fact that repeated dieting and consequent yo-yo weight levels are considered by many experts to be a significant health hazard that may shorten life expectancy—not to mention making permanent weight loss all but impossible. As for evolving *nutritional* theories regarding the treatment and prevention of obesity, to resort to the vernacular: Forget about it.

Fourth, doctors allowed obesity and eating disorders to grow to epidemic proportions by rejecting every possible causation except patients' presumed overeating and laziness—even though several studies to the contrary have been widely publicized. Examples include an *American Journal of Clinical Nutrition* report in 1988, which proved that obese women actually eat, on average, less than thin women—just as we claim to; a study of identical twins at Quebec's Laval University by Dr. Claude Bouchard indicating the strong influence of genetic heredity on weight levels; and various other data suggesting the strong possibility that obesity may be caused, and/or exacerbated, by heredity, food intolerances, insulin resistance, maladaptive brown adipose tissue, and other physical factors.

Fifth, they forget nature's decree that some degree of fatness is beneficial to women, especially for child-bearing. Examples of this reality, cited in "Rethinking Obesity," include preserving menstruation in young women (because, as most anorexics, some bulimics, and many athletes have learned, when the level of body fat drops lower than approximately 15 per cent, hormonal disruption can cause this monthly process to cease) and reducing osteoporosis in older women (because severely limited body-fat levels can result in the loss of bone density); and lowering the incidence and/or severity of cancer and certain respiratory, infectious, and cardiovascular diseases. There has also been speculation that healthy people who *steadily* carry extra body weight may produce the same strengthening effect on bones, joints, the heart, and other muscles that happens when body-builders strap on artificial weights during their workouts. I'm no scientist, but I consider myself living proof of this because my strength and stamina—for walking, swimming, and stair-climbing, among other activities—often exceeds that of my thinner friends, and even my younger sister, who has always been slender.

And sixth, doctors who specialize in weight-loss surgery do so in defiance of frightening research results indicating not only the potential danger of the operations themselves, which can multiply an obese patient's mortality risk ninefold, but the fact that the failure rate, in terms of weight loss, is as high as 50–75 per cent. Additionally, some experts contend that each type of weight-loss surgery (including intestinal bypass, gastric balloons, and stomach stapling) carries the risk of at least two dozen different complications, including liver damage and severe malnutrition.

I was lucky enough to have escaped these terrifying complications when I had my stomach stapled in 1985. Unfortunately, the only permanent result of the surgery was, not weight loss, but the necessity of making myself throw up at least once a week, when food fails to "navigate" properly to its destination, either because of its texture or because I haven't paid enough attention to the copious chewing that's necessary to prevent internal "gridlock" on the way down. And, I assure you, you haven't lived until you've had to induce vomiting in a public restroom at a restaurant and then return to the dinner table trying to conceal your red face and watery eyes.

Worst of all is reflecting, at such times, on the fact that, in my case, stomach stapling was an entirely inappropriate procedure in the first place. When this type of surgery does work, it's generally because it averts voluminous eating, especially of dense food such as meat. Had my surgeon thought to interview me about my eating habits and preferences—rather than automatically assuming that my excess weight was caused by "standard" gluttony—he would probably have realized that, because I've never been a big eater and am practically a vegetarian, I was an unsuitable candidate for stomach stapling. Thus, like the untold number of women whose situation resembles mine, I could have been spared undergoing a major operation, having an unsightly 10-inch scar on my midriff, and enduring a lifetime of being obliged to make myself throw up.

The third ugly term that must be applied to far too many physicians is *greed*. Of course, the mother of all profit-makers in this context is weight-loss surgery. The number of intestinal bypasses leapt from 0 to 30,000 by 1980, and to 50,000 just two years later in the United States and, for variety, there was the insertion of gastric balloons, and then stomach stapling. Although initially mandated only for the "morbidly" obese (whose weight is twice as much as average), before long it was full speed ahead and damn the side-effects and failure rates described above. Even women whose weight was as low as 154 pounds received the operations.

When enthusiasm for weight-loss surgery flagged because of the failure rates and related deaths, along came liposuction (the mechanical sucking out of fat), which quickly became the most frequently performed cosmetic operation in history. Complications, such as infections and lung embolisms from dislodged balls of fat, gradually brushed some of the bloom off the rose. And then, in the mid-1980s, after some twenty deaths occurred, not to mention unsightly puckering, drawing, bumps, and unevenness for many of those who survived, liposuction's popularity drooped. Whereupon some genius promptly came up with modifications such as a smaller fat-sucking tool (cannula), and an equally refined new name: liposculpturing.

(By the way, sample fees for liposculpturing done in Canada range from $1,800 to $5,000. A "tummy tuck" will set you back $3,500 to $5,000, while similar work on your derriere will cost $2,000 to $6,000; and tightening up those inner thighs will whittle $2,000 to $6,000 from your bank balance.)

To illustrate how outrageous the situation has become, liposuction is now so commonplace that sales and discount days are being advertised—such as a recent one for the Zollman Center in Indianapolis, boasting: "27% Off Large Volume Liposuction. . . . " And a recent full-page ad for liposuction and other cosmetic surgery available at Jewish Hospital in Louisville, Kentucky, featured a photographically bloated "before" picture of Michelangelo's *David* beside an unretouched photo representing "after." What next? Two-for-one gastric balloons? Double-your-stomach-staples for one low, low price?

Collusion is another negative term that must be discussed in this context. What else can we call it when, every time the anti-fat profiteers dream up a new weight-loss scheme, thousands of doctors allow themselves to be courted, seduced, and kept in style by its marketers? When metabolism-boosting amphetamines were all the rage, for example, they were pre-scribed by the *billions*, despite such alarming side-effects as hypertension and insomnia. Eventually, these complications drew enough heat that the pills fell out of favour.

But in the early 1990s, new versions of "fat" pills once again began flooding the market. These include fenfluramine, which is suspected of causing brain damage in monkeys; and dexafenfluramine, which—according to health authorities in France—was killing between twenty and forty women per year until its use was restricted in 1995. Yet, the fol-lowing year, while dexafenfluramine was already in widespread use in the United States—and a potent new form of it called Redux* was approved by the FDA—the drug's complicity in some seventy-eight incurable cases of a lung disease called primary pulmonary hyperten-sion was under investigation in France.

When some sadist came up with jaw-wiring, physicians stampeded to buy the necessary tools. When the absolute bonanza of human chori-onic gonadotropin (HCG) injections came along, they had their patients literally lined up by the dozens every hour of the working day—and all it took was a minute or so with each one to weigh 'em, jab 'em, and head 'em out. Liquid-protein fasts represented the same kind of labour-saving jackpot in that patients simply zipped in to their physicians' offices every week to be quickly weighed (usually by nurses) and sold another batch of expensive powder, and then zipped back out. Figuring in routine initial lab tests brought their total tab up to $54.75 for every pound (temporarily) lost on the protein-sparing regimen, according to a report published in *American Health*.

Of course, devoting one's practice to these simple assembly lines left

---

*Weight loss industry observers currently project that Redux's annual revenues will run to $8 billion.

plenty of time for writing gimmicky best-sellers—scores of them have been published by doctors since Twiggy inadvertently let the genie of avarice out of the bottle in the late 1960s.

Still another way for enterprising doctors to clean up is to use their medical credentials to get on the boards of big-bucks marketers—and in line for the gravy train of research grants. With a little luck, nobody will breathe the nasty words "conflict of interest." But somebody did when NAAFA executive director Sally E. Smith tipped over this rotten-apple cart in a hard-hitting piece in *USA Today* in 1995. She named several prominent American physicians who frequently express pro-thinness opinions and—surprise!—just happen to be on the payroll of such anti-fat profiteers as Optifast and United Weight Control. Smith also reported that the ostensibly impartial 1991 conference of the North American Association for the Study of Obesity was actually funded by no fewer than eighteen diet-product and pharmaceutical biggies, including Jenny Craig, Weight Watchers, Nutri-System, Eli Lilly, Upjohn, and Hoffman-LaRoche.

As for psychotherapists, I doubt that Sigmund Freud ever modified his most famous question to "What do *fat* women want?" But if he were to travel from his time to ours and ask me to clue him in, I know exactly what I'd say: What we want, Herr Doktor, is simply respectful, informed, sincere help from those who followed in your footsteps.

It's certainly not what we're getting now. In fact, when troubled Fat Chicks are desperate enough to seek psychological lifelines, we frequently encounter the same sorts of disservice meted out by medical doctors. We ask (and pay) for help, but usually all we get are tranquillizers, antide-pressants, diet sheets, and lectures. Or years of expensive therapy aimed towards goals that are either impossible or reprehensible: lose enough weight to conform with society's unreasonable and unrealistic demands, or "adjust" to the role assigned us, which is basically two parts pariah to one part laughing-stock. With the result—which bears repeating yet again—that eating disorders, depression, and general misery have reached epidemic proportions within the female population.

Also eminently blameworthy are the assorted research authorities whose studies form the foundation for so much of the foregoing injus-tice. We, the desperate public, are drowning in contradictory messages from researchers who are evidently more interested in one-upping each other and playing yet another round of Duelling Grant Proposals than in buckling down to solving, or even alleviating, the problems and the paradox of obesity. Rambunctious *Stop the Insanity* author Susan Powter does a hilarious rap on this phenomenon to the effect that, every day, we're told something like: *Eat* lemons! And then, the next day: *Don't* eat lemons!

We've all seen exactly this kind of argument ping-ponging through headlines about (to name only a smidgen) margarine, oat bran, and pasta. And an even worse example of this sort of stalemating occurred when the National Institutes of Health first declared that yo-yo weight levels are lethally dangerous and, later, opined that they are not. Given the host of negative complications from this process described above, this callous shilly-shallying about practices that have a significant impact on the health and lives of millions of people seems like unforgivable irresponsibility.

Why the miasma of confusion? To a great extent, because of the disgusting fact that many research studies are sponsored by companies (or whole industries) with financial stakes in the outcome of purportedly objective scientific investigations. Shocking examples cited in an eye-opening book by Cynthia Crossen titled *Tainted Truth: The Manipulation of Fact in America*, include a research report "proving" that white bread does not cause weight gain—a study that turned out to have been sponsored by the Wonder Bread company. Another equally outrageous report—to the effect that chocolate inhibits tooth decay—was funded by a dubious organization called the Princeton Dental Resource Center, which was financed by the candy company that manufactures M&Ms and Mars bars.

The contradictory messages that reach the public thanks to this double-dealing have resulted, to a dangerous extent, in a "What the Hell" syndrome. It's a mental process by which we say to ourselves, consciously or subconsciously: Hey, as long as nobody can manage to tell me conclusively what I *should* or *shouldn't* eat, or when, whether, or how much to exercise, what can I do but let myself off the hook, and just do what I please? Might as well order up that double-cheese pizza with extra garlic butter. Who knows? Tomorrow, they might be saying *that's* what's good for us.

Bottom Line

I could go on and on about other ways in which physicians and other professionals in the health and fitness industries have failed to stop, or even denounce, the anti-fat propaganda machine and, instead, have lent it legitimacy by going for the gold themselves. Instead, let's end this lengthy indictment by quoting some of the criticism that's beginning to be expressed about their mistreatment of overweight patients. The Institute of Medicine, for example, in a recent policy statement calling for "a fundamental change in public thinking about obesity," reported to the U.S. Congress that "perhaps most lay persons, health care providers and even obese individuals themselves do not perceive the metabolic nature of the disease and thus view obesity as a problem of willful misconduct."

And concern about the epidemic levels of excess weight prompted Dr. William Dietz, director of clinical nutrition at the New England Medical Center in Boston, to take the extraordinary step of denouncing his colleagues in a recent op-ed piece in the *New York Times*. In it, he deplored the fact that "there is no commitment to obesity as a public health problem. We've ignored it, and blamed it on gluttony and sloth."

Yet another doctor, psychiatrist Theodore Isaac Rubin, broke ranks and defied collegial ethics two decades earlier with this scorching indictment in *Alive and Fat and Thinning* in America: "There is an increasing number of so-called doctors who run weight-reduction mills and inflict on their innocent victims all kinds of extreme, fad, and inappropriate diets. Weight reduction has become an ugly, multimillion dollar business, both inside and outside the confines of established medicine."

But, rather than obeying their Hippocratic oath to "first, do no harm," thousands of physicians have chosen instead to simply imitate the see-no-evil monkey. In so doing, they and their related health colleagues have allowed the anti-fat epidemic to rage out of control, garnering millions when Rubin wrote his book, and billions today spent by desperate people who've been convinced, beyond question, that—at all costs—they must be thin.

CHAPTER FIVE

Mind Warped

How does it *feel* to belong to the only group in contemporary society that's still considered fair game for prejudice, exploitation, and outright cruelty? What's it like to live exempt from the laws and standards of communal behaviour that now protect every other minority? It's like this, day in and day out:

Seven A.M.: "And finally, folks, this just in. According to a recent poll, 11 per cent of those surveyed say they'd choose abortion rather than have babies who were prone to obesity. There ya go. Better dead than fed."

"Jeez"—the disc jockey chortles to the news guy—"if only Roseanne's mom and dad had thought that way, we wouldn't have to watch her waddle to the fridge for another tub of that *loose meat!*"

"Yeah," cracks the sports announcer, "whadja think's in that stuff anyway? A jillion calories of *ugly?*"

All three laugh as, somewhere in the listening area, a plump hand reaches out and switches off the radio. The woman rises and pads down the hall. Showers, does her make-up and hair. Avoids all but superficial glances in the mirror. Better *not* to see what even she's been brainwashed into loathing.

Casts a wary eye at the scale, but resists the compulsion to step on it. For once, she'll stick to her vow not to begin every day with a guilty verdict from a hanging judge.

To her closet. Hot weather is forecast, but she chooses something that conceals the maximum amount of detested flesh. Snips out the double-digit size labels that testify against her even though the chance of anyone seeing them is zip. Curses the compromises she's been forced to make in style, colour, and price. You take what you can get.

Rouses and feeds the children and hustles them out the door. But not before battling another refusal to eat from her slender adolescent daughter. "I'm getting as, uh . . . as *big* as a pig, Mom." And not before being reminded that even her children think the word "fat" is an obscenity.

Drops the youngsters far enough from the schoolyard so other kids won't get the opportunity to embarrass them with nasty remarks about their mother.

Drives to her fitness centre, where she's blatantly stared at and whispered about from the time she hits the locker-room to the moment she heads back to her car. Oh well, she consoles herself for the umpteenth time, at least it's not as bad as her old club in Montreal. It forced members to swim underwater to the pool it shared with an adjoining hotel and then to remain submerged to the neck to spare hotel guests the sight of excess avoirdupois.

Rushes to a doctor's appointment. Tries to ignore the usual morons puffing out their cheeks and gesturing at her from other cars. Tries not to bite the doctor's head off when he bluntly implies that her sore throat is somehow the result of obesity. Decides not to ask him about a suspicious lump because that would mean undressing and being seen and touched by someone she obviously repels. Bad enough that he seemed annoyed at having to hunt for a large-size blood-pressure cuff.

To work. Not a great job, and certainly an unfairly meagre salary. But the only one she could get after being fired under rather suspicious circumstances. But two lawyers said she'd be a fool to sue. Her credentials landed her interviews for better jobs than this one, but her appearance got her crossed off the candidates' lists at first glance.

So what if her co-workers here exclude and avoid her as if they thought obesity was a communicable disease? So what if almost no one seems to see or hear her in meetings? So what if she has to remember not to turn so quickly that she catches colleagues gauging her girth? So what if the occasional wag anonymously sends her the latest Ann Landers column complaining that overweight people take up too much room on public transportation?

So what? It's a paycheque, and she needs it more than ever since her husband made good on his threat to walk out if she didn't get back to what she weighed when she was twenty. Funny how he forgets that, back then, he said she was too skinny.

One P.M.: Today she's got a rare lunch date with a friend. So at least the gang at the company cafeteria won't be checking out her tray. It isn't as embarrassing when she doesn't actually know the diners who peer disapprovingly over their menus and glare when she squeezes between their tables.

Five P.M.: To group therapy. "What can I do about my constant anger, doctor? . . . Why can't they understand that just because we haven't succeeded doesn't mean we haven't tried our hearts out? . . . Why don't they just tell us not to *breathe* and be done with it?"

Six P.M.: Her hair is sorely in need of a trim, but she's sick of having everyone stare when she refuses to change into a smock that's way too small. And she's tired of wondering whether the stylist will obey her instructions or just butcher her hair with a rush job, because who cares what a Fat Chick looks like?

To the mall. Total immersion in the unkindness of strangers. And she's in such a hurry today she can't manage the mincing, controlled steps that minimize both her jiggling and the corresponding catcalls.

To the book shop. Past all the shrieking magazines. "Take Off Stubborn Pounds." "Firm Your Butt Fast!" Tries to ignore the "joke" greeting-cards featuring naked 300-pound women eating cake. Pretends she hasn't heard a couple of jerks paraphrasing the title of a recent best-seller for her benefit: "Should be 'Women Who *Waddle* with the Wolves.'"

A quick dart into a department store, then a long hike down to the large-size women's clothing department, somewhere between the gerbils and the lawn mowers. What a surprise—apologetic polyester pup tents are still in this season. With ruffles.

Tries on a few things. Snarls to the unsympathetic mirror that designers obviously think chubby women have Arnold Schwarzenegger's shoulders, King Kong's arms, and Phyllis Diller's taste. Buys an unreasonable facsimile of what she needs. Tucks the telltale shopping bag inside the bookstore sack for camouflage.

Hurries past window after window of attractive, appropriate clothes. Remembers that, not so long ago, their regular sizes ran big enough to fit her. Now they stop at 14 or smaller. But, hey, that chic blue tunic looks kind of roomy. Maybe she'll . . . No, better not risk it. Last time she ventured in there, a clerk stomped clear across the store to snarl, "We wouldn't have anything for *you!*"

To the supermarket. As usual, muffled snickers pursue her all the way to the check-out. As usual, everyone stares at what she's tossing in her cart. Band-Aids, broccoli, or butterscotch cookies, it doesn't matter. They all draw the same disdain. At least this time nobody reaches in, snatches out something they think is fattening, and tells her—"for her own good"—that she shouldn't buy it.

Home. Nutritious dinner for the kids and low-fat frozen goo for herself. She eats four bites and has to vomit, thanks to a stomach-stapling operation that left only her bank balance slimmer. "Why did I mutilate myself like that?" she wonders, for the zillionth time. Then she remembers how desperately hopeful she was back when she still believed her naturally *zaftig* physique could be perma-shrunk down to "the ideal."

Decides to cut her night class. Can't face the professor making her the butt of yet another "friendly" jest. Decides not to jog or ride her bike, even though she'd love to work off some tension. Neighbourhood teens have taken to oinking and mooing whenever she passes by.

Phone rings. A reasonably nice guy, asking for a date. She puts him off. Non-stop rejection makes it tough to trust even someone who seems to appreciate her. Besides, nowadays she flinches if anyone so much as pats her fleshy arms.

Quiet at last. Her stomach growls to protest the lost dinner, so she peers into the fridge and cupboards. Then decides that hunger pangs will be easier to cope with than guilt feelings. Settles for yet another of the eight glasses of water her nutritionist insists she gag down every day.

Sinks exhaustedly onto the sofa and skims a magazine article about being obese. Stops when she reads: "The thought of anyone parading nude in front of a mirror at 190 pounds literally makes me gag."

Peruses a psychological self-help book someone recommended, but slams it shut when the author states: "I have always been repelled by fat women. . . . How dare they impose that body on the rest of us?"

Scans the local paper. In the news section, "Eating disorders triple in last decade as more than 11 million North American women and girls become bulimic or anorexic." On the editorial page: Yet another cartoon using fat to symbolize evil. In the TV listings: Tomorrow's talk-show topics—fat, fat, fat. In the companion ads: Wanted—slim, slim, slim. In the Business section: "Profits of weight-loss industry soar."

To bed. Maybe a little TV to help her relax. She slides in a video she's been saving as an antidote for the late-night blues. Usually, she loves the Royal Canadian Air Farce. But tonight they've got Luba as a grotesquely obese Rita MacNeil, and Roger in a disgusting fat suit as Luciano Pavarotti. She snaps off the VCR and turns to David Letterman: Fat Oprah Winfrey joke. Jay Leno: Fat Elizabeth Taylor joke. Some other clown: "Didja see where Roseanne . . . " Click.

And so to sleep. Perchance to dream that tomorrow won't be quite so full of hostility, humiliation, and hopelessness. Or that the miracle everyone's demanding of her will somehow happen overnight and she'll wake up slender.

This "day from hell" is an amalgam of experiences suffered by millions of large women, including me. All of its horrid moments don't happen every day, thank heaven. But many do, and none more frequently than having your clock radio start the day off by letting you know you haven't a prayer of living prejudice-free any time soon and, at day's end, falling asleep to TV's version of the same cruel "humour." And, in between, being clobbered by hostile stares and vulgar comments that head straight to your heart and stay there forever.

To be a target for *this* much grief, you probably have to weigh quite a lot, as I have for most of my life. But the essential point is that no one is propaganda-proof, whatever she weighs. The brainwashing is ubiquitous, and is perfectly characterized by Susan Douglas in *Where the Girls Are* as being bombarded with non-stop images of "smiling, air-brushed, anorexic, and compliant women whose message seems to be 'Shut up, get a face-lift, and stop eating.'"

And whenever we succumb to these outrageous slings and arrows by punitive dieting, "we turn our bodies into metaphors for all of our bad feelings—and we find confirmation for doing so everywhere we look," according to Jane R. Hirschmann and Carol H. Munter in their insightful book, *When Women Stop Hating Their Bodies: Freeing Yourself from Food and Weight Obsession.*

Has everyone gone crazy? Well, what else can we call it when
• we believe the body types of roughly 95 per cent of the female population are abnormal and only the other 5 per cent are acceptable;
• we act as if eating was perverted, antisocial behaviour instead of something we all must do to stay alive;
• we blame the 95–98 per cent failure rate of diets on dieters instead of applying basic cause-and-effect logic;
• we're oblivious to the epidemic of eating disorders and the plague of prejudice that's all around us;
• we're blind to the fundamental logic that if *any* of the diet schemes actually worked, all the others would go out of business;
• we're deaf to the messages of medical researchers about the counter-productivity of dieting and the implacability of genetic heredity;
• we ignore the elementary contradiction that, by trying to get thin, we're actually becoming fatter;
• like a nation of automatons, we epitomize the most basic definition of insanity—doing the same things over and over but expecting different results.

All this *sounds* like madness, but it's really just the logical result of three decades of brainwashing. Certainly, it's no accident that these mass delusions flourish within a culture in which the mightiest industry of all manufactures anxiety, rather than steel or any other tangible. But the hucksters who monopolize the mass media with their sheer spending power have managed to create, escalate, and perpetuate something far worse than mere anxiety about attractiveness or social acceptability. During the post-Twiggy era, they have fostered epidemic levels of not only the psycho-physiological illnesses of anorexia, bulimia, and compulsive eating, but also the emotional maladies of depression, intolerance, and body hatred—both self- and other-directed.

No one under forty remembers it, but size diversity was just a fact of life until the No Fat Chicks credo hooked us. Sure, some women have always been considered more attractive than others, and those others have always yearned to be deemed attractive. But until recently, the less favoured were never actually demonized or driven to psychological and physical self-destructiveness.

Today, Fat Chicks are the most *blatantly* reviled, ridiculed, and punished people in society. Fully twenty-five years after the women's liberation movement galvanized us into achieving our potential in so many other ways, the most treasured goal of the majority of women—according to numerous surveys—is *not* personal fulfilment, professional success, or wealth, but simply becoming as tiny as the bogus beauty icons paraded past us every waking moment.

Yet, incredible as it seems, no authorities are monitoring the emotional toll on the millions of women whose response to the societal demand for thinness is extremely dangerous behaviour. The resulting dearth of data forces me to extrapolate from general psychological research on women—which, in itself, is extremely sobering. The fact is, North American women suffer major depression and manic-depressive disorder at twice the rate of men (25 per cent, as compared with 12 per cent) and receive an estimated 83 per cent of all antidepressants prescribed by psychiatrists, and an incredible 90 per cent of tranquillizers and other psychotropic medications prescribed by other types of doctors, according to a shocking book, *Outrageous Practices: The Alarming Truth about How Medicine Mistreats Women,* by Leslie Laurence and Beth Weinhouse.

What I know personally about being a Fat Chick, together with everything I learned in the course of researching this book, convinced me beyond doubt that a huge number of large women are among these millions of depressed, psychologically maltreated patients. In fact— given that we are often humiliated on a daily basis from childhood onward, and then deprived of fulfilling lives—the psychological cost is, arguably, even worse: We have a sky-high rate of severe depression, an abysmally low level of self-esteem, and a profound sense of hopelessness.

And Fat Chicks also pay a concomitant physical price, as evidenced by a recent study at the University of California at Irvine, which determined that chronic emotional distress is an even worse health risk than smoking, and actually doubles a person's chances of incurring serious disease.

Why such a heavy toll? "Because you can't measure up to [the] cultural ideal, you feel unworthy. You just want to go away and hide," explains Judith Jordan, PhD, director of the Women's Treatment Network at McLean Hospital in Belmont, Massachusetts. "But you can't—when you're overweight, it's broadcast to the world. And you get caught in [a] spiral of social withdrawal, becoming more isolated and ashamed."

What's the best way of communicating how helpless all this makes an overweight woman feel? Maybe by borrowing a dramatic technique used in a crisis shelter near my home. To give volunteers and visitors some insight into the perplexing question of why women stay in abusive relationships, staffers haul out a huge stack of heavy wool blankets. Someone steps forward and is gradually covered by blanket after blanket after blanket, until she can no longer see or hear anything outside her dark cocoon, until she can hardly breathe, and until the weight is so heavy she cannot move, let alone find an escape route.

The blankets represent the layers of fear and psychological undermining that insidiously trap abused women. In our fat-phobic society, large women are just as entangled inside layers of prejudice and emotional distress. But, unlike other psychological maladies, the effects of living in a society that hates you and teaches you to hate yourself garner very little serious, or even respectful, professional attention. Why? Because the Fat Chick's problems are thought to be voluntarily incurred, personally remediable, and essentially trivial.

Eloquent testimony about the toll all this takes turned up in many of the responses to my Internet queries and *USA Today* ad:

GAIL: They taught me to see myself as grotesque. That's not accurate but it's apparently what they see, and that's all that counts in this world.

TESS: What's toughest for me is realizing that this whole thing has kept me from appreciating my own good qualities: I don't smoke, drink, carouse, gamble, overspend, or emotionally abuse anybody. I'm healthy, strong, honest, brave, idealistic and I have tons of will power. Yet others' perception of me is the opposite, so I keep thinking: How can I be right and the rest of the world be wrong?

CARRIE: I read about a Scottish study of how depressed people get when they don't win the lottery. And I thought: that's one of the reasons it's so devastating to keep on trying to lose weight. Every time you step on a scale and see that you haven't lost anything, you feel more hopeless than the time before.

Identity Crises

"I am . . . invisible . . . simply because people refuse to see me. . . . When they approach me, they see only my surroundings, themselves, or figments of their imagination—indeed, everything and anything except me."

So wrote renowned novelist Ralph Ellison about being black fifty years ago. But his eloquent description applies equally well to Fat Chicks. When you're noticeably overweight, you suffer the double whammy of disappearing, as far as your real identity is concerned, yet remaining all too visible as an object of disgust. It's a very disorienting clash of feelings—like being naked in public and feeling humiliated because of it. Yet, at the same time, you feel as though what people are seeing isn't the real you. It's a disguise you never chose, yet it's attracting more punishment than is heaped upon anyone else in our society, be they swindlers, murderers, rapists, or even child abusers.

> JUDY: They refuse to recognize who you really are. It's like you're invisible even though everybody's staring at you in disgust. And even if they do finally see you, they insist that you be what they insist on seeing. And they can get very angry if you won't play along.
>
> DENITRA: There are only a few acceptable roles for us: buffoon, whipping girl, object lesson. And about all people will tolerate from us is if we're jolly or obsequious.
>
> DEIRDRE: It's gotten to where I feel so disconnected from this body everybody hates that I've stopped wishing to be thin. Now I want to be invisible, just pure spirit.

Many Fat Chicks respond to the condemnation we endure in this "looks above all" world by attempting to do psychological penance. It is extremely common for fat women to accept our designation as cultural criminals and to sentence ourselves accordingly to virtual solitary confinement. This consists of not just isolation from others, but also putting our lives "on hold" in what Geneen Roth has dubbed the "When I'm Thin Fantasy." "We've told ourselves that the reason we're not loved properly is our fault for not being thin," she writes in *When Food Is Love*. "Blaming ourselves gives us a feeling of some control [and] the illusion that when we're finally thin, we will be loved properly." Until that magical day arrives, many of us unconsciously fend off every opportunity that might lead to husbands, children, and normal social lives.

And why is our need for control so intense? Because to be obese is to feel out of control, to know that you are considered unstable by others, and to be defied by your own body, which refuses to obey, no matter how hard you drive it. Also, of course, our sexist, market-driven culture guarantees that all women's bodies are considered common commodities.

> PEGGY: How can women have the slightest hope of recovering from the disease of body hate when we live in a culture that's completely toxic?
> FRAN: It offends me that women are supposed to be so small—not just skinny, but really teensy. I always remember what Roseanne says: that women should get bigger, not smaller, until we take up so much space that we'll have to be taken seriously.

There is no escape from the scrutiny, even if you're talented, famous, and successful. Just ask Canada's only female prime minister, Kim Campbell. Vulgar comments about what was actually very moderate pudginess were zinged by colleagues and the media throughout her short-lived administration, according to Sydney Sharpe, author of *The Gilded Ghetto: Women and Political Power in Canada.*

Or ask Monique Bégin, whose rapid 60-pound weight gain after she was appointed a federal cabinet minister was sarcastically chalked up to pregnancy—not only to her face by journalists, but also in a House of Commons exchange—by Campbell's predecessor, Brian Mulroney, who then had his jest stricken from *Hansard.*

Or check with actresses Sharon Gless and Tyne Daly, whose mutual weight gain, though modest, was widely remarked when they reprised their *Cagney & Lacey* series as a TV special in 1994. Or the lead singers of Heart and Fleetwood Mac, whose respective chubbiness was the subject of far more comments than their voices when their groups reunited recently. Or country singer Wynonna Judd, whose size is often a target for snide or pitying remarks in popular magazines, and who was humiliated in front of millions of people recently when *Tonight Show* host Jay Leno inexplicably tried to pick her up after she sang a song—and both of them tumbled to the floor.

Linda Ronstadt's plumpness as she nears age fifty is mentioned by practically every disc jockey who introduces her records. Even when *Mirabella* magazine published an otherwise flattering article about her recently, writer Karen Schoemer and her editors chose to include a put-down that revealed their own class bias: "Ronstadt has put on a good deal of weight, and in workout clothes she more closely resembles a woman in front of you in the supermarket checkout line than the most successful female pop star of the seventies."

> CONNIE: What kind of a sick world is it where the only "legitimate" accomplishment for a woman is denying her most basic needs and starving herself so she'll get smaller and smaller?

Other plus-size women—especially those whose self-esteem is comparatively intact—grapple with different psychological obstacles. Some long to be slender but bitterly resent the pressure to conform. So our answer to those who tell women to squeeze themselves into ever-tinier packages is a defiant no. But this means that, in our own minds, we're damned if we do lose weight and damned if we don't.

Then there are the deal-makers, whose state of mind is eloquently expressed by Pam Houston in *Minding the Body—Women Writers on Body and Soul*: "For a good part of my life, I would have quite literally given anything to be thin . . . a finger, three toes, the sight in one eye. Now I find it only mildly surprising that for the majority of my lifetime I would have traded being ugly, deformed, and thin for being pretty, whole, and fat."

Similarly, a University of Florida study of women who'd lost weight after intestinal-bypass surgery reported that virtually all said they'd rather be blind, deaf, or have a leg amputated than ever be fat again. If this seems incongruous, remember that, today, the highest form of compliment is congratulating a woman for squashing herself to a smaller size.

But Why Is Everybody Else So Mad?

The other side of the coin, in terms of what the "billion-dollar brainwash" has wrought, is the intense anger so many people feel towards Fat Chicks. Certainly, other minorities face deplorable prejudice. But, when you're overweight, the hostility feels more personally directed. After all, nobody is told flat-out to switch religions, or to change the colour of her skin or the shape of her facial features. The disabled aren't ordered to walk, and those with diseases aren't told to simply snap out of it. Society has finally evolved to the point where alcoholics, drug addicts, and the mentally ill are treated with compassion instead of contempt. But the overweight are still regarded as *deserving* of abuse and exclusion.

The fact is that we have been deliberately conditioned to be repelled by the very sight of a fat woman. And this knee-jerk reaction is constantly reinforced in the media—both information and entertainment—by means of the hundreds of images that surround us during an average day. Yet a stroll through any traditional art gallery will confirm that this is a conditioned, rather than a primary, response, and that it is of very recent vintage.

Oddly enough, however, appearance *per se* isn't the most significant element of the taboo against obesity, according to many psychological authorities. Rather, the hostility has more to do with the presumed breaking of rules that others feel compelled to obey. Given that most women are not naturally skinny, especially as they age, achieving this body image takes prodigious effort and self-denial. Yet only rarely do we hear such women characterize this as the extreme sacrifice it is. And even when they do hint at it, they blame *themselves* instead of the ruthless pressure to accomplish the impossible. In fact, it's often as if a societal ventriloquist is at work when they alternately apologize for eating and concoct absurd rationalizations for consuming even innocuous amounts (as Fat Chicks also often feel compelled to do).

What's the reaction when someone who has gone to punitive lengths to be thin sees someone who evidently has not? Anger, because the Fat Chick appears to be enjoying the pleasures her slender sisters are denying themselves. Even worse is the implicit assumption that she's not only not playing the game, but actually repudiating the rules and ridiculing those who abide by them. So, as feminist scholar Susan Bordo phrases it in *Unbearable Weight: Feminism, Western Culture and the Body:* "If the rest of us are struggling to be acceptable and 'normal,' we cannot allow [the obese] to get away with it; they must be put in their place . . . humiliated and defeated."

KALLI: The truth is that very, very few people have enough will-power to starve themselves for years and years, let alone do all the other stuff I do to lose weight. Yet I'm treated as if I'm a lazy slug with no self-control at all.

PAULA: I keep trying to think of a way to buttonhole these people who obviously hate how I look and say: You're wrong. This is not the body I gorged my way up to, it's the one I got by a lifetime of starving to please you.

The resentment is exacerbated when an overweight woman seems to be contented with her size, or when her demeanour indicates that she expects to be treated respectfully.

KATH: Nobody expects blacks to shuffle any more. But if [fat women] just have a normal amount of self-confidence or dignity, people are outraged. How dare we expect to be treated like human beings?

These comments probably explain a peculiar incident several years ago, when a magazine story I wrote won a Canadian Author's Award. No one even informed me that I'd been nominated, let alone invited me to the awards ceremony. My certificate just turned up in the mail one day. It's tough enough to achieve amid all the negativity that's directed at Fat Chicks, and the lack of reinforcement when you do succeed, but this sort of pointed exclusion has the psychological effect of actually negating what, for anyone else, would feel like a triumph.

Another basis for anger-inducing anti-fat prejudice is what I call the "Dorian Gray Syndrome." Remember Oscar Wilde's famous tale about a man who remained handsome while the physical evidence of his depravity appeared on an increasingly hideous portrait? Well, I believe this scenario is reenacted whenever slim people project onto Fat Chicks the qualities they've been brainwashed into believing are the ugliest, but fear they themselves embody. What qualities? Gluttony, sloth, selfishness, asexuality, lack of control, lack of self-respect, unfemininity. The inference is that "anyone who allows herself to be or become fat is exhibiting in a public way weaknesses or flaws in her basic nature," as Jane Rachel

Kaplan explains in *A Woman's Conflict: The Special Relationship between Women and Food,* adding that "persons who exhibit such imperfection are not living up to the standards of decency followed by all other members of the society, and therefore do not deserve to share equally in the rewards offered by the system."

This process of "trial by appearance" is often subconscious. But many slender women embrace the No Fat Chicks rule itself quite consciously— which brings to mind what crusader Elizabeth Cady Stanton said of those who opposed female suffrage in the late nineteenth century: "It is too bad that these women are begging to be left in their chains."

> CINDY: We've got to realize that all this insistence on women having perfect bodies is as insulting and regressive as if we suddenly had to start coming up with dowries of so many cows or goats.

Even Losers Can't Win

Ironically, a Fat Chick can incur anger from others even when she does manage to "go with the flow" by losing weight. A troubled patient named Connie, for example, told the authors of *When Women Stop Hating Their Bodies* that, after losing quite a lot, she realized "that not only have I been eating differently, I've been acting differently as well. . . . [And] I suspect that [the] real problem has more to do with the fact that I'm not as compliant as I once was. . . . "

It wasn't Connie's new figure, but her newfound self-respect that landed her in hot water at home. As strange as it seems, Fat Chicks' significant others—even those who insist upon slimness—often try to sabotage the dieting process as soon as results reach a significant level. This may take the form of warning a dieter that she's endangering her health, insisting she looks better when she's heavier, criticizing her for not providing adequate meals for other members of the household, and/or inundating her environment with fattening food. One of the reasons I found it necessary to move away during my *Chatelaine* diet series was that the (previously abstemious) man I lived with suddenly began hauling home donuts and other "treats."

Why the contradictory signals? Because the perception (which may be conscious or subconscious) is that the balance of power in relation-ships will be upset if the woman no longer considers herself inferior. And the status quo will be equally threatened if her popularity outside the home increases.

So even when a Fat Chick succeeds in losing a substantial amount of weight, her problems are far from over. Among the challenges she'll likely face are not only coping with relational hostility, but also combating the physical fail-safe mechanism described in Chapter 3, and fighting to overcome the residual psychological fear and bitterness instilled while she was a target for prejudice. And she may also have to wrestle another demon called "body-image distortion." The most extreme form of this inability to see the new body that's *really* reflected in the mirror affects anorexics, who somehow perceive phantom flab where there's actually nothing except skin and bones. But other formerly fat women can also have a tough time believing their eyes, and therefore appreciating that they've reached their cherished goal.

This kind of confusion happened to me in a clothing store when I was searching for something to wear for a TV appearance following my *Chatelaine* diet series. Holding a dress three sizes smaller than anything I'd worn since my teens, I panicked when I saw a sales clerk approach. Years of being insulted or ignored by her ilk made me jump to the con-clusion that she was going to snatch the dress out of my hands and revile me for thinking it would fit. Instead, she smiled graciously and suggested I needed an even smaller size. She was right, yet somehow I still couldn't see my body realistically.

The Worst Punishment

Ironically, cruelty from an increasingly intolerant world isn't actually the worst part of being overweight. Even more painful is the internalization of the No Fat Chicks edict that leads obese women to feel guilty, ashamed, and worthless every day of our lives—an experience that feels, to quote an e-mail note from a woman named Molly, "like swimming upstream in a river of burning molasses."

Even Oprah Winfrey, the most successful and admired woman on tele-vision, felt psychologically crushed when the weight she lost so publicly during her liquid-protein fast crept back. "I'm 180 pounds," she wrote in

1990 in one of many such journal entries. "Now I wake every morning hating myself." When she won an Emmy award, Winfrey says she felt so ashamed of her appearance she didn't want to go onstage to accept it.

But even those whose innate good sense lets them reject most of the ghastly qualities projected onto overweight women are still vulnerable to the negativity of the people in our lives who do think this way and treat us accordingly—especially in all the ways described in the foregoing "day from hell." Care to guess whether *that* helps? Never mind. Psychologist and eating-disorders specialist Susan Wooley has come up with the heart-breaking but definitive answer: "If shame could cure obesity, there wouldn't be a fat person in the world."

To Eat or Not to Eat

The mere presence of food can sometimes spell psychological torture for Fat Chicks. To eat or not to eat is the question that can buzz incessantly in the brain. Why? Because food can simultaneously represent the temptation of a taboo, as well as both the catalyst for your persecution and the source of consolation from that persecution. So the murky emotional ratio of hating, loving, and needing food means that simply knowing it's nearby can induce subliminal panic similar to that we face before a crucial exam. In conflicted moments like this, we often feel as if we're walking a tightrope and it is a given that we'll eventually fall. The suspense of whether this will happen sooner, rather than later, can be unbearable.

But what about the millions of North American women whose response to societal pressures is to develop clinical eating disorders, including anorexia (refusal to eat), bulimia (bingeing, followed by purging), and compulsive eating?

Paradoxically, large women whose compulsive eating has become out of control actually represent the flip-side of an anorexic's rejection of food. Both are eating-disorder victims who believe this is the only arena in their lives over which they have control. But the skinny woman says no to food, while the fat one is often saying yes, not out of gluttony, but out of a need to mentally counterbalance all the other no's she hears from society because of her size.

Other Fat Chicks form a powerful dependence on foods that represent "comfort." Why? One illuminating answer comes, not from an unhappy housewife in the hinterlands, but from a rich, beautiful, celebrated actress—Elizabeth Taylor, whose weight nearly doubled during her unhappy marriage to a politician. "The large amounts of food I ate were a substitute for everything I felt I was lacking in my life. But what was really starving was my self-esteem. . . ."

As for anorexia, there are many theories about the cause, including the one that seems most obvious to me: simply "overconforming" to society's demand for thin women. As historian Joan Jacobs Brumberg writes in *Fasting Girls: The Emergence of Anorexia Nervosa as a Modern Disease* (the pre-eminent book in this field): "Given our longstanding and extravagant collective worship at the shrine of slimness, it is no wonder that so many contemporary young women make dieting an article of faith and that anorexia nervosa has become the characteristic psychopathology of the female adolescent of our day."

And the tragic ultimate stage for an anorexic, as psychotherapist Kim Chernin writes in *The Obsession: Reflections on the Tyranny of Slenderness*, is "a feeling of profound humiliation that the body exists at all."

About bulimia, which authorities say is even less curable than anorexia, there seems to be a virtual consensus that the behaviour is a psychological "adjustment" to the pressures of fat-phobia. Chernin focuses on bulimics, to powerful effect, in another of her excellent books. In *The Hungry Self: Women, Eating and Identity*, she quotes a study of normally functioning college women who "[experience] their hunger as exaggerated and obscene," and describes the eating obsessions of many of her patients. The most compelling case-study is that of a patient Chernin calls Anita, who told her that, because of the all-consuming pressure to be thin, "[women] are vomiting our guts out to let them know we just can't stomach it." The day after singer Karen Carpenter died of anorexia, the patient told Chernin: "Now they'll *have* to take it seriously."

Sorry to say it, but Anita was wrong. A decade after *The Hungry Self* was published, the number of North American women and girls with eating disorders has risen to more than 11 million, according to the National Eating Disorder Information Centre in Canada, and the National Association of Anorexia Nervosa and Associated Disorders in the United States. Many of these women—especially those of college age—admit that staying slim is their motive for starving themselves or vomiting much of what they eat, and that they frequently accompany this behaviour with laxative and diuretic abuse and compulsive overexercising—not to mention swelling the ranks of the fastest-growing category of smokers on the continent.

"Restrained eating" is considered by some authorities to be a fourth kind of eating disorder. But, as asserted by University of Toronto researchers Janet Polivy and C. Peter Herman, who coined the term, the practice of permanently limiting your food intake to less than you desire is now so commonplace that many experts (not to mention the general public) don't think of it as a disorder at all. "The meaning of a phrase such as normal eating," the duo wrote in an article in the *Journal of Consulting and Clinical Psychology*, "is no longer obvious [because] 'normal' eating for North American women is now characterized by dieting." To which Elizabeth Gleick added, in a compelling article in *New York* titled "The Fat Mind," that "even 'normal' women have completely lost their perspectives . . . [and are] sunk in a mire of lusts and prohibitions about what [they] eat, how [they] eat it and with whom."

And what's the effect of obsessive restrained eating—always saying no to yourself and feeling permanently deprived? I can think of no better answer than to quote another of Oscar Wilde's brilliant observations. You've probably heard the first line many times, but the second part—which is so significant in this context—is rarely repeated: "The only way to get rid of temptation is to yield to it. Resist it, and your soul grows sick with longing for the things it has forbidden to itself."

The Big Question

No discussion of the psychological toll exacted by the "billion-dollar brainwash" would be complete without addressing the basic question that seems to mystify so many normal-weight people, and prompt so much prejudice: Why do Fat Chicks *choose* to be miserable misfits by staying so much bigger than we "should" be? Answer: We don't. In fact, the ultimate defeat for Fat Chicks is that incessant dieting actually keeps us fat—a process I described in Chapter 3.

The Big Lie—that obesity *must* be voluntary because anyone who tries hard enough can be thin—is one of the most cunning ploys adopted by the anti-fat profiteers. But the rock-bottom truth is that the media version of slenderness is simply *not* a possibility for many body types. Dr. Jane Blouin, a psychologist at Ottawa Civic Hospital's eating-disorder clinic, says she often has to deal with "the myth that we can force our bodies into the shape we think they ought to be. [But] it doesn't work that way any more than you can force your foot into the size of shoe you want. . . . "

Think about it. What could possibly be more psychologically devastating than to keep doing what everyone in the world is demanding, over and over again, year after desperate year, only to have the supposed solution turn out to be an inescapable trap?

Undeniably, the current epidemic of obesity, eating disorders, and depression are chiefly the result of deliberate disinformation, carefully instilled fat-phobia, and the inescapable imperative for incessant dieting. Yet, just as obviously, there *are* other complicated causes. Physically, excess weight is often the result of such factors as genetic heredity, food intolerances, and insulin imbalance.

In many other cases, the paramount causation is emotional, with obesity and eating disorders being not so much the problem as the sad solution. Such cases include survivors of sexual abuse—possibly as many as 50–60 per cent of the total, according to a study cited by Dr. Kathryn J. Zerbe in *The Body Betrayed: Women, Eating Disorders and Treatment.* Not only do such women consider eating the safest source of comfort, they also know that, in our current culture, nothing advertises a woman's sexual unavailability, or repels potential admirers, more effectively than a protective layer of fat.

> SANDRA: I've come to think of my body as my disguise. It's my cave and
> my bomb shelter. And it's my walking rebuke to those who inflict
> Barbie doll demands on all women.

An inability to handle anger appropriately can also result in overeating, so that women try to "stuff" their rage down deep. Why are they so angry? According to many experts, it's frequently because of physical, sexual, and emotional abuse or neglect, especially in childhood. The logical outcome of feeling betrayed and abandoned, as author and former compulsive eater Geneen Roth puts it in *When Food Is Love*, is the fear "that if I didn't eat . . . I was giving up an opportunity, maybe my last, to fill the part of me that was forever hungry, forever desperate for relief. I could never honestly say that I had enough because although my body was full, I was empty."

Substituting food for emotional nurturance that's otherwise unavailable is also aptly described by an overweight woman in Marcia Millman's *Such a Pretty Face: Being Fat in America*: "I'm trying to be a good neighbor and a good daughter and a good parent and a good wife and a good teacher and a good scholar and a good friend and the one thing that will take care of me is food."

Psychiatrist Theodore Isaac Rubin provides yet another description of the motivation for overeating comfort foods in *Alive and Fat and Thinning in America*: "In an attempt to ward off depression, fat people will eat . . . to counter sadness with pleasure . . . to feel love and warmth symbolized by foods and memories of maternal care expressed through feeding. . . . Thus, eating binges are often . . . defenses against depression. . . . "

Makes sense, right? But let's get real here. How many people *don't* equate food with nurturance and use it to assuage emotional turmoil? Yet those whose extra pounds make us walking advertisements for this elementary human dynamic are treated as if our behaviour—but *not* that of people who seek emotional relief in smoking, intoxicants, sexual promiscuity, or violence—is destructive, aberrant, irresponsible, and unforgivable.

And the kicker is that, even though eating, as Zerbe points out in *The Body Betrayed*, "functions as a form of self-medication against painful feelings . . . [in people who] suffer mightily in many areas of their lives," bigotry has deprived so many of us of *other* rewarding life experiences, including having companions or children. Yet the one source of consolation that's available on every corner—food—is what we alone are expected to do without.

IRENE: What I hate most are all those makeover articles in the magazines. It's like we're surrounded by all this stuff telling us how to be somebody else. And, of course, on all the other pages, it's diets, diets,

diets on one side of the page and humongous pictures of food on the other side. It's crazy, but nobody even notices the contradiction.

Yeah, but . . .

Okay, fine, but why do the remainder of Fat Chicks eat? To stay alive. That sounds ridiculously obvious, but think about it. Somewhere along the way, we seem to have forgotten that—however much she may regret, or be despised for, her appearance—the Fat Chick cannot quit "cold turkey." She *must* eat, 365 days a year. Just like everyone else.

Beyond that is the inescapable social obligation and familial ritual of eating. When do we ever get together for a cup of nothing? Or sit around a nice empty table celebrating a holiday? As a prominent food anthropologist puts it: "In all societies, both simple and complex, eating is the *primary* way of initiating and maintaining human relationships."

Mustn't we agree, then, that the Fat Chick's basic motivations for consuming food match those of every other human being since the beginning of time? Ah, but not everybody eats enough to get fat, right? Actually, a growing percentage of us do, especially since regular sit-down meals have been all but supplanted by frequent "grazing" on fast and fatty foods. And this has been exacerbated by the dramatic decrease in physical activity in modern times to the point where millions of North Americans now weigh at least 20 per cent more than is currently deemed to be "average."

So Fat Chicks aren't abnormal after all. We're simply the most visible products of our culture and our cultural conditioning. Left unchecked, the marketers who manipulate these forces will continue manufacturing all the consumers they need for their worthless wares.

Bottom Line

The foregoing illustrates what a sea of psychological trouble Fat Chicks are forced to swim in every day. And, just to make it worse, when we turn to medical or psychological practitioners for help with the sharks that besiege us, all we usually get are insults, lectures, and diet sheets (as we saw in Chapter 4).

Even enormously famous and successful women are unable to escape the No Fat Chicks imperative. Those whose resultant eating disorders have become public knowledge include Princess Diana; actresses Jane Fonda, Sally Field, Lynn Redgrave, and the late Gilda Radner; dancer/choreographer Paula Abdul; the late Karen Carpenter; *Beauty Myth* author Naomi Wolf; actress Tracey Gold, who was fired from the *Growing Pains* TV series because of uncontrollable anorexia; and *Married with Children* star Christina Applegate, who recently told *People* magazine that she eats only when she's "doubled over and passing out."

In the introduction to this book, I described the abrupt psychological shock of losing my "golden girl" status when I became fat in prepubescence. Until then, it seemed as if everyone loved me—and, afterwards, that no one did, or ever would. As I continued writing, I forced myself to review the many cruel words and gestures that have stayed with me for a lifetime. Soon even bitter memories I'd managed to repress for decades floated back into my consciousness. Example: At age twelve, being so ashamed of my tubby tummy that I secretly kept a tight, rubbery girdle on under my pyjamas at my first slumber party. I was so uncomfortable and afraid that the other girls would find me out that I couldn't sleep all night and crept away at dawn.

Another unwelcome recollection cost me a few nights' sleep when I reflected on, not just my childhood pain, but the consequence of being among the high percentage of fat teenage girls who are too demoralized to pursue higher education. Why? Because of humiliations that begin in grade school and never stop. Example: Being forced to compete in grotesque sports competitions, called "field days." I was inevitably among the least-capable pupils attempting compulsory races, jumps, and other feats that were far too difficult for those of us who were overweight, puny, or congenitally uncoordinated. The ordeal was intensified by always being scheduled last, which meant that, with our families and the entire student body watching, we were an annual spectacle in the small southern Alberta town of Calmar. And whichever of us came in last— often me—was taunted by the other kids throughout the following year as the "worst of the worst."

I was forcibly reminded of how hurtful it is to be just such an overweight child while watching a recent television special called *Growing Up Fat.* A dozen or so teenagers who had spent many summers trying to lose weight at "fat camps" were filmed as they watched a videotape showing a class of five-year-olds boisterously exhibiting the anti-fat prejudice that had already been instilled in them. The teenagers' expressions as they listened to the younger kids shouting that stupidity, ugliness, and even mutilation are preferable to obesity were utterly heart-breaking.

The fact is, the "billion-dollar brainwash" has created communicable forms of madness to which precious few are immune. So unless it can be stopped, life will continue to be emotionally anguishing and needlessly restricted for any of these youngsters who grow up to be Fat Chicks. That's the whole idea—because every time they respond by trying to reduce, somewhere a cash register will ca-ching up another chunk of the unconscionable profits that derive from mass delusion.

CHAPTER SIX

Hungry for Work

A nurturer of severely retarded children is denied work unless she loses weight. A lawyer quits her firm after being told too many times that clients "see her differently." A health-food clerk is rejected because slicing cheese, stocking shelves, and working the cash register are considered "too much" for her.

The first female prime minister of Canada is a frequent target for anti-fat potshots when she gains a bit of pudge. A nursing student is hounded out of school because she refuses to starve for her education. Flight attendants are grounded for fulfilling their chronological destiny. A police woman is denied promotion for tipping weight scales her male colleagues don't even have to step onto.

A hotshot saleswoman can't get her foot in the door—even at a large-size women's clothing company. The most popular actress on a hit TV series is sacked, although fans don't object to her growing rotundity. A talented editor who built an impressive résumé before her weight hit 200 is reduced to working as a typist in an out-of-sight work ghetto. A seventeen-year-old secretary, despite being well qualified, healthy, and energetic, is fired from her first job—at a life insurance company—because she weighs 30 pounds more than their mortality tables allow.

If fat women really were as jolly as their reputation, they might see macabre humour in the absurdity of the "Too Fat Polka" that's been number one on the workplace charts ever since the "billion-dollar brainwash" began manipulating the attitudes of millions of people. But there's nothing funny about being literally forced to go hungry to obtain or retain a decent job. Or the fact that fully 60 per cent of overweight North American women say they've been denied employment solely because of their appearance—or rather, because of prejudice against their appearance. And it's distinctly unhumorous that almost a third say that, when they do land jobs, they are routinely passed over for promotions and raises. Or that 78 per cent say rampant cruelty and injustice have undermined their professional confidence. Or that they earn, on average, $6,700 less per year than thin women.

Extrapolating the percentages revealed in the most comprehensive survey ever done in this context—by the National Association for the Advancement of Fat Acceptance (NAAFA) in 1987—means that approximately 2.5 million Canadian women, and at least 17 million of their American sisters, are the victims of employment discrimination that is now illegal for every minority except the obese.

NAAFA's empirical proof came as no surprise to the legions of women affected by workplace discrimination. What was a shock was that the situation had become outrageous enough, by November 1992, to land smack dab on the front page of the *New York Times*. In what was undoubtedly the first time such respectful, high-calibre attention has been paid to the severity of what amounts to an epidemic of prejudice against the obese, the *Times* published a series called "Fat in America," which ran on page one for three days.

There it all was, in sickening detail: Overweight workers are penalized $1,000 in salary for every "extra" pound. Obesity results in poverty for at least a third of women workers. The vast majority of the overweight have been laughed at on the job and derided by fellow employees. Concluded series writer Natalie Angier, "People who would never publicly confess to racism have no qualms about expressing revulsion for the obese."

Added Dr. Susan C. Wooley, director of the eating-disorders clinic at the University of Cincinnati: "We're running out of people that we're allowed to hate and to feel superior to. Fatness is the one thing left that seems to be a person's fault—which it isn't."

The commendable *New York Times* series was balm for many a broken heart and extended temporary dignity to many a reviled anti-fat victim. What it wasn't was enough of an eye-opener to make a difference. Today it takes a severe, public, nowhere-to-go-but-up epiphany to legitimize even blatant inequities. With sexual harassment of women in the workplace, for a prime example, it required nothing less than a psychological gang-rape on national television.

But chronically unemployed, underemployed, and exploited fat women are still awaiting their Anita Hill. Before enough outrage is crystallized to begin redressing our oppression, the equally repugnant, equally routine mistreatment of one of us will have to wind up in an equally illuminating spotlight.

Until then, candidates for this dubious honour are mostly enduring their employment ordeals in private. Name an industry—from high finance to health care, aviation, electronics, communications, law, and even law enforcement—and you'll find abuse. Some are instances of bare-faced prejudice. Some are flimsy smokescreens based on fallacious health-insurance rationales. And some are just so ludicrous they defy analysis. Or, rather, they beg the question so movingly answered by Robert F. Murphy's *The Body Silent*, an examination of the prejudicial atmosphere in which a group whose oppression parallels that of the obese is forced to exist: "The disabled serve as constant, visible reminders to the able-bodied that the society they live in is a counterfeit paradise, that they too are vulnerable. We represent a fearsome possibility."

Top of the Heap

It's hard to imagine more odious evidence of anti-fat bias than what turned up in a recent attitudinal survey of 1,139 top-level CEOs, presidents, and executive vice-presidents—none of whom is overweight. The results clearly demonstrate that both halves of the "lean and mean" metaphor have been transmuted into literal reality by the folks at the top. Epitomizing the overall tone was this nasty remark from Donald Lennox, former CEO of Navistar International Transportation: "I don't like fat people. If I were recruiting and some guy waddled in with a big gut, he'd be dead before he opened his mouth."

And a fat female candidate would be unlikely even to get the chance to "waddle" into Mr. Lennox's august presence, according to University of Pittsburgh psychology professor Dr. Irene Frieze. "Grossly overweight females are penalized more severely than men with the same problem," she concluded upon completing a study of 1,200 MBA graduates for her university. Results for the males: Upper-level managers who are 20 per cent overweight earn approximately $4,000 a year less than their average-weight counterparts. Results for the 350 female MBAs: Non-existent—

there were too few fat women in top management to be statistically significant!

"Bosses interpret weight gain in a woman employee," said Frieze, "as a signal that she's abandoned any hope of rising higher." Of course, the fallacy in that "interpretation"—though the bosses would doubtless deny it—precisely parallels what George Bernard Shaw said long ago in a similar context: "The American white relegates the black to the ranks of shoeshine boy and then concludes that the black is good for nothing but shining shoes."

Summing up the attitudes towards obesity among powerful and influential executives, psychologist Leonard J. Donk, a California counsellor to Fortune 500 companies, says, "The profundity of the narrow-mindedness . . . is incredible." To which Lynn Smith, president and CEO of St. Louis's Dunhill Personnel, adds: "I've had employers say to me, only half-jokingly, 'Can't you find us someone who's blond, blue-eyed, and has a flat stomach?'"

The picture gets no brighter as you climb down the corporate ladder or venture farther from the mega-power bases.

Sales

Take what happened to saleswoman Diane Wildowsky when she weighed 230 pounds. Granted, her profession is one of the most notoriously image-conscious. But with a successful track record in cutthroat New York City, she thought she'd be a shoo-in as a representative for an apparel company in the northwest. "Over the phone, they liked everything they heard," she recalls. But in her face-to-face interview, Wildowsky was "stunned. Here he was trying to get me out of his office. I was never even considered."

The product was large-size women's clothing.

But even this degree of self-defeating executive stupidity is standard practice in sales, according to personnel authorities. "Anyone who's supposed to meet with customers and is more than 40 pounds overweight is going to have a big-time problem," says Connecticut-based Peter Floyd, of Personnel Corporation of America. "Managers assume that overweight people don't have the energy or drive to operate in the field as salespersons," adds Chicago outplacement executive James E.

Challenger. "Not only is it harder for fat people to get jobs, they tend to lose them faster."

These assessments are amplified by a recent study of the effects of obesity on service careers, such as sales, done by Professor Michael L. Klassen, of the University of Northern Iowa. The overweight, he found, are considered (in rank order): "lazy, unkempt, jolly, lacking self-discipline, lacking self-care, unhealthy and insecure."

And, says Martin Everett, general editor of *Sales & Marketing Management*, the crowning irony of the fact that "most sales executives won't look twice at a fat candidate" is that the bias is flourishing "despite mounting difficulty in finding field sales talent."

Law

No eye-popping studies such as Klassen's have been done of the legal profession, probably because discretion is the bedrock for attorneys. So it's not surprising that, even though the *American Bar Association Journal*, and several other professional publications, have reported that disenchanted female attorneys are quitting the law in droves, only one has gone public about what it's like to be an overweight lady lawyer.

"All fat people are 'outed' by their appearance," wrote Buffalo, New York, attorney Jennifer A. Coleman in a recent *Newsweek* "My Turn" column. "But . . . I really believed I could infiltrate the ranks of the nonfat and thereby establish my worth . . . by a regimen of swimming, cycling and jogging that put all but the most compulsive to shame. I ate only cottage cheese, brown rice, fake butter and steamed everything. . . . " Coleman's weight didn't budge and, "fit but still fat," she queried: "How was it I was still lazy, weak, despised, a slug and a cow? I finally realized: It didn't matter what I did. I was and always would be the object of sport, derision, antipathy and hostility so long as I stayed in my body." So, after hearing much too often the veiled insult from superiors at the large firms for which she had always worked that "clients looked at me differently," Coleman told me she'd decided to become a sole practitioner. Her new speciality: employment discrimination.

To be scrupulously fair, however, is it possible that what appear to be straightforward cases of size discrimination are actually hard-headed business decisions? In some cases, the deplorable but true answer is yes. A study of business students, for example, shows they flat-out hate being served by overweight people (of both genders). Does this justify not hiring the obese? Social commentator Lindsy Van Gelder has this eloquent answer: "If a business claimed that it needed to discriminate against Jewish workers in order to protect its image with its anti-Semitic customers, no one would suggest religious conversion as a solution to the problem. But an 'unattractive' job applicant? The onus instantly switches to what she should do to 'fix' herself."

Which brings us to the broader context in which employment discrimination against Fat Chicks flourishes. It's actually just the latest chapter in a very old story: backlash against the emancipation of women. In the all-too-recent past, the male powers-that-be fought tooth and nail to keep women out of their exclusive domain—the workplace. When the battle was lost, at least from the point of view of the most dim-witted "old boys," a cunning way was found either to disqualify the female usurper at the starting-gate or to undermine her success and self-confidence when she did land a job. The new deal: whatever the position, the prerequisite for females would be attractiveness. Why? As Naomi Wolf expresses it in *The Beauty Myth*: "Employers did not simply develop the beauty backlash because they wanted office decoration. . . . The triumph of 'beauty' ideologies . . . came about as a result of real fear on the part of the central institutions of our society about what might happen if free women made free progress in free bodies throughout a system that calls itself a meritocracy."

So, to ensure that the hordes of women flooding the workplace were anything but free to threaten the existing power structure, what Wolf calls a "third shift" was added. Women would now be coerced into a daily grind of not just one professional shift, as men have, and not just the two they had already been holding down at home and at work, but also a third shift, which consisted of maintaining a standard of appearance that had previously been demanded only of professional beauties, such as models and actresses.

Thus was born the concept of jobs as never-ending beauty contests—a notion whose ludicrousness becomes instantly obvious if it's applied to men. But the fact is, it almost never is looked at that way. Women—

aided and abetted by many of the same profiteers who convinced every-one that "fat" equals "ugly"—fell for the self-defeating ruse hook, line, and (especially) sinker.

Now, rather than insisting that their worthiness be judged solely by the official BFOQ—bona fide occupational qualification—rule that was established in the name of equal opportunity, as Wolf writes, "women . . . are persuaded to trim their desires and self-esteem neatly into the dis-criminatory requirements of the workplace, while putting the blame for the system's failures on themselves alone."

Blimpos Anonymous

That induced sense of self-blame ran like a disturbing undercurrent beneath the tales recounted during a recent meeting of an all-woman obesity support group in a small Midwestern city. Like children feigning courage by whistling past the graveyard, these women call their group "Blimpos."

"If you can see the humour and the defiance in that name," explained the group's founder, "then you're ready for Blimpos." Tess* then called for someone to kick off what she called a "moan and groan" session, devoted, on this occasion, to employment experiences.

Tugging her thigh-length shirt away from her hips and stomach, in a defensive gesture that's second nature to large women, Daisy steps to the front of the room. "I'd like to frame my comment tonight into a literary context," she says, in a quietly defiant voice. "As some of you know, I had a damn good career going as a magazine editor when I was slim. And now all I can get is word processing, at a third of my former salary. Well, this is how Virginia Woolf described the psychological effect of that kind of squashing in *A Room of One's Own*: 'always to be doing work that one did not wish to do, and to do it like a slave . . . and then the thought of that one gift which it was death to hide . . . perishing and with it my self, my soul. . . .'"

There's a smattering of applause. And then a voice from the side of the room. "I know exactly what you mean," says Gillian. "I'm holding onto my crummy job as a factory assembler because I'm a realist, but I

---

*The names used here are pseudonyms.

feel like I'm just withering. Whenever I read the classifieds, all I see are companies that wouldn't even let me in the door. Anything to do with food, forget it. They'd see me as a walking advertisement why customers shouldn't buy their product. And ditto for anything that's based on image—like sales or receptionist."

"Aw, come on," objects Annie from the other side of the room. "What isn't considered an image job these days?" After an explosion of affirmative expostulations, Tess asks for specific examples of job discrimination.

Ginny recalls the division of labour when she worked in the ad section of a publication. "Only the thin women were allowed to go out and make cold calls and, of course, that's where the big commissions are. All the overweight girls were kept in the office on lowly telephone sales."

"Sure, and how about me?" queries Katie. "I've been working with an employment agency for months now, looking for something in desktop publishing. My counsellor says, if anything, I'm overqualified and any employer would be lucky to get me. But she hasn't sent me on any interviews in the last two months. When I asked her why, she got all embarrassed. Then she sort of whispered, 'I know I shouldn't tell you this because I could get in trouble. But the last place I sent you, that advertising agency, told me they'd snap you up in a minute—if you weighed 50 pounds less.'"

"Yeah," says Nancy. "They've even got a code for that. If they write 'NFO' on your file, it means 'Not Front Office.' In other words, they won't even bother sending you on interviews unless your appearance is up to snuff. And we know what that means, don't we?"

"Well, I've tried and tried to talk myself out of believing this," muses Shannon. "But when I had a great job as a paralegal, I ended up making a very bad enemy. He obviously felt that I should be obsequious and apologetic just because I was fat. I reported him [to upper management], but eventually it got so bad that I felt I had to quit. They had to assign, literally, three and a half people to do what I had been doing. But when the creep left a few months later and I tried to get my job back, they wouldn't even take my calls. I know I was good at what I did, so what reason other than prejudice could they have for just letting me go like that, even when it costs them big bucks?"

"Just about the same thing is happening to me right now," adds Paula. "I know I'm excellent at what I do and I've worked like a maniac to get where I am. So I try to behave like the other people at my management level, you know, like I expected to be respected and listened to. But it's just not happening. It's as if everybody's demanding that I act like some kind of fool and then they get furious when I don't."

"But it isn't just about getting a job," pipes up a younger woman named Chris. "It's also about what it's like every day at work if you're overweight. This might sound picayune but there's this manager who always comes into my department with donuts for everybody. And almost every day he says something at the top of his voice about how I really shouldn't have one. I never do, but people keep laughing, so he keeps on saying it."

Rejoinders come flying from all over the room. "I was sexually harassed for over a year until I finally quit. But, to this day, nobody believes it could have happened just because of the way I look."

"Three of us who are overweight were the constant butt of jokes everywhere we went in the plant and, one day in the cafeteria, some jerks actually threw food at us. But the union wouldn't do a thing."

"My company now has a really good program to help people with alcohol or drug problems. They don't even lose pay or seniority when they go to dry out. But fat is supposed to be your own fault, so all you ever get is grief for being a lazy, disgusting slob."

"Sure, but that just shows you how bad it is for all women who have to get tarted up to keep a good job and compete with each other for crumbs in terms of money and promotions."

See You in Court?

None of the women described so far, including attorney Coleman and saleswoman Wildowsky, has chosen to take her justifiable grievances to court. And the brave women who have done so have experienced decidedly mixed results.

Elder Care: Sandra Davison, of Melville, Saskatchewan, is the only fat Canadian woman so far whose employment-discrimination case has hit the headlines. At age twenty-seven, weighing about 280 pounds and standing 5' 4", she applied for a job as an aide at a local nursing home in 1989. The interviewer told her point-blank that she "didn't have a chance" of being hired because obesity would make her unable to

handle the required physical exertion. Davison rebutted with three argu-
ments: (1) She'd been on her feet and exceptionally active for seven years
at a dental office (from which she had just been laid off because of
government cutbacks); (2) She was qualified as a personal-care aide; and
(3) The nursing home's mandatory six-month probation period would
afford a risk-free opportunity to assess her ability to do the job.

The interviewer refused to even consider Davison's remarks and,
instead, hired a barmaid and a friend of her niece's, neither of whom had
pertinent qualifications. Meanwhile, Davison took her case to the
Saskatchewan Human Rights Commission, which spent four years fighting on her behalf at various judicial levels. In the end, she lost because of
what can only be described as a Catch-22 trap.

The only specified groups that are protected under the disability por-
tion of the provincial Human Rights Code are those with "natural"
problems such as deafness, blindness, or paralysed limbs. Because
Davison suffered none of these, and a doctor testified that the cause of
her obesity was "unknown," the ruling went against her. That she'd been
denied employment because the interviewer perceived her as disabled
was deemed to have no bearing on the court's decision.

Melville attorney Brian Graff, who argued the case on behalf of the
nursing home, told me it is the inference that obesity is entirely voluntary
that clouds legal cases such as Davison's. To date, none of the scientists
who believe that as much as 70 per cent of obesity may indeed be genetically caused has yet been given the opportunity to testify in court. Graff
believes, however, that the wording of the judicial opinion that went against
Davison left the door open for future employment-discrimination cases
to be brought by obese plaintiffs in Saskatchewan, and that the wording
of Human Rights Codes in several other provinces, as well as at the federal level, seems to provide equal leeway.

As for Davison, she was later denied another job at a local dental clinic,
despite the fact that she is a certified dental assistant. That employer
chose instead to hire a cook with no relevant qualifications whatsoever.
The best Davison has been able to do for employment since she lost her
case is to work part-time as a clerk in an appliance store and to babysit
whenever an opportunity arises.

Another example of the inescapable Catch-22 trap that permeates weight-discrimination cases snared a Michigan nurse's aide in the case of *Krein* v. *Marian Manor Nursing Home*. After satisfactorily tending to the nursing home's elderly patients for five years, Melanie Krein was fired because of her obesity. She attempted to sue Marian Manor, but the suit was dismissed by the trial court. When Krein appealed, the state supreme court concurred with the lower court that "the mere assertion that one is overweight or obese is not enough to make a person a member of a protected class."

Translation: Most courts, in both Canada and the United States, maintain that obesity is not a disqualification, and therefore is not covered by human-rights safeguards for minorities. But employers who wish to contend that obesity *is* a disqualification are completely free to fire, refuse to hire, or professionally squelch overweight workers.

Mental-Health Care: Even in a case where the clients couldn't possibly be presumed to have anti-fat sentiments, a large woman can experience employment discrimination. For five years, Bonnie Cook had satisfactorily performed her work as an aide at a Rhode Island residential centre for severely retarded children. Her daughter's illness forced her to resign for a time and, when she reapplied for her former position, she was refused it because of her 320-pound weight.

When Cook sued the state Department of Mental Health, Retardation and Hospitals, Dr. Mark O'Brien testified that he had turned her down because her "morbid obesity" made her "susceptible" to a host of health problems. But the doctor's hypothesis was shattered by the fact that Cook's weight was exactly the same when she reapplied as it had been when she was considered a satisfactory employee.

In the first such victory in an American federal appeals court, Cook won her job back, plus retroactive pay and seniority, and $100,000 in punitive damages. Says Rhode Island American Civil Liberties Union executive director Steve Brown: "The irony of this is that we have an agency that has worked hard to change public attitudes toward the mentally disabled, and here they are discriminating against someone based on all the stereotypes of obesity." Echoes Cook herself: "All I can say is that people shouldn't judge others because of how they look. What's important is whether or not they can do the job."

Retail Clerking: Across the continent, in Santa Cruz, California, Toni Cassista applied for a clerking job at a health-food store called Community Foods. When she got the old don't-call-us routine and later saw the job readvertised, she launched a one-woman counter-attack that eventually grew into a state-wide *cause célèbre*.

"I started small," she recalls, "by simply asking why I wasn't hired." She says the response was that "a fat person could not work on [her] feet eight hours a day, forty hours a week, and that slicing cheese, working the cash register or stocking shelves would be too much for me." Knowing that the employee-owned health-food store had a progressive reputation, Cassista first tried sweet reason, trying to raise store personnel's consciousness about size-diversity issues. When they turned a deaf ear, she filed a complaint with the California Department of Fair Employment and Housing.

Community Foods then offered to settle out of court, but Cassista refused. "This is not about money," she insisted. "Everything that I am— my self-worth, my self-respect and my dignity—are at stake. Employers need to get a strong message that any applicant who walks through the door should be treated equally . . . that if certain physical abilities are necessary to do the job, a test of those abilities should be incorporated into the hiring process."

Cassista eventually won what so far is a purely pyrrhic victory. The California court that heard her case made legal history when it decreed that the burden of proof in employment-discrimination cases should shift from the plaintiff to the defendant. If the state supreme court concurs, Cassista and Community Foods will head back to the courtroom. But, this time, the health-food store will have to prove it didn't discriminate, rather than Cassista having to show the opposite.

At the federal level, however, the situation was made gloomier for all categories of job-discrimination plaintiffs in 1993. Two years earlier, in what the *Los Angeles Times* and others called "a clear slap at the high court," Congress enacted an amendment to the Civil Rights Act to make it easier for mistreated employees to pursue employment-discrimination cases. It also made them eligible to have jury trials and to claim damages. But the U.S. Supreme Court tipped the teeter-totter once again by upholding the "reverse onus" situation that places upon plaintiffs, rather than defendants, the burden of proving that bias was the cause of their dismissal.

Incidentally, while the Cassista case was in the spotlight in Santa Cruz, California's first public forum on appearance discrimination was staged there. Spearheaded by NAAFA and the city's Human Rights Task Force, the debate drew national attention to what boors delighted in calling "a freak show." On one side were proponents of size acceptance such as Michael Coonerty, who stated: "Appearance discrimination cripples businesses because they aren't hiring the best qualified people. They are hiring for ridiculous, unrealistic reasons."

On the opposite side was chief opponent Louise Rittenhouse, who snarled: "If [the anti-discrimination ordinance passes] and I have two equally qualified candidates for employment, one thin and well dressed [and] the other obese and dirty . . . I have to discriminate against the thin, clean one or I go to court."

When the ordinance did pass, influential media pundit Rush Limbaugh—a 300-pounder who apparently misunderstands the nature of glass houses—cast a characteristically insensitive stone. "I want an ordinance," he thundered from his radio-bully pulpit, "prohibiting ugly people from walking on city streets during daylight hours."

Law Enforcement: Since there are so few laws protecting the overweight, it's not surprising that even law-enforcement workers can be tagged for obesity. In the case of *Donoghue* v. *County of Orange*, a female police-department clerk decided to train for a deputy-sheriff position. Carole Donoghue underwent the same boot-camp conditions as the male candidates. But the daily weigh-ins were mandatory only for her and for the one other woman in the program. After incurring repeated reprimands for exceeding the women-only weight limit, she was ultimately terminated.

Donoghue filed a complaint with the Equal Employment Opportunity Commission (EEOC), which found in her favour, concluding that males who were even more overweight than she were not punished or penalized, let alone terminated. She also prevailed at trial on the grounds that her civil rights had been violated. It's important to note, however, that this case was essentially a victory against sexual, rather than weight, discrimination.

Jury Duty: No lawsuits have yet been brought against him, but at least one officer of the court does whatever he can to keep overweight women off his juries. San Diego deputy district attorney August Meyer was recently quoted in the *San Diego Union* as contending that not only does it take a man "to make the tough decisions," but the obese "don't have the sort of social contact and work-together skills of someone I would like to [have] on my jury. They tend to be outcasts and unhappy people."

Military: In the United States, as the military looks for ways to trim ranks now that the Cold War is over, a quiet little "police action" is being waged against overweight personnel. The experience of Nyleen Mullally, who had served for thirteen years with the Minnesota National Guard, is typical. Without warning, she says, she was suddenly chewed out by her commander for "getting away with" excessive weight for too long. He froze her advancement for three years of what she calls "hell" until she resigned. Then, as if in an attempt to place one final blow, eight months later, Mullally recalls, "I was called to involuntary active duty in Operation Desert Storm. The war was short and I was discharged [without going to the Middle East], but I was never weighed. I was just told that the weight standards had been 'waived' for the duration."

Nursing: Sharon Russell is an overweight woman whose professional problems, and exemplar status, were dramatic enough to interest even *60 Minutes* and *People* magazine. Now a successful nurse in Florida, she was nearly prevented from getting her RN because of size discrimination. Russell, while an A-student at Rhode Island's Salve Regina College, was expelled for failing to comply with an edict to lose 2 of her approximately 300 pounds every week. Why the career-threatening ultimatum? Because school administrators ostensibly feared she would "lack credibility" in counselling patients on the subject of nutrition.

Russell completed her nursing degree elsewhere and sued Salve Regina for breach of contract. She won a $44,000 award at the first trial, based on a judgment that she had been dismissed "because she was obese and for no other reason." But the school, whose lawyer put forward the non sequitur: "I don't know of any blind people who are nurses [and] doctors don't write charts in Braille," appealed all the way to the

U.S. Supreme Court. There, on a jurisdictional technicality, Russell's victory was overturned and sent down to the First Circuit Court in Boston, where it is still stalled as of this writing.

Aviation: Another category of well-publicized court cases involved thousands of women who weigh far less than Sharon Russell, but whose careers were even more jeopardized by weight gains. The flight attendants of American Airlines, Pan American, United, USAir, and Delta fought plucky but protracted battles to get punitive weight policies rescinded. Not until federal EEOC attorneys entered the fray did the hostility in the so-called friendly skies towards ageing and thickening flight attendants grab the spotlight.

Even now, when those loathsome "fly me" slogans have been jettisoned, the employment manual of, for example, American Airlines still states that "a firm, trim silhouette, free of bulges, rolls, or paunches, is necessary for an alert, efficient image." But, countered the EEOC, women who don't gain some weight as they pass age forty risk health problems.

The parting shots in the fracas have gone to a variety of judges over the past few years. Pan Am (now defunct) was ordered to pay $2.35 million to 116 female flight attendants and to reinstate those who had been fired. Chided Judge Thelton E. Henderson: "the Court finds Pan Am's weight policy perpetuated a sexual stereotype that female flight attendants must be slim-bodied, attractive women, rather than competent employees."

Succumbing to the "Weigh my performance, not my body" rallying cry of furious flight attendants, American Airlines relaxed its archaic weight restrictions to an allowable maximum of 145 (up from 129) pounds for flight attendants aged forty to forty-four. And both Delta and USAir stopped weigh-ins for flight attendants altogether. Yet insiders predict that, though this particular battle was won, the war for flight attendants may yet resume.

Entertainment: There have been two spotlighted cases of weight discrimination in Hollywood in the past few years but—probably because so many people think slenderness is automatically a BFOQ for actresses—neither had the sort of "Anita Hill effect" I believe will one day begin turning the situation around. Delta Burke, who played the most popular character (Suzanne Sugarbaker) on the *Designing Women* TV series, was hounded about her escalating weight by her producers, humiliated in the press, and ultimately fired. Three years later, however, secret behind-the-scenes negotiations created a new role for Burke. With what looked like every one of her "extra" pounds intact, she went on to star as a congresswoman on *Women of the House*—a comedy series that was developed by Linda Bloodsworth Thomason and her husband, the same duo who had previously sacked Burke.

Kathy Bates, the only large woman ever to win a best-actress Oscar (for *Misery*), was denied the movie version of her Broadway success in *Frankie & Johnny*. Instead, the role of the depressed, down-at-heels waitress went to the least logical candidate—glamorous, rail-thin Michelle Pfeiffer. Actually, Bates was accustomed to this process by then, because she'd also been passed over for the film versions of two of her other stage triumphs: *'Night Mother* and *Crimes of the Heart*, both of which went to reed-slender Sissy Spacek.

And, more recently, actress Janeane Garofalo was amazingly candid about what it took to land a starring role in the film *The Truth About Cats and Dogs*: losing 35 pounds. Nothing too unusual about that in showbiz? Maybe not. But Garofalo's pre-movie weight was only 140 pounds—and she played a woman who is called an "ugly bitch" and considers herself so unattractive that she can't bring herself to reveal her identity to the man she loves, instead coaxing a skinny model to stand in for her. Hollywood's "imagery of the 'plain' person," says Garofalo, "is galling. I don't feel I've done the right thing, [and] I don't condone what I've done. It's just a reality. . . . "

Electronics Technology: One of the few cases in which the irresistible force of justice has met the immovable object of prejudice—and the object moved—occurred in the vital field of electronics technology. It took ten tenacious years, with setbacks every step of the way, but Catherine McDermott ultimately trounced the mighty Xerox Corporation.

After succeeding in similar positions elsewhere, the 249-pound systems consultant had been hired by Xerox. But she flunked the pre-employment physical solely, as she proved in court, because of her weight. Xerox, which submitted no evidence that McDermott's size was an impediment to her work performance, was ordered by the New York State human-rights board to hire her, with equivalent back pay.

But that decision was overturned on appeal by the same application of Catch-22 reasoning that defeated Sandra Davison and Melanie Krein: Since McDermott had proven that she was not disabled, her obesity was deemed a "voluntary condition," and therefore she was not among the groups whose human rights are protected in the context of employment. Of McDermott's later victory in a higher court, the *Labor Law Journal* remarked: "It is significant to note that Xerox forthrightly claimed that nothing was wrong with her, but that it was concerned about the 'potential' impairments she might develop in the future. Similar concerns have been increasingly voiced by other companies [which] see people like McDermott . . . as a burden. . . . "

Health Insurance—No Laughing Matter

Isn't it funny how such burdensome "potential impairment" scenarios apply only to the Catherine McDermotts, and not to, say, bungee-jumpers, motorcyclists, hot-air-balloon enthusiasts, or even smokers, all of whom incur health risks far more voluntarily than do the obese.

The *Labor Law Journal* actually hit the health-insurance nail squarely on its head in characterizing one of the earliest lawsuits in the context of weight discrimination as "merely" the first red flag that signaled the interest of employers in having an . . . illness-free and claim-free labor force. . . . " NAAFA co-founder William J. Fabrey agrees with that, but adds that "all too often, the employer's real reasons for not wanting to hire fat job applicants lies in the area of aesthetics—they feel the fat person would be bad for the corporate image."

Even so, the crisis of mushrooming health-care costs is certainly no laughing matter, and the legitimate health consequences for any employee group—the overweight included—cannot simply be disregarded. At this writing, the rules of the American health-insurance game are being vociferously debated, while, in Canada, a dearth of funding seems to be producing a scary decline in services. However, what probably won't change in either country is the employers' right to establish general eligibility standards for the health-insurance coverage they provide.

Overweight workers essentially have no problem with that. At least so long as the criteria applied to them are as fair as those applied to other workers, and are not just knee-jerk, prejudicial assumptions about their capabilities and the amount of money they might cost in health-insurance claims. Currently, however, as pioneering obesity specialist Dr. Albert Stunkard, of the University of Pennsylvania, told the *New York Times* in the "Fat in America" series: "The extent to which overweight people have difficulty in obtaining work goes far beyond what can be justified by medical data and must be due to discrimination."

A striking case in point was provided in September 1995, when the first jury ever to go this far financially awarded an obese San Francisco man $1 million in damages. Pundits everywhere hooted derisively when they heard that John Rossi had been fired by an auto-parts store because he weighed 400 pounds. What most of them didn't hear—or didn't even consider—was that Rossi had held the job from which he was fired for ten years, and had taken a grand total of three sick days in all that time.

Another Wrinkle

For Canadians whose employment opportunities are limited by this sort of bare-faced bigotry, a new wrinkle was added to the debate in Alberta in April 1994. The case involved an Edmonton man named Delwin Vriend, who was fired by The King's University, a Christian college, for wearing a pink-triangle pin that identified him as a homosexual while he was working there as a lab coordinator. Vriend ended up suing, not his former employer, but the provincial government because it refused to allow the Alberta Human Rights Commission to pursue his claim of wrongful dismissal.

The decision that was ultimately handed down by Madam Justice Anne Russell ruled that Alberta's Individual's Rights Protection Act (IRPA) must henceforth include homosexuals among the protected classes. While there have so far been no specific challenges raised to clarify whether the employment rights of the obese are also covered by the act, its author, Senator Ron Ghitter, is on record as declaring that "the IRPA is for everyone who faces the indignity, the blows to their self-esteem, the paralysis of bigotry and the cruelty of discrimination."

Shades of Things to Come?

Keeping all of the above in mind, consider how much outrage would explode in this country if a high-profile corporation began docking $5 per paycheque from all workers who were, say, Progressive Conservatives, or whose spouses were Progressive Conservatives—until they stopped being Progressive Conservatives.

Substitute the word "fat" for "Progressive Conservatives" and you've got the exact situation that U-Haul International began imposing on its workforce in 1990. Some 13,500 employees were required to sign statements swearing that they, and their spouses, would either comply with the company's so-called wellness weight level or consent to a salary reduction. The penalty for lying: immediate dismissal.

U-Haul's policy scarcely made a news ripple, even though the American Civil Liberties Union denounced it as "barbaric . . . unconscionable . . . [and] outrageous." But corporate beancounters were paying attention, and not just to U-Haul's punitive ploy, which conceivably could chop $250,000 off the company's annual salary expenses. Beady-eyed bottom-liners also evidently noticed the national indifference towards oppression of the obese.

And now authorities such as the *Labor Law Journal* predict that "more than half of the major corporations will [soon] implement such programs [as U-Haul's]." Plus, looming in the not-too-distant future, according to various employment authorities: genetic pre-employment testing to winnow out applicants with a predisposition to obesity.

Yet companies who find U-Haul's example enticing would do well to think about the broader implications. For sheer practicality, employee policies must be considered from the perspective that more than one-third of the North American population—including the available labour pool—is now at least 20 per cent overweight, while millions of others are even heavier, and overall obesity has been on the rise for the past few decades.

Add to that the calculation by census bureaus on both sides of the border that, beginning in 1996 and lasting for the next eighteen years, a North American will turn fifty every 7.5 seconds. By the turn of the century, the members of this age group—known *ad infinitum* as the Baby Boomers—will number in excess of 80 million. This will make them the biggest—in both senses of the word—demographic group of all. The Boomers' economic and sociological clout has already enabled its members to rewrite the social contract in many significant ways. In the context of employment, it seems entirely predictable that, both as workers and as consumers, they will demand a new definition of "normality."

To illustrate the point, two giant companies serve as perfect examples of how abstemious employee policies would decimate profits if adopted as general business practices. Coors workers, and their counterparts at Hershey, now know that, if they chug enough of their employer's beer or munch enough of its chocolate bars to sprout soft flab, they'll pay for it in hard cash.

At Hershey, 650 non-union employees were recently ordered to report to a health screening site to be weighed, measured, and quizzed about their diet and exercise habits. Those found "least fit" stand to lose $1,404 per year in company health benefits. Similarly, at Coors, only those employees who meet management's "wellness" standards are eligible to have 90 per cent of their medical bills covered by the company-subsidized health-insurance plan.

But don't expect to see this Big Brotherly attitude creeping into either of these companies' advertisements any time soon. Consumers will be encouraged, to the tune of millions of ad dollars, to keep eating and drinking without regard for the consequences.

Another comestibles corporation, Stouffer Foods, was the target of what is thought to be the first class-action suit ever brought by overweight workers in North America. But this time it was management that had to dig into its pockets because of strict anti-fat policies. In 1993, Stouffer's parent company, Nestlé, was forced to settle out of court with fifty-one obese job applicants who had filed a federal discrimination suit after being turned down because of their weight. The company ended up paying a plump $303,000 to forty-five of the overweight complainants and hiring six of those it had previously rejected.

Unfortunately, the suit's potential fizzled, both as a legal precedent and in terms of publicity, because it never went to court, and also because the claims of the obese applicants were rolled in with those of a larger group of racial-minority workers who had also been turned away by Stouffer.

Is Legislation the Answer?

For all intents and purposes, weight discrimination is simply not against the law anywhere in Canada. The same is true in the United States, at the federal level and in thirty-nine states. In eleven other states, light has been glimpsed at the end of the tunnel, with either the enactment or the introduction of legislative antidotes to the anti-fat plague spread by the "billion-dollar brainwash." These include California, Colorado, Illinois, Maryland, Michigan, Nevada, New York, North Dakota, Rhode Island, Tennessee, and Texas.

Michigan led the way with its sweeping Elliott–Larsen Civil Rights Act of 1977. The pioneering legislation decreed that "an employer shall not: fail or refuse to hire, or recruit, or discharge, or otherwise discriminate against an individual with respect to employment, compensation, or a term, condition, or privilege of employment, because of religion, race, color, national origin, age, sex, height, weight or marital status."

It took New York State sixteen years to catch up with Michigan. But Bill A.3484, which was proposed by Assemblyman Daniel Feldman in the spring of 1993, is now being touted as a model for other jurisdictions. Feldman persevered despite ridicule from (among many others) the generally compassionate then New York governor, Mario Cuomo, who publicly called the proposal "one law too many."

Feldman responded by appearing at a press conference called by NAAFA to endorse and publicize his bill. "For too many years, people have experienced blatant prejudice because of size," said Feldman. "This may be the last form of discrimination that conventional thinking accepts—but that acceptance must be ended." Added NAAFA executive director Sally E. Smith: "We are a society that prides itself on equal opportunity for all and a society that likes to believe that anyone can reach for the American dream. Assemblyman Feldman's bill will go far to ensure that this dream is available to all people, regardless of body size."

As the New York anti-discrimination act awaits passage, the overweight there and elsewhere—in both Canada and the United States—remain as vulnerable as were women and racial minorities until the advent of equal-opportunity employment policies, and sharp-toothed laws to back them up. Unless and until that scenario is extended to the obese, say legal authorities, there is only one legislative umbrella to shelter them from the storm of prejudice: the federal Americans with Disabilities Act (ADA).

Until passage of the laudable ADA in 1992, American employers were as free to ignore and exploit the disabled as they still are with regard to the obese. Now, however, it's a whole new ballgame for the physically challenged, with Uncle Sam acting as a stern umpire. In essence, the ADA legally protects the disabled from any employment discrimination that isn't based solely on reasonable job-related qualifications. That, of course, is all the disabled, the overweight, or indeed any other workers, need ask.

So, in light of the burgeoning scientific data indicating that as much as 70 per cent of obesity may be genetically caused, some see the ADA as legal salvation for the overweight in employment, housing, and many other contexts. Says attorney Jennifer Coleman: "It is my conviction that obesity is a clinical condition, not a moral fault. And that's exactly what the ADA is all about." A recent article in the *Labor Law Journal* concurred with her: "Protecting the obese, who suffer discrimination due to untrue stereotypes, comports with [the] legislative intent."

In practical terms, and in the absence of specific protective legislation for the obese, both of these opinions are correct. But if ever the term "double-edged sword" had a perfect application, this is it. If Fat Chicks accept the protection of the ADA in the United States, or any future human-rights legislation in Canada based on disability, we must—by definition—accept being defined as "disabled." But the truth is that, for all but the truly huge, and for almost all job categories, extra weight is not disabling.

Kim Campbell's performance as prime minister was not affected in the slightest by her modest weight gain. Sandra Davison had a mandatory probation period in which to prove whether or not she could function efficiently in the Saskatchewan nursing home that refused even to consider hiring her. And that seventeen-year-old secretary who was fired from her first job—whose name was Terry Poulton—could surely have managed to type, file, and take dictation without dropping dead because of 30 extra pounds.

The fact is, whatever incapacity pertains in most employment-discrimination situations—be it weight, disability, sex, or race—is literally in the eye of the beholder. Yet, even for her own protection, we would scarcely think of applying a "disabled" label to, say, an aboriginal citizen who lost an employment opportunity because of prejudice. Labels—particularly those that diminish and are not legitimately applicable—are the problem for Fat Chicks, not the solution.

What *would* be fair and effective? In my opinion, simply adding overweight people to the existing categories of employees whose mere outward appearance prompts the kind of blind prejudice that leads to illegal labour practices.

Bottom Line

The foregoing is just a small sampling of the deluge of size discrimination currently occurring all over North America, and only a tiny whiff of the wholesale, transparently veiled prejudice that utterly fails the "sniff test."

In Canada and in 80 per cent of the United States—despite the Americans with Disabilities Act, the embryonic precedent of the Stouffer class-action suit, Alberta's Individual's Rights Protection Act, and the handful of other partial victories detailed above—the obese are fundamentally still on their own, prey to whatever punitive actions anti-fat employers care to dole out.

So, at least in the near future, the vast majority of pudgy plaintiffs are doomed to learn an expensive lesson: The social, psychological, and legal groundwork simply hasn't yet been laid for significant numbers of weight-discrimination cases to prevail. Before that happens, anti-fat victims will have to wage the same sort of militant battles as did other oppressed groups, who marched in the streets to make it worthwhile to stride into the courtrooms.

CHAPTER SEVEN

Life with Laugh-Track

In a world where people agree on less and less as time goes by, there are two things we're unanimous about: Fat people are hilarious, and Fat Chicks the most amusing of all. The only thing that's funnier still is a Fat Chick who actually thinks she's entitled to enjoy her life like a normal person. Laugh at *this* deluded loser and the world will laugh with you.

To a certain extent, this is just business as usual here on Planet Earth. The nature of the human beast seems to be that we always need a designated punching-bag. So, if it's not a racial, ethnic, or religious minority, it's got to be some individual trait we can use to relegate *somebody* to lesser status than ourselves. Remember Newfie jokes? Polish jokes? Little Moron jokes? Mercifully, most of us have finally evolved to a point where compassion has consigned such mindlessly cruel barbs to, if not extinction, at least a degree of odiousness that punishes with a disapproving frown anyone who still repeats them.

Some of us welcomed this overdue attitudinal transformation, which goes by the unwieldy name of "political correctness" (PC). Others had to be dragged to enlightenment, kicking and screaming about reverse discrimination every step of the way. And some are unrepentant still, though they've wised up enough to lower their voices and make sure they're among like-minded bigots before indulging in their nasty little knee-slappers.

But, thanks to the "billion-dollar brainwash," we've all still got one allowable whipping-girl left: our faithful, oh-so-useful friend, the Fat Chick. Stereotypically, she's sloppy, lazy, greedy, stupid, gross, clumsy, sweaty, smelly, insensitive, antisocial, self-indulgent, hostile, loud, sarcastic, and oversexed. All of which means she's still fair game for any degree of cruelty anyone cares to inflict, especially if it's cloaked in the guise of humour. And the best part is: she won't fight back. She can't—there is no defence for all the negative qualities she represents.

So when she's a little girl, it's okay to trot out the time-worn "Fatty, fatty, two by four, couldn't get through the kitchen door." It's perfectly fine to make her sit red-cheeked and squirming through the many children's movies that include a stock fat-kid character who's not only always eating, but too dumb and food-obsessed to care what others think. *Little Giants*, say, or *Richie Rich*. Or *Casper*, in which the grossest of a trio of evil ghosts gobbles voraciously every moment it's on screen.

When the Fat Chick becomes a teenager, it's completely acceptable to hurl such "jests" as "Porker," "Tubbo," "Lardo," and "Blimpo" at her. If she doesn't like it, she can just stay home on prom night—when she certainly won't have a date anyway—and perhaps watch *Jurassic Park*, in which the chubby computer programmer played by Josh Mostel is a slob who constantly munches, speaks with his mouth full, strews his work area with food wrappers, and ends up betraying the good guys. At school, amid the inevitable post-prom giggling about the assorted weirdos who were absent, someone will make sure there's an audience to catch the Fat Chick's reaction to an old pop song that's carefully passed from generation to generation:

> I don't want her, you can have her
> She's too fat for me
> She's too fat, she's too fat
> She's too fat for me.

When the Fat Chick reaches adulthood, the jokey taunts can take on a whiff of sexual innuendo—"thunder thighs," "bubble butt," and the necessity of "pushin' through cushion"—just to make sure she doesn't miss the point about how far from ideal her body really is. "For a fat girl, you sure don't sweat much," she'll be told by way of flimsily veiled insult. Other lessons regarding her status will be reiterated in non-stop comic quips during the course of any average day. When she's watching TV, for instance, she'll learn that

• being overweight automatically negates achievement. So not even the first female prime minister of Canada could escape crude jokes about her figure. And David Letterman has no qualms about cracking fat jokes about Oprah Winfrey—even after she lost weight. (What kind of jokes?

To pick just one in an outrageous onslaught: That Oprah's TV studio is plastered with zoo-like signs saying "Please Don't Feed the Host.");

• if the writers of the *Royal Canadian Air Farce* series are stuck for innovative material, they'll fall back on fat jokes, put Luba Goy and Roger Abbot into fat suits as, respectively, Rita MacNeil and either tenor Luciano Pavarotti or TV newsman Mike Duffy. And to make it even funnier, both actors will stuff their mouths non-stop throughout the sketches;

• comedian Joan Rivers, apparently forgetting she's on record as saying that "the psychic scars caused by believing you are ugly leave a permanent mark on your personality," will think nothing of claiming—among a flood of similar insults—that a photograph of Elizabeth Taylor on the cover of *People* magazine "looks like she devoured her previous husbands."

The lessons will continue even when the Fat Chick reads a book about losing weight:

• In *Diary of a Fat Housewife*, she'll note that author Rosemary Green takes Joan Rivers to task, albeit mildly, for joking about Elizabeth Taylor's weight, but only because she used Taylor's real name—implying that it's perfectly fine to ridicule fat people anonymously.

When the Fat Chick reads a newspaper, she'll learn that

• students at The Citadel military academy in South Carolina were free to fight off female usurpers with purportedly humorous bumper stickers mocking wannabe-cadet Shannon Faulkner's famous extra 20 pounds: "Save the Males—Shave the Whale";

• newspaper editors who need to round out a page with "filler" thank their lucky stars when something like this comes over the wire: "(AP) Seattle—A 410-pound death-row inmate is too fat to be hanged, a federal judge ruled . . . because he might be decapitated. . . .";

• or maybe it'll be a squib numerous news organizations found funny enough to print about an insensitive Florida teacher who got laughs by forcing an overweight student to wear a "Wide Load" sign. If the Fat Chick is lucky, this won't remind her of any humiliations in her own school days. (But if she's the author of this book, she'll remember a painful incident in the seventh grade when her gym teacher became angry because she had trouble learning to square-dance. She'll still see him stopping the music, rushing towards her, grabbing her, and roughly shoving her through an intricate step. And when she kept on stumbling, how he stopped abruptly, stomped back up to the stage, and said to the entire class, "It's like trying to push a bull moose around.")

If the Fat Chick listens to a radio talk show, chances are good that she'll hear someone like

• Michigan talk show host Ted Heusel inviting a representative of the National Association to Advance Fat Acceptance to talk about the fitness walk they've planned for International No-Diet Day (see Chapter 10), only to use his guest as the butt of simple-minded jokes. "So, are you gonna take an ambulance with you?"

Seeking a little comic relief, she'll find it hard to avoid cartoonists such as

• *B.C.*'s Johnny Hart, who created a horrendously aggressive character called "the fat broad" so he could make fun of her, decade after decade.

Browsing at the bookstore, she'll likely notice

• how much of the humour section is devoted to fat jokes. In a single book by Milton Berle (*Private Joke File*), there are no fewer than seventy. "She was so fat she went on her honeymoon in a U-Haul." "When she wears white she looks like a bandaged whale." "She never met a meal she didn't like."

Although it'll be small comfort, the Fat Chick will see that chunky men don't get off scot-free either:

• Watching the 1995 Academy Awards, she'll wince when host David Letterman kicks off the evening with a tasteless, unfunny joke about portly film critic Roger Ebert devouring all of *Forrest Gump*'s notorious chocolates.

• Or she may be reminded of being fascinated as a child by the way Americans obviously loved to utter the full title of their leader: "the President of the United States of America," they'd say, always in respect-ful tones. But not today. Bill Clinton's weight has been average for his body type ever since he moved into the White House, and he jogs every morning, rain or shine. But obesity is the ultimate leveller. So the myth that he's an out-of-control glutton has served as profitable fodder for comedians ranging from TV biggies like Leno, Letterman (again!), and the *Saturday Night Live* gang, right down to wee-hours deejays. And the print media are no better. In a typically gratuitous swipe, a recent fitness article in *Vogue* sarcastically denounced "the leader of the free world's

double biceps curl—Quarter Pounder in one hand, slurpee in the other. . . ."
Even when Clinton *did* lose a few pounds, *People* magazine smirked:
"Where's the blubba, bubba?"

Laughing All the Way to the Bank

Whether or not we applaud the PC taboo against victimizing minorities,
we have to notice that fat people are the *only* group that's still totally
exempt from such social protection. But if this contention strikes you as
far-fetched, even in light of the foregoing examples, try substituting *any*
racial, ethnic, or religious minority as the target of all these "jokes." Then
ask yourself two questions: (1) Do the allegations implicit in each of the
instances cited above—which include being ugly, unlovable, greedy, contemptible, gluttonous, cannibalistic, bestial, feeble, and belligerent—*still*
seem like harmless fun? And (2) Would such assertions be socially toler-
ated in any other context?

The universal contempt that preserves Fat Chicks' status as society's last allowable laughing-stock didn't just happen. Certainly many
individuals, both famous and private, revel in ridiculing the obese for
fun and profit. But the lion's share for deliberately escalating and
perpetuating anti-fat bigotry undeniably goes to the weight-loss profiteers. They saw that there was a fortune to be made by exploiting one
of the baser human inclinations, which is enhancing self-esteem by
denigrating "inferiors." Or, as novelist Daniel Pinkwater describes this:
"There is nothing we humans like better than abusing and reviling
others for perceived faults of which we are guilty ourselves—but are
getting away with."

Thus, turning up the cultural heat on Fat Chicks coerces us into
spending every penny we possibly can in an attempt to escape the
orchestrated punishment. And that vivid object lesson, in turn, pressures
smaller women into spending whatever it takes to avoid being included
in the vilified group. Meanwhile, the remainder of the population also
absorbs anti-fat messages and responds to Pavlovian reinforcement
right on cue by mocking the obese at every opportunity. Media wordsmiths get in on the fun by concocting sneering phrases such as "gravi-
tationally challenged," "horizontally challenged," "human heftiness,"
"diametrically disadvantaged," and "St. Oprah of the Stairmaster."

Finally, the mindless monkey-see-monkey-do tradition is passed on to children. Result: Everlasting profits are guaranteed to roll in.

But exactly which mental buttons are being pushed when someone jeers at a Fat Chick and someone else laughs? Mark Breslin believes a couple of them serve the "billion-dollar brainwash" perfectly. As founder of the cross-Canada Yuk Yuk's Comedy Club chain, he says he's noticed that a lot of humour springs from "fear that our body will betray us at any minute by spiralling out of control—whether it's through sex or size." Breslin also believes that ambivalence about breaking rules is another of our psychological buttons. He's been watching audiences for a long time now and knows the exhilaration people feel when societal conventions are flagrantly flouted. "But it all depends on who's doing it," he told me. "Some people can get away with it and some can't."

One who can't, at least in the view of her legions of irate critics, is comic actress Roseanne (formerly surnamed Barr and Arnold) because she pushes both of these mental buttons, according to Breslin. "She's just too much for most people to take. She's overweight, has a big mouth and presents herself as working class. Yet she earns a gazillion dollars and enjoys all the rewards that are 'supposed' to go to svelte, conventionally attractive women."

Comedian Kathi Maio couldn't agree more. And she believes that what also makes Roseanne a target for intense anger is that she broke a crucial silence. As Maio writes in *Revolutionary Laughter: The World of Women Comics*, before Roseanne "entered our living rooms . . . like an invading army of Amazons . . . women of substance led a shamefaced, completely secondary existence in our culture. . . . [She] exposed the female experience by exposing herself. . . . And she made it clear that she wasn't going to put up with any bullshit about her jeans-size. . . ."

Bingo! To people who've been carefully brainwashed to believe that Fat Chicks should sit down, shut up, and have the decency to be ashamed of ourselves, Roseanne's exuberant defiance is so bewildering it makes the arrows on their mental compasses gyrate wildly. If she's allowed to get away with that attitude, nothing in their lives will make sense any more. There'll simply be no way of knowing which way is up.

⌐

Now try another swap. Insert into the bumpy scenario of Roseanne's career the name of anyone who personifies an excluded minority. Then ask yourself if the virulent response to Roseanne's refusal to accept her assigned role (i.e., shamefaced Fat Chick) isn't *identical* to the mental process that produces every other kind of prejudice. If "these people" aren't put in "their place," p.d.q., we're afraid our little world will wobble so violently we won't know who's who any more. Or, more to the point, whether *we* are still happily occupying the high hierarchical rank we desire—and have convinced ourselves we deserve. Far better to take no chances, and nail everything down with a clear understanding of the rules, an agreement among ourselves to abide by them, and severe penalties for anyone who disobeys.

But how can we disseminate and enforce these vital rules? Simple—just ape the technique of demagogues since time immemorial, be they ambitious dictators, callous royals, unscrupulous politicians, religious fanatics, or advertising moguls. First, decide what you want and who you're most likely to swindle it from. Then designate that group as an "enemy of the people" and shout it from the rooftops. If you demonize and dehumanize your target convincingly enough, rather than being outraged everyone else will be so relieved they're not among the outcasts they'll do everything in their power to maintain the status quo. After which you won't have to lift a finger—except, of course, to count your profits. Thy will *will* be done until earth becomes heaven for you and hell for your victims.

Makes sense. But isn't "demonize and dehumanize" a tad strong? Not at all. Let's take the most obvious example of all: war. History is drenched with bloody examples. Somebody covets somebody else's land, or gold, or oil, or widgets. So the first somebody hauls out the biggest sabre available and starts rattling it passionately. That so-and-so has no right to those widgets! He/she/it is nothing but a useless, worthless, disgusting blankety-blank.

And everybody *knows* blankety-blanks eat their young, despoil our precious world, and slither on their bellies like reptiles! A reptile doesn't deserve widgets, now does it? *We* deserve them because we embody everything the blankety-blanks do not. We're clean, upstanding, hard-working, virtuous, brave, and, above all, human. Which means not only that we are vastly superior to the dastardly blankety-blanks, but that the Almighty is automatically on our side—and *wants* us to show those wicked, serpentine, Almighty-less blankety-blanks who's who. And we *must* strive to deserve the Almighty's favour by doing the Almighty's will. Which is to trounce the blankety-blanks once and for all and take the widgets that are rightfully ours. And that means war, my friends. Forward, ho!

Fattening 'Em Up for the Kill

Now we'll fill in the blankety-blanks and see how well humour acts as one more big gun in the arsenal of weapons the pillaging propagandists use to swipe the Fat Chicks' treasure and that of her slimmer sisters. Let's start by deconstructing a few anti-obesity gags:

• A fat, well-dressed, ultra-dignified woman is strolling down a boulevard when she notices a bedraggled, extremely inebriated man staring at her and chuckling. "Lady," says the drunk, "you are the fattest person I've ever seen." "And you," she replies in her snootiest tone, "are the drunkest person I've ever seen." "Yeah," the wino replies, "But I'll be sober in the morning."

• A sleazy strip joint in the Midwest carves out a cachet for itself by advertising "50 Beautiful Girls and 3 Ugly Ones." How ugly are we talking? Well, to be honest, the only strippers who answered the ads weren't all that bad-looking. But they *are* pudgy, so management is home free. The joint is guaran-damn-teed to go hog wild when these gals doff their duds and let it *all* hang out!

• A neophyte comic climbs on stage at a club whose clientele is accustomed to more seasoned acts. It looks like disaster time when his ho-hum shtick bombs and a heckler down front revs up his harassment. Then the comic spies an escape route. He'll just aim his half-baked barbs straight at the heckler and keep tacking on "ya fat pig." It works. His jibes bring the house down, and everyone goes home happy.

What's really going on here? And how do such scenarios fatten the anti-fat profiteers' bottom lines? By using what virtually amounts to a new form of Esperanto in which accusing someone of being obese is understood to be the equivalent of exposing their dirty little secret and shattering their "pretense" of respectability.

It's the same kind of detestable mind game that used to be considered acceptable in the context of racial, ethnic, and religious minorities. Belly laughs could always be won by simply imitating, or alluding to, gross stereotypes. And gutter epithets acted as shorthand that instantly communicated a reprehensible subtext: It's okay to laugh because the blankety-blanks aren't like "us." They're a lesser species. They must be, or everyone wouldn't be laughing so hard. By inference, this makes everyone who doesn't belong to the target *du jour* superior—no matter how much evidence there is to the contrary. Even if we're hopeless drunkards, pot-bellied strip-club patrons with nowhere better to go, or dullard descendants of the bear-baiters of yore hanging around comedy clubs. Hey, at least we're not despicable blankety-blanks. So all's right with the world.

F—The Last Scarlet Letter

A halt to this kind of cruel, divisive, culture-coarsening bigot humour has been called by the PC movement. But the sole remaining variation on the theme—that Fat Chicks are the worst blankety-blanks of all—remains intact thanks to three decades of incessant anti-fat propaganda. Consequently, any transgressor who dares to buck "accepted wisdom" is rocking the profit boat and must pay a heavy price.

Roseanne is at the top of the list of Fat Chicks whose refusal to be cowed threatens the aggressively entrenched scheme of things. The worst venom was, of course, sprayed after Roseanne's parody of ballpark anthem singers went awry a few years ago. But vituperation also reached a fever pitch after her appearances on the cover of *Vanity Fair* magazine, wearing scanty lingerie and unmistakably in-your-face expressions. Displaying such a large body so shamelessly was regarded as tantamount to committing a crime. Theft, most likely, because everyone knows the covers of popular magazines are reserved for women who have the decency to do what they're told, which is whittle their bodies down to skin and bones, complemented by big, surgically augmented breasts.

As a two-fer who was both fat and a minority, Oprah Winfrey has no business being so talented and hard-working that she's predicted to become the first African-American billionaire in U.S. history. So pundits crowed when she first lost weight and then began regaining it, while the tabloids chronicled every pound. "Oprah passes 200!" But slimming down again only compounded her perceived impertinence—infuriating, rather than placating, the anti-fat forces. Why? Because if Fat Chicks achieve mega-success, theories about our inferiority will fly out the window and the whole hoax may be exposed.

Does Winfrey feel she's been punished accordingly? Definitely. She kicked off a show in early 1994 gazing at a TV monitor as videotape rolled from several of the series that have lampooned her the most mercilessly: *In Living Colour, Seinfeld, Saturday Night Live,* and, of course, the *Late Show with David Letterman.* And this is to say nothing of the thousands of jokes still told around the continent about her formerly rotund figure.

Rita MacNeil might be considered a four-fer (if there were such an ungainly term). She's a fat, middle-aged, working-class Maritimer. She's also the favourite singer of thousands of Canadians, who dote on her soaring voice and down-home style. Does the combination have the effect of painting a big bull's-eye on her back? You bet. The most egregious shots have been taken on the *Royal Canadian Air Farce* TV series, as described above. But other anti-fat bigots went ballistic after a humiliated MacNeil had the gall to actually fight back—reportedly refusing to appear on her own TV series until their mutual network, CBC, persuaded the *RCAF* stars to cough up an apology. Result: A raft of cruel jokes soon began making the rounds. Sample: Did you hear Rita contracted that horrible flesh-eating virus? Yeah, she has only twenty-five years to live.

Fun 'n' Games on the Flip Side

Until these three admirable women achieved monumental success—on their own terms—Fat Chicks who could successfully fend off the orchestrated onslaught of bigot humour were few and far between. But here comes the good news: The tide is now turning big-time (*double entendre* purely intentional). Other facets of what's gradually becoming an exciting fight-back revolution reminiscent of women's liberation and the civil-rights movement are included in Chapter 10. But I've clustered some of the most humorous of the ongoing efforts here as a bracing antidote to the heartless "comedy" described above.

Welcoming Back Womanly Sized Women

Plump playwright Wendy Wasserstein, whose highly regarded Broadway productions include *The Heidi Chronicles*, somehow managed to mesmerize *Harper's Bazaar* into printing a fable that contradicted pretty much everything the posh magazine stands for. Mind you, it was scarcely a coincidence that the piece ran just a few months after Tina Gaudoin's detestable denial that portraying only ultra-thin models encourages eating disorders. Wasserstein's fantasy was titled "Goodbye Waif, Hello Bulge." The heroine of the hilarious what-if story (which coincidentally resembles my own McScrawny tale in Chapter 9) is a Junoesque, 183-pound model named Wanderful who transforms the fashion scene after being discovered while wolfing down biscuits and gravy.

Before long, "hips and thighs return to American couture in a big way" and formerly successful supermodels like Cindy Crawford steal away "to fat farms, where they binge on cholesterol. . . . " Meanwhile, the fashionable new "bulge look makes thin women feel [so] embarrassed about their flat tummies . . . that they [begin] gorging themselves on Heath Bar Crunch ice cream and duck sausage while avoiding exercise." Wasserstein's welcome parody ends with a goofy but pointed refutation of Gaudoin's own words: "Eating disorders don't come from fashion. They are a dysfunction of dysfunction . . . [and] the fact that thin women are unable to be happy with their well-toned bodies has nothing to do with the current bulge trend. . . ."

Waving Goodbye to the Waifs

Jay Leno's audience cracked up one night in the spring of 1995 when a female guest told what may well be the world's first *bona fide* anti-bulimia joke. It concerned something that sounds like, but is not, a gag in itself: Several of the skinniest supermodels (Elle MacPherson, Naomi Campbell, Claudia Schiffer, and Christy Turlington) recently opened a restaurant at New York's famed Rockefeller Center. Logically enough, it's called the Fashion Café. Here's the joke: "A customer comes in, sits down, and orders a lima-bean shake. It's so nauseating that she calls the waiter over and says: 'I feel like I'm going to throw up.' And the waiter replies: 'Exactly!'"

Crimes of Corpulence

Large and lovely Kathy Najimy, who was so appealing as the relentlessly upbeat nun in the two *Sister Act* movies that she was tapped to star in the opening dance number at the 1995 Academy Awards, and included as one of *In Style* magazine's "heavenly bodies," recently tipped off late-night TV talk host Greg Kinnear about Los Angeles's anti-fat laws: "If you're five pounds overweight, you only have to pay a $5 ticket. Being 15 pounds overweight gets you a $15 misdemeanor ticket. But 20 pounds is a felony. And 50 pounds automatically means the electric chair."

Mind Over Matter

Writer Mickey Guisewite turns out to be just as amusingly perspicacious as her cartoonist sister, Cathy. The duo recently collaborated on a book of comic essays titled *Dancing Through Life in a Pair of Broken High Heels*. Arguably the best chapter is "I Think, Therefore I Am Fat," which begins: "The reason men will never understand women's weight anxiety is because men have never had to get on the same scale we do: The one that is in our brains. The one that tells us every morning that we're fat. The one that reminds us all day long that we're fat. . . . The one that makes us overeat because, what the heck, we're already fat."

Destruction by Deconstruction

For the past five years, a uniquely activist Vancouver troupe has used caustic humour to help subscribers to its eponymously named *Adbusters* magazine become "media literate" enough to perceive the ghastly under-side of many of the most ubiquitous ad campaigns. Logically enough, much of their efforts concern the work of anti-fat profiteers. A favourite target is Calvin Klein, whose advertising for Obsession perfume the group has metamorphosed into a soft-focus, black-and-white photo of a woman's nude torso. "Obsessed" reads the headline, with the credit line going to "Calvin Swine." On second glance, you realize that the ad brings bulimia right out in the open, because the woman is crouched over a toilet.

Adbusters shot a TV version of this hardhitting, advertising-offending spot and pitched it, without success, to CNN. CBC TV first accepted it, but later changed its corporate mind. Adbusters took the network all the way to the B.C. Supreme Court, only to receive a judgement that CBC had the right to reject any ad it deemed to be in bad taste. However,

Adbusters publisher Kalle Lasn told me that, having since adjusted its "advocacy advertising policy," CBC has now consented to air the bulimia busting "Calvin Swine" ad.

Bottom Line

Anti-fat humour is not harmless fun; it is the sole surviving form of socially acceptable discrimination. To complain about it is not simply to throw a "pity party" for Fat Chicks. For what's so destructive about this brand of bigot comedy isn't *just* that it hurts the feelings and restricts the lives of large females, young, older, and yet to be born. It also damages and limits the rest of our society, helping to keep us divided into sparring factions—and nothing could be more useful to the imagemeisters than this classic divide-and-conquer technique.

The welcome "reverse humour" trend promises to be a very effective revolutionary tool over time. It also seems like such good, therapeutic fun that I can't resist trying my own hand at it.

THE SCENE: *Some late night in the sweet by and by in beautiful downtown wherever, at the popular If the Tables Were Turned comedy club. Onstage is a jolly jokester who's just winding up the last set of the evening. Let's listen.*

"But seriously, ladies and germs, you've been a great audience—for skinny folks! Yeah, I know what your problem is. You're afraid your scrawny little bones'll shatter if you crack up, right? And who's got enough energy to applaud when all you're eating is a couple of lettuce leaves and half an eye of newt— hold the dressing? And that's only on days starting with a W! Ba-boom.

"Anyhoo, let's wrap it up tonight with a really cheap shot. How cheap is it? It's sooooo cheap you can afford it even after you've paid your dues at Jenny Watchers, or wherever the hell you go to make sure your ego doesn't get too healthy. It's sooooo tasteless that even those yucky diet-shake makers won't use it as an ingredient. Ready? Here goes.

"'Two gals walk into a restroom. They take one look at their bony little bods in the mirror, shake their heads in dismay, head into the stalls, and stick their fingers down their throats. Between heaves, one manages to gasp: "You know what I can't believe?" "What?" croaks the other. "That only one diet doctor has been shot to death so far!"'

"Ba-boom."

CHAPTER EIGHT

Starved for Affection

Her suitor was amorous and persistent. He had proposed marriage over and over again, but she always turned him down because she cherished her independence and her stage career, to say nothing of her international reputation as the most desirable woman of the 1890s.

Today, however, the big man with the huge diamond in his cravat was determined to hear "yes." He strode into her parlour, took one look at her cornflower-blue eyes, peaches-and-cream complexion, and the 200 pounds of dimpled flesh flowing into a perfect hourglass, and decided to play his trump card.

"Sit down, darling," said Diamond Jim Brady to Lillian Russell. And when she did, he poured a million dollars into her capacious lap.

Her answer was still no. But that didn't end their liaison, and they continued doing all the things they enjoyed most. High on the list was eating together, and one of their favourite pastimes was ordering up tray after silver tray of sweet corn, and devouring their fill.

Luscious Lillian wouldn't fare quite so well a century later. Instead of being celebrated as "sonnets of motion," her ample curves would be so despised and denigrated by others that she'd probably detest the sight of them herself. Her chances of meeting, let alone attracting the love of, a top tycoon would be zilch. Star status and international admiration would be out of the question. And if she allowed herself to gorge on corn or any other favourite food, it certainly wouldn't be in the company of a man whose esteem she valued. Anyway, she'd probably either force herself to regurgitate her feast, or loathe and berate herself for eating it in the first place.

All in all, if Lillian Russell *were* somehow transported to the 1990s, her first response to the new world would probably be utter incredulity.

Since the beginning of time, her explicitly fertile body type has been favoured by nature, men, and artists. But today she'd be told in no uncertain terms, and by any number of sources, that she represented the epitome of ugliness—simply because her weight was almost twice what's now allowable for any woman who wishes to be considered attractive.

In our day, Lillian would have to look long and hard to find *any* successful, celebrated, or abundantly beloved women whose girth remotely resembled hers. Flipping through magazines or newspapers wouldn't do it. And if she figured out how to turn on a TV set, she'd likely recoil in horror at the sight of the skeletal, near-naked young women who slither and grind through music videos. Then she'd channel-surf until her thumb got sore, looking for large ladies. Zap: Skinny women and girls fretting about their shameful appetites. Zap: Skinny women in peril after abusive peril. Zap: A skinny blonde excitedly flipping alphabet letters. Zap: Skinny, yet strangely busty, women prancing in bathing suits. Zap: Skinny women reporting the news. Zap, zap, zap: More of the same.

With luck, though, Lillian might stumble upon a performance by Aretha Franklin or Canada's Rita MacNeil, the only large female stars left in North American music. Although Lil wouldn't know it, there used to be others: Kate Smith, Mahalia Jackson, Sophie Tucker, Mama Cass, and, in Canada, Maureen Forrester and Marg Osborne. But not now.

Zapping onward, Lillian might catch large-and-lovely Liz Torres, who plays Mahalia Sanchez on *The John Laroquette Show*. Or ample Elaine Miles as Marilyn Whirlwind on *Northern Exposure*. Or stout Conchata Ferrell as Dr. Madeline Stoessinger on *Hearts Afire*.

But, as something of an expert on romance, Lillian would surely notice that these substantial women hardly ever get to play love scenes. (In fact, when a character Ferrell played in a different TV series—*L.A. Law*—married an extremely handsome man, the other cast members expressed incredulity because of her size. Sure enough, one plot twist later, it turned out that the marriage was just a sham to get the man a "green card" that allowed him to remain in the United States.)

If her timing was right, however, Lillian would discover *Roseanne*, the only series in the history of television starring (and created by) a Fat Chick whose weight doesn't relegate her to the status of self-deprecating buffoon, or pitiful spinster, or both. The show is also unique in that it depicts a married couple who are both hefty but whose size is incidental to the plot lines, and whose love and sexual attraction for each other are unmistakable.

Alternatively, Lillian might catch *Avonlea*, in which Lally Cadeau (who plays Janet King), while certainly not a 200-pounder, does resemble the well-rounded women of her character's Edwardian era, and enjoys an obviously amorous relationship with her screen husband.

But if Lillian became encouraged enough by these few shows to assume she'd find similar dynamics in any other media images today, she'd be disappointed. And bewildered—because on the street, in stores and offices, on public transportation, and everywhere else, she'd see more real women who do look like her than scrawny waifs who do not.

"What in tarnation," she might well ask us, "have you done to yourselves in a hundred years?"

What we've done is surrendered even such a fundamental of human life as love to the forces of commercialization. Beauty is still in the eye of the beholder, just as it was a century ago. But the minds that see through those eyes have been brainwashed to condemn and exclude every physical quality that doesn't serve the interests of marketers. In the 1990s, even though we *think* we're the freest thinkers in history, our psyches and libidos are virtually *owned* by the big-bucks industries of diet, fitness, fashion, beauty products, and cosmetic surgery.

So, above all, men must not find heavy women desirable, because that might stop us from spending billions of dollars on whatever promises corporeal salvation. Above all, women must not consider themselves attractive unless they're clones of the emaciated, painted, surgically and photographically enhanced beauty icons who now dominate all forms of popular culture.

That leaves rather a lot of us out in the cold.

For the record, there are some large women who are happily attached. They and their significant others are to be congratulated for staying sane while the rest of us succumbed to the "billion-dollar brainwash."

And succumb we did, body and soul. Three decades into the No Fat Chicks era, the vast majority of adults, teenagers, and children now believe that large women are disgusting, unforgivable, and—in the context of romance—a caste of untouchables.

Does that statement strike you as exaggerated? Then consider a recent survey of male college students concerning what type of woman they'd be least likely to marry. Fat Chicks "won," ranking as less appealing than cocaine users, shoplifters, embezzlers, and ex-mental patients.

Or you could check out the personals ads in your local newspaper and count how many male romance-seekers specify slim, thin, fit, or variations on the theme. More than 80 per cent of the personals ads in a recent edition of the Louisville, Kentucky, *Courier–Journal,* for instance, included such demands. There was also one that thundered: "No fatties" need reply.

According to a recent study by the Harvard School of Public Health, large women are at least 20 per cent less likely to marry than their thinner counterparts. Divorce and marital discord are also disproportionately prevalent for fat women, according to a welter of anecdotal evidence (although no scientific studies appear to have been done).

Advice columns frequently feature letters similar to a recent one to Ann Landers from an Arizona man who complained that he'd been "forced into celibacy" for the past ten years because his wife had gained weight. Another man was convicted in Tennessee of attempting to have his wife killed (on Mother's Day!) because she hadn't lost the weight she put on during pregnancy.

Two men who appeared on a recent edition of the *Carnie* (Wilson) TV talk show—entitled "They Hate Me Just Because I'm Fat"—stopped short of murder, but bald-facedly maligned their romantic partners for gaining weight. The first grouched that "she's done the most unforgivable thing a woman can do to her man." But when his wife strolled onto the set in shorts, she appeared to weigh no more than 130 pounds. The other man, insisting that his fiancée was "a beautiful person" but that he just couldn't "deal with the fat," had recently invited her to lunch, but taken her instead to a fitness centre, where he'd secretly signed her up for membership. The tall woman in question looked to be a statuesque 160 at most.

Granted, those are extreme examples of fat-phobia. But it's equally sad and wasteful when so many other heavy women endure lifetimes of romantic exclusion—from not receiving valentine cards in grade school to missing proms in high school, to being wallflowers at college mixers, to being ignored or insulted in singles spots as adults. And, of course, this kind of ostracism is often in addition to being left out of the kind of everyday social life that affords opportunities to meet potential mates.

Small wonder that, as Roberta Pollack Seid remarks in *Never Too Thin: Why Women Are at War with Their Bodies*, "many women regard their weight as the central issue of their lives, the primary obstacle to self-realization, the matter that must be resolved before other issues, such as careers or romance, can be addressed."

The Fat Lady Vanishes

Overweight women are punished and penalized for our appearance in many facets of our lives. But as tough as it is to lose out in economic, social, and practical matters, being disqualified from romantic relationships can be even more devastating. "Because 'beauty' lives so deep in the psyche, where sexuality mingles with self-esteem," Naomi Wolf explains in *The Beauty Myth*, "to tell a woman she is ugly can make her feel ugly, act ugly, and . . . be ugly, in the place where feeling beautiful keeps her whole."

Put another way, as Whitney Otto writes in *Now You See Her*: "The inside soon listens to the outside and the next thing you know, you're a ghost." This perceptive novel actually chronicles what often happens as women age, another branch of the "billion-dollar brainwash." But Fat Chicks frequently respond in the same self-defeating way to the inescapable message that we are undesirable and unwanted. That is, we retreat into the "ghosthood" of protective isolation and living only "from the neck up."

So, if no man can get anywhere near us, we eliminate the risk of being rejected. If we never go near "date bait" bars and restaurants, we won't be subjected to cruel critiques of our appearance—or, even worse, crude jokes about the sexual insatiability of women who appear to have large appetites.

Whatever situation we happen to be in, we're extremely careful to avoid the appearance of flirting, lest it provide fodder for yet another cruel jest. This motivation can extend as far as actually reassuring any man we're talking to—using a variety of verbal and non-verbal techniques—that we know there's no possibility he will find us sexually attractive. In this context, I remember my closest friend scolding me that, when we were at social gatherings, she would usually see me erecting an invisible, man-repelling barrier of defensiveness around myself as if to say: Don't even *think* about approaching me because I know, and you know, that nothing will come of it.

In an attempt to avoid painful misunderstandings in such situations, Fat Chicks often spin out whole social scenarios in our heads of how a romantic catastrophe might occur. We write all the dialogue, control all the imaginary action, and inevitably cast ourselves as losers. Logically enough, this can lead to habitual isolation.

Such protective reclusiveness can, in turn, become a self-perpetuating trap that makes any kind of social contact—romantic or otherwise—more and more intimidating as time goes by. In extreme cases, such isolation can turn into a condition closely resembling an agoraphobic's panic about leaving home.

But at least that's not as self-destructive (or physically dangerous) as the degrading promiscuity to which desperate loneliness sometimes drives overweight women. And too many of the men they attract are on the look-out for women whose frail self-esteem makes them highly exploitable.*

Others find different ways to hide. "When I was thin, I couldn't say no to my husband if he wanted sex. If I looked gorgeous—which meant thin—I assumed my body belonged to him," a woman named Lisa told the authors of *When Women Stop Hating Their Bodies.* "Somehow when I'm fat," she continued, "I'm not Daddy's little girl in the same way. I worry that if I lose weight, I'll lose myself again."

The I-Deserve-It Syndrome

For heavy women who've been too demoralized to defend themselves any other way, being alone affords plenty of time to come up with corroboration—and therefore comprehensible justification—for the prejudice that envelops us. In other words, if we can find a way to blame ourselves, the pain and prejudice will make some kind of sense and be infinitesimally easier to bear.

Which sometimes leads us to think such thoughts as these: "I happened

---

*A particularly appalling example of this dynamic recently occurred in Toronto when a physician lost his medical license for, among other offences against his obese female patients, coercing a woman into having sex in return for getting her stomach stapled.

to glance down at my body," wrote Margaret Atwood in an illuminating novel, *Lady Oracle*, "[and] there, staring me in the face, was my thigh. It was enormous, it was gross, it was like a diseased limb . . . it spread on forever, like a prairie photographed from a plane . . . with veins meandering across it like rivers. It was the size of three ordinary thighs."

The operative word in Atwood's insightful passage is, of course, "ordinary." Large women have been just as brainwashed as everyone else into denigrating any manifestation of "ordinary" or "normal" that doesn't match the media's standard. And if you're so convinced your body is disgusting that even appearing fully clothed can be an ordeal, the prospect of revealing your naked body—even for lovemaking—can seem like an utter impossibility.

So even if a Fat Chick is in a relationship, the shame she's internalized can poison the couple's sex life. A brave woman named Michelle Hrabak, for example, recently told *Ladies' Home Journal* that, when she weighed 257 pounds, her husband "still wanted to make love, but I could barely get undressed in front of him, let alone deal with having him touch my hip bulges. Then, I'd only make love with the lights out. . . . Finally, I just shut down—wasn't interested in sex at all."

Similar body anxiety is expressed in an intriguing article about posing for a photo exhibition "exploring the erotic possibilities of an unconventional body" in a recent issue of *Extra!* A San Francisco writer named Laura Fraser, who participated in the exhibition, points out that "many of us have spent more time in bed pulling our stomachs in than letting our passions loose." If that sounds a tad preposterous, let me remind you that, not so long ago, *Cosmopolitan* magazine published an article with detailed instructions about the best ways for women to pose and position themselves during lovemaking so they won't look fat!

Many of the women who responded to my Internet bulletin and *USA Today* ad expressed crushing sexual inhibition because of their appearance. This was scarcely a surprise, since the Eating Disorders Centre estimates that fully 90 per cent of Canadian women feel bad about their bodies, no matter what they weigh. That leaves only a tiny minority whose sense of attractiveness *hasn't* been so undermined that their sexual confidence is in tatters.

The authors of *Feminist Perspectives on Eating Disorders* describe this kind of psychological damage: "The tyranny of the ideal image makes almost all of us feel inferior. An internal voice rages at us: 'You are fat. You are ugly. Your thighs are like jelly. You have cellulite. You have pimples. You have vaginal odor. Your hair is drab. Your skin is dry.' We are taught to hate our bodies, and thus learn to hate ourselves."

He's Ashamed to Be Seen with Me, and Other Sad Tales

Several of my respondents reported that their partners are ashamed to be seen with them in public or among male friends or professional colleagues. And I, too, remembered "only-in-the-dark dating," as a woman from New York termed it, and especially a boyfriend with whom I lived for several years who—on the rare occasions when he didn't succeed in keeping his acquaintances from meeting me—habitually introduced me as his "tenant."

Some women described how they passively put up with various degrees of abuse for fear of losing their husbands or lovers, and then not being able to attract anyone else. And more than one said her husband had admitted feeling short-changed because his partner didn't measure up to the "trophy woman" image he's been conditioned to feel he deserves.

Darla, from Charlottetown, wrote about how devastated she felt the first time she made love with a man she'd yearned for for years, only to hear him say, "as if he never noticed til then, that I was 'a really big girl.'" Sandy, from Austin, said that whenever she tried to visualize herself "getting intimate with someone, my fantasy would be shattered because I knew I couldn't find lingerie that would make me look even halfway like I should." Caroline, from Seattle, described the lengths to which she goes to avoid letting men she's interested in see her from the rear. "Even if it's time for me to go home, or if I urgently need to go to the bathroom, if I can't get out without keeping my back to the wall, I just sit there."

Carol, from Atlanta, said that "there are only about two days a year when I don't hate my looks so much I'm afraid to set foot out my door."

And a correspondent from Toronto, who identified herself only as "Wasted," cracked a bitter joke about being "a double virgin now, because every cell in the body is renewed over seven years, and it's been fourteen years since I've had sex."

He Must Be Crazy If He Thinks I'm Attractive

Other respondents reported being unable to accept or trust men who do appreciate their looks. Which reminded me of a time when I was a young secretary in a law firm in Toronto. There was a client who was so crazy about my chunky legs that, every time he had an appointment with my boss, he'd arrive, say, "Hi, Terry," stare at my legs, and walk right into the wall. Any other woman would probably have been flattered. But all I remember thinking was, "What's wrong with this weirdo?"

A large woman in an extraordinary documentary film called *Fat Chance* (discussed in Chapter 11) goes much further in this same vein: "I've been told so many times that I have 'such a beautiful face' that now, when I hear it, I want to mutilate myself so people will stop saying it." As sad as this statement is, it nevertheless demonstrates that the woman has not bought into the ugly-duckling-becomes-gorgeous-swan fairy-tale that's implicit in the non-stop make-over features that permeate women's magazines.

Marcia Millman explains the entrapping effect of the before-and-after fantasy in a moving book called *Such a Pretty Face: Being Fat in America*: "The need to be extraordinarily beautiful is related to the need for unconditional love. So severe was the original rejection and injury, that it is not enough to be average."

The internal and external obsession with women's appearance, which is deliberately instilled by the weight-loss and beauty industries, is reflected in all of these comments. Which brings to mind Anaïs Nin's famous axiom: "We don't see things as they are, we see them as we are."

Many of the conflicted feelings expressed by my respondents also shine a big spotlight on a 1989 survey by *Vogue* magazine in which a majority of the women participants stated that, in return for having "ideal figures," they would willingly give up their husbands and boyfriends (as well as their careers and money). This defeat-the-purpose attitude shows just how far from human verities we have been dragged. The age-old practice of trying to attract a mate by looking beautiful has been co-opted into a pathetically self-contained, self-focused effort that has lonely, exhausted, obsessed women running in place and getting nowhere—except to the gym and the mall.

What about Men?

Men who've absorbed the No Fat Chicks credo are all too numerous, not to mention all too vociferous on occasion. Of course, having an attractive woman on their arm has been a status symbol for men for hundreds of years. But if there are any Diamond Jim Bradys left in North America today, they're keeping mighty quiet. In fact, the very thought of an Edgar Bronfman or a Donald Trump becoming besotted with a woman the size of, say, Roseanne seems even less likely than the notion that either of these multimillionaires will toss all his money off Place Ville Marie or the Empire State Building.

But there *are* some men who've managed to resist the brainwashing and are attracted to large women despite—or because of—their size. The bravest of these guys say so right out loud. And a few lionhearts actually say so in front of their buddies, knowing that the resulting flak, raucous remarks, and innuendo about their masculinity are bound to be brutal.

A couple of these independent thinkers have even written books about their love for plus-size women. In *Fat Is Not a Four-Letter Word*, for instance, physiologist Charles Roy Schroeder states that his wife, whom "most people in our culture would consider to be fat," was wearing a bathing suit the first time they met. "And before I ever said a word to her," Schroeder recalls, "my hormones started bubbling."

One of William Fabrey's motivations for helping found the National Association for the Advancement of Fat Acceptance was that, while applying for their marriage licence, his plus-size wife-to-be was asked by a clerk who could possibly be interested in marrying her.

Fashion photographer Ken Mayer is another bold soul who has backed up his beliefs in a book and in many media appearances, including a memorable *Donahue* show during which he spiritedly defended his fellow "fat-admirers," many of whom, he said, remain "in the closet because society discriminates against them. . . ." In *Real Women Don't Diet: One Man's Praise of Large Women & His Outrage at the Society That Rejects Them*, Mayer muses: "I think I'm a throwback to what men are all about." He also gets deliciously truculent (from a Fat Chick's point of view, that is) in his denunciation of a culture that "worship[s] the too-thin, childlike female body [and] limits our happiness at every turn."

As we'll see in Chapter 10, large women and the men who find them attractive have recently begun coming up with creative ways of finding each another. But, even though Schroeder's and Mayer's stout defence is music to a Fat Chick's ears, such men don't have an easy time breaking down the defences of women who've been scarred for life by anti-fat prejudice.

Dan Davis, an accountant whose views are similar to those of Mayer and Schroeder, recently focused on this stumbling-block in a revealing article in *Radiance* magazine: "Fat women are often harder to approach than thin women. Because of the psychological battering inflicted on them by society, many . . . become defensive and withdrawn. Suspicious of compliments, they may be annoyed or baffled by even the sincerest admirer [whereas] thin women are much more likely to accept male attention as their due. . . ."

And How about Children?

There may be no sadder result of the "billion-dollar brainwash" than the logical fact that, if heavy women have fewer marriages and romantic relationships than their slimmer sisters, they're also bound to have fewer children. Actual statistics in this context proved as impossible to elicit as did many other aspects of my research for this book. In fact, many of those to whom I put my queries either couldn't fathom what I was getting at, or responded in such sarcastic tones that they may just as well have come out and said what they obviously were thinking: "Who cares about fat women anyway?"

Compounding the cruel social attitudes that prevent Fat Chicks from bearing their own children is the fact that obesity is viewed so negatively by many adoption authorities—who spout the same fallacious health issues as do the employers discussed in Chapter 6—that extra pounds are frequently considered an automatic disqualifier.

Bottom Line

Zaftig Kathy Bates was asked in a recent interview how it felt to be passed over in favour of slimmer actresses for the movie versions of several roles she triumphantly created on stage. The multi-award-winning Bates gave a thoughtful answer that extended well beyond her own self-interest: "We've been taught to accept this very narrow definition of what is beautiful for women, and we are missing the humanity in people because of what someone may happen to look like."

Her eloquent remark resonates powerfully in the context of romantic love, as it is experienced by—and withheld from—large women in the destructive wake of social conditioning since the exploitation of Twiggymania. Throughout most of recorded history, Rubenesque damsels were deemed the ideal "squeeze." But today, when even the most intimate relationships between human beings have been commodified, and manipulated accordingly by media images, millions of women who resemble the celebrated Lillian Russell lead lonely, loveless, conflicted lives, and are often bereft of husbands, children, and grandchildren.

The profitable plundering of psyches has affected both sides of the romantic equation. Yet most of the men who feel repelled by Fat Chicks are merely behaving as they've been deliberately trained to do over the past three decades. And many large women, who've been equally hood-winked, are blind to both their own innate worth and to the admirers with whom they might find fulfilling relationships.

Geneen Roth explains the sad logic of this process in an invaluable book called *When Food Is Love*: "We mistake the longing to be loved and healed and valued for the longing to be thin. It's an enormous, life-altering mistake."

Roth's remark is appropriately poignant in this context. But, as a Fat Chick who was duped into squandering most of her life, and all of her child-bearing years, I know there's something that must be added. The "mistake" that keeps millions of women like me from both giving and receiving love is not accidental; it is the intentional *modus operandi* of the anti-fat profiteers.

CHAPTER NINE

On the Rack

One morning, Kate and Cindy and Shalom and all the other fashion models in New York suddenly received pink slips from their modelling agencies.

"Sorry, babe. But your brand of bony, long-legged beauty is obsolete. Ciao!"

Kate and Cindy and Shalom and all the other fashion models in New York galloped to the nearest newsstand—and discovered, to their horror, that it was true!

A thousand magazine covers had been launched by a valentine-faced twelve-year-old who stood just four feet tall and boasted a ten-inch waist. She was Scottish and came from the latest cultural mecca, Flinging Edinburgh.

Her name was McScrawny.

At first, the fashion world was aghast. But, recognizing a lucrative bandwagon when it oom-pah-pah-ed along, they hopped aboard and began singing McScrawny's praises, morning, noon, and night. And decreeing—for everyone who's anyone, darling—the teensy tartan ensembles that complemented her miniature charms.

Soon it became impossible to stroll down a street or snap on a TV set without seeing images of McScrawny. She became everyone's ideal.

Meanwhile, Kate and Cindy and Shalom and millions upon millions of other women sank into a deep depression. Not only did they look terrible in tam-o-shanters, they just couldn't measure up—or rather down—to McScrawny. Yet their every waking moment was bombarded by messages that any woman larger than McScrawny was unforgivably disgusting, grossly unlovable, and utterly worthless.

So they begged their doctors to chop five or six inches from their shins. They clamoured for a waist-cinching, Victorian-era operation in which the bottom ribs are removed to produce a true wasp waist. They paid electrologists fortunes for reshaping their hairlines to match McScrawny's deep *widow's peak. They bought every pill, potion, gadget, and gizmo they could get their hands on. Some forced themselves to throw up nearly every morsel they ate. Some smoked their heads off. Some popped laxatives, diuretics, and amphetamines as if they were vitamins. And—it goes without saying— they dieted and exercised frantically.*

But nothing worked. The harder the woebegone women tried to shrink themselves to McScrawny's size, the more stubbornly their bodies resisted.

And, just to make it worse, they couldn't find any decent clothes. They simply weren't being made any more in sizes larger than 2. Which left nothing but the dowdy duds at down-market shops that made them feel they'd died and gone to Polyester Purgatory.

All the females in the land came to hate themselves, despise each other, and meekly accept the rising tide of contempt being orchestrated against them, day by day, pound by pound, dollar by dollar.

Sound preposterous? Think again. Much of my McScrawny fable actually took place when the "billion-dollar brainwash" kicked into high gear in the late 1960s. And, since then, even women who wouldn't dream of mutilating their ribs, shins, or hairlines succumbed, to one extreme or another, to the virtual commandment that all women must be thin.

Joining them in what amounts to a mass flight from reality was the women's apparel industry, which squandered a fortune by kowtowing to the waif-worshipping bigwigs of the fashion world. Baffled clothing moguls couldn't understand why their bottom lines were dwindling to the wispy dimensions of the gaunt models who came to dominate the mass media. But the reasons were right under their noses.

Any demographer could have told them that the skinny icons who were sashaying down the runways and cavorting onscreen represented, at most, 5 per cent of the female population. Any woman of average proportions would gladly have pointed out that apparel shopping was becoming more infuriating than enjoyable. And any plus-size woman who hadn't been cowed into silence would have eagerly explained why the literally slim pickings in the stores were forcing most of her clothing budget to remain unspent.

But, seduced by increasingly shrill songs touting increasingly slim sirens, manufacturers and retailers failed to even ask the pertinent questions.

Instead, they meekly allowed their size ranges to stop at precisely the point where the average North American woman's body begins—and wound up spurning, by the mid-1980s, an estimated 40 million consumers with a combined buying power of $6 billion. By 1995, this total would grow to at least 50 million women, who spent an estimated $12 billion on the plus-sizes that *did* fit them.

While influential stores along New York's Fifth Avenue and Toronto's Bloor Street were busily swapping their realistically sized mannequins for scrawny Twiggy clones, no one noticed that frustrated women were scurrying out the door in droves.

Let Them Not *Eat Cake*

The last time anything like this had happened was back in 1947, during the now forgotten rebellion against Christian Dior's "New Look." After a century or so of wrapping, strapping, and cinching themselves to obey fashion's dictates, women had gratefully discovered comfort in the relatively relaxed clothing they wore during the Depression and the Second World War.

Suddenly, new marching orders were issued from Paris. In a radical bid to reassert the primacy of French couture, Dior had conjured up the sort of hourglass silhouette that hadn't been seen in decades. He demanded that hemlines plunge from the knee to the ankle, that shoulder pads be shucked, and that waists be whittled by—yes, a return to corsets.

Pandemonium raged in Paris when Dior presented his first collection. Princess Elizabeth, the Duchess of Windsor, and a host of other celebrities deplored the retrogression. Across the ocean, 300,000 American women, complaining that Dior's decree "shows everything you want to hide and hides everything you want to show," formed a national protest club and vowed to resist the New Look no matter what. In just a few months, according to a *Time* cover story titled "Counter Revolution," the women's clothing industry "fell into a frightening slump. . . ."

Dior was undaunted. Even when dozens of Dallas women picketed Neiman Marcus while he was inside accepting a fashion award that autumn, he remained calm. His English may have been fractured when he opined that "I know well the women," but his prophetic prowess was right on the money: "You can never stop the fashions."

Cheered on by everyone in the clothing industry because it obliged women to scrap their entire pre-war wardrobes and spend lavishly on replacements, the lucrative New Look swept to supremacy. And women obediently squashed themselves once again.

Two decades later, in the dizzying wake of Twiggymania, a similar crisis for womanly sized women occurred when *de rigueur* duds were rapidly downsized. This time, women *wanted* to comply, but the apparel industry itself made following fashion's edicts well nigh impossible for anyone who wasn't as narrow as an arrow.

It happened fast. Before mini-skirts pranced onto the scene in the mid-1960s, regular clothing had routinely run to size 18 in nearly every women's store. Size 20s were frequently tacked on to the most popular lines. And for those who were even larger, half-sizes were readily available, albeit generally designed with an older, not particularly fashion-conscious woman in mind.

But, just a few years later, anyone larger than size 16 began to feel like a forgotten woman as she scoured the shops, boutiques, and department stores in search of *au courant* clothing. Before long, the cut-off point for mass merchandise would drop to size 14 and stay that way well into the 1990s. Meanwhile, *haute couture* creations generally ran only from size 4 to size 10.

Some of the styles that paraded through the next two decades were absurd and some were hideous. But others—especially the sophisticated pantsuits introduced by Yves St. Laurent—were wonderful to look at and comfortable to wear, and seemed to epitomize how emancipated women wished to present themselves. Fanciful "flower child" styles gave way to the more authoritative fashions that were ideal for the millions of women who'd flooded into the workplace by the end of the 1970s, when, for the first time in history, more North American women were working outside the home than remaining in it. And the need for appropriate clothing leapt exponentially, along with female purchasing power.

But size 16-and-ups were strictly wallflowers at the fashion show, forced to sit out trend after trend. Industry insiders who gave any thought at all to this sector held onto hoary assumptions that large women had little money to spend, and even less taste, and habitually postponed clothes shopping because they were perpetually planning to diet. Consequently, the options for Fat Chicks shrank to plus-size specialty chains such as Pennington's in Canada and Lane Bryant in the United States; smaller stores with godawful names such as Oink Inc. and Catherine's Stout Shops; or trekking to the nether regions of department stores, where the ironically monikered "women's" departments were inevitably hidden.

Wherever large women went, the sparsity of styles was exceeded only by the dowdiness of clothes that always seemed a year or two behind the current fashions, and were generally limited to cheaply produced "trailer-park" polyester. (I've never forgotten the outrageously callous answer a department store buyer gave me when I interviewed her in 1978 for an article about Pennington's for *Canadian Business*. Asked why plus-size shoppers were stuck with a plethora of polyester, she replied: "Well, they eat a lot, right? And they probably spill so much they have to keep washing their clothes. So why not give them polyester?")

Even when imitations of the most popular items from the "misses" market *did* turn up in large-size stores, they were usually all wrong—just ill-fitting, blown-up balloons, in pallid pastels where dark colours were called for, and vice versa, not to mention bows, ruffles, and assorted gewgaws tacked on at random by indifferent designers.

Intimate apparel was even worse. Bras and girdles were heavy, hot, industrial-strength monstrosities. Sleepwear was itchy, bulky, and often macabre enough to guarantee nightmares. Pantyhose, after taking forever to be produced in large sizes in the first place, were overpriced, yet lacked both quality and colour range.

Sportswear was either too juvenile or too boisterously butch. Swimsuits were usually ugly and uncomfortably boned. Evening wear often consisted of gaudy muumuus with sequins and satin furbelows plopped in peculiar places. But the kind of attractive, high-quality, natural-fibre clothes that smaller women took for granted were nowhere to be found.

All in all, plus-size choices for most of the 1970s "added up to a big yech," as Una Abrahamson expressed it in a contemporary *Chatelaine* article titled "Women's Clothes: What's Wrong?" But her timely advice—that whoever offered large women "well-made, correctly-sized garments designed with some pizzazz . . . [would] strike pay dirt"—fell on deaf ears.

How awful *was* it to shop at these establishments? Well, they did keep Fat Chicks from wandering around in gunny sacks, or sewing everything we wore from scratch, so maybe we should have been grateful. But I remember peering furtively over my shoulder to make sure no one I knew was around, darting inside with the stealth and speed of a bank robber, and always making sure I had a shopping bag from some "respectable" place in which to stash the tell-tale plus-size sack.

To this day, a chic acquaintance of mine, who lost a lot of weight, still uses quick trips to a certain plus-size chain as "aversion therapy" to reinforce her determination to stay on the straight and narrow. And two of the women I interviewed for *Canadian Business* said that, after reducing enough to fit into regular-size clothing, they'd celebrated by ceremoniously cutting up their Pennington's charge cards.

But the worst effect for large women was that it became nearly impossible to maintain a dignified appearance—and all too easy to be perceived as the contemptible, stereotypical slobs the imagemongers insisted we were. Truth be told, human beings almost always judge books by their covers. So, as Fat Chicks were increasingly accused of having the most reprehensible covers of all—and simultaneously rendered less and less able to combat negative impressions—hostility towards us intensified as the years went by and the drumbeats of the "billion-dollar brainwash" grew louder and meaner.

Fashions Become Unwearable and a Plot Is Hatched

But shopping also became problematic for smaller women as the 1980s spiralled into an orgy of conscienceless consumption. The trouble was essentially that designers had become superstars, according to Grace Mirabella, who succeeded Diana Vreeland at *Vogue*. Several were now so rich and autonomous that, as Mirabella recalls in her autobiographical *In and Out of Vogue*, "fashion came to be about nothing more than itself [and] degenerated . . . into a self-referential game full of jokes and pastiches that amused the fashion community enormously and did nothing at all for [women]."

Photographers, models, and even editors also began basking in the limelight, and no longer seemed to care about anyone else's preferences or requirements. Logically, female consumers *should* have been in the driver's seat as never before, thanks to their new financial clout and increased need for appropriate clothing in which to pursue burgeoning employment opportunities.

And certainly some designers, including Donna Karan, Liz Claiborne, and Anne Klein, were practical enough to capitalize on this situation.

But the fashion élite and the fashion press—which are, directly or indirectly, bankrolled by many of the No Fat Chicks profiteers—blithely reversed the emperor-has-no-clothes formula to an arrogant assumption that designers' creations no longer needed emperors, let alone ordinary women. As time went by, they drifted farther and farther into the realm of fantasy. But not the right fantasies, as far as the majority of modern women were concerned.

The zenith of this clash is generally reckoned to be the 1986 "Baby Doll" collection of French designer Christian Lacroix. In reality, the average North American woman was now thirty-two years old, weighed about 143 pounds, stood no taller than 5' 4", and was eager for clothes reflecting her true identity. But Lacroix chose to spotlight her exact antithesis. Wobbling down the runway on teetery spike heels were towering teenage skeletons wearing ridiculously pouffed mini-skirts below cinched-in bustiers, out of which their silicone-filled breasts threatened to spill. The fashion press swooned, retailers snapped up Lacroix's designs, and dress prices jumped by as much as 30 per cent during the following year.

But no one had bothered to ask women if they *wanted* this return to what the industry called "high femininity." And no one had grasped the significance of polls indicating that—whatever their size—80 per cent of them had come to detest wardrobe shopping. But women made their opinions obvious by steering clear of clothing stores during the following year and, instead, spending their money on more houses, cars, and restaurant dinners than had ever before been bought by their gender. Result: Women's apparel sales plummeted and the so-called Year of the Dress turned into a débâcle.

And things just got worse as the narcissistic 1980s lurched into the nervous 1990s, and recessionary realities rocked many a boat. On both sides of the border, profits in the regular-size clothing industry were vanishing so rapidly that designers *should* have done some soul-searching and asked whether, by snubbing the majority of women, they'd become their own worst enemies. Instead, encouraged by assorted anti-fat hucksters, they drifted so far from reality they may as well have been creating with extraterrestrials in mind.

All the over-the-top tastelessness added up to the stuff movies are made of, thought director Robert Altman, who flew his film crew to Paris in 1993 to capture the madcap collections and the eccentric personalities for what later became *Pret-à-Porter* (*Ready to Wear*). Whereupon *crème de la crème* designer Karl Lagerfeld showed just how out of touch designers had become by fretting that the film might misportray the fashion world as "a nightmarish cartoon."

But chaos was already running amok on the runways, as increasingly tarty-looking models tottered out in sky-high skirts, slinky pants with derriere-revealing cut-outs, and breasts either bared under transparent tops or clad in vulgar metallic cones. Then there were Vampira-type rubber dresses, the weird underwear-as-outerwear look, bustles, dunce caps, dog collars, and Wild West gear—and cyberspace punks decked out in a hodgepodge of clashing colours and prints. Then it was on to a tawdry parade of fake-fur skirts worn by models with multihued hair and painted-on black eyes.

None of the cynical nonsense bolstered the fashion industry's bottom line. So, in 1992, desperate designers evidently decided to try a bit of *déjà vu*. Crossing their fingers and hoping what worked so well in the late 1960s might get the black ink flowing again, they sent out wave after wave of gaunt, dead-eyed waifs wearing little-girl frocks and carrying teddy bears. Sure enough, *Newsweek*'s John Leland dubbed the trend "Back to Twiggy." Noting that yet another scrawny English teenager was leading the pack, he nailed the key connection: "We'd describe [Kate Moss] as four straight limbs in search of a woman's body, a mini-bosom trapped in perpetual puberty, the frail torso of the teenage choirboy—except that *Newsweek* already used this prose to describe Twiggy back in 1967."

Precisely what relevance this disinterment was meant to have for the millions of women whose age was now closer to the real Twiggy's (forty-two) than to that of little Miss Moss went unexplained. Magazine editors like *Harper's Bazaar*'s Elizabeth Tilberis—who gushed that the waifs looked like "angelic little boys"—straightfacedly foisted all this bunkum on their readers and then wondered why subscriptions were sagging.

The worst was yet to come. But when it did, it was just idiotic enough to jolt retailers and manufacturers into delivering an overdue comeuppance. Swiped from the rock stars whose seedy anti-style had wafted from the mean streets of Seattle, it was aptly called the "grunge" look. And it consisted of little more than rag-bag jeans and torn flannel shirts accessorized by scruffy sandals, greasy hair, and make-up-free faces.

Designers preened and hung $155 price tags on shirts that sold for a tenth of that at Kmart. The fashion press churned out copy hailing this exciting new "scaled down," "reality-based" trend. But exasperated apparel moguls cut right to the chase. Exactly what part of this no-look look, they asked, can we *possibly* alchemize into socko sales? And when a fed-up flock of other marketers—representing cosmetics, jewellery, accessories, footwear, and hair products—began shouting the same cogent question, a crisis was secretly declared.

Scuttling together "like characters in an Agatha Christie novel," according to *New York Times* fashion writer Amy M. Spindler, a group of insiders set out to resuscitate profits by "deal[ing] a death blow" to the grungers and waifs. At the helm was *Vogue*'s latest editor, Anna Wintour, whose publisher talked turkey to the *Times*: "Retailers weren't moving product . . . [and] if you can't sell it, you can't advertise it."

So what *would* sell better than waifs and grungers? Glamour, glamour, and more glamour, the alleged collaborators allegedly told the finally humbled designers. Give us the works, top to bottom: fancy hair, extreme make-up, super clothes, jewellery, handbags, spike heels, as many accessories as possible in between, and as much lavish lingerie as possible underneath.

All of which were duly trotted out during the spring fashion shows in 1993, even though designers had to scramble so quickly that much of the new stuff didn't make it to the stores on schedule. Not to worry. *Vogue* had it covered. Not only did the magazine take the unprecedented step of actually co-financing some of the shows (according to Spindler), but Wintour devoted her May issue to "discovering" what she termed the switch to "Strong and Sexy." Whence had this new look "spontaneously" emanated? According to her editorial: women she'd seen on the streets of Paris and New York.

An ambiguous postscript was added by Tilberis when *Harper's Bazaar*, and many other publications, began going with the flow: "A lot more people will be thanking us for this look than [for] the waif." Whom she had in mind was left dangling. But one thing was clear: Nobody in 1993—or, as it turned out, 1994 or 1995—was asking the female rank and file if spike heels, thigh-high skirts, skintight suits, waist-crushing patent leather belts, bare-it-all slip dresses, lilliputian sweater sets, daytime diamonds and sequins, push-up bras, garish make-up, and out-to-here hair was really what they needed at this stage of the game.

Fashion-industry thinkers (arguably an oxymoron) could have saved themselves time and grief just by checking out the *Cathy* cartoon strip drawn by Cathy Guisewite, who can always be counted on to skewer absurdities. Her take on the spring 1995 collections was neatly expressed in a panel showing an ecstatic salesclerk praising the switch to styles "designed to torture not one, not two, but every single cell of the female body!"

The Wallflowers Are Finally Asked to Dance

What was happening for Fat Chicks during this phantasmagorical frenzy? Plenty. As it turned out, there *was* life after size 14 after all. We were still being forced to sit on the sidelines watching a bewildering parade of *haute couture* styles that—love 'em or loathe 'em—didn't exist in our sizes. But while the regular clothing sector was foundering, aesthetically and financially, the plus-size market had begun experiencing double-digit growth. The irony was scrumptious, considering how the mainstream had so callously abandoned everyone larger than size 14, and that even those who *did* pay attention pretty much treated us like cheap dates they were ashamed to be seen with.

If a single person can be accorded the lion's share of the credit for wising up the apparel community, it's got to be a size-22 Californian named Carole Shaw. Sick and tired of not being able to find good clothes, she dreamed up the first magazine for and about large ladies—*BBW: Big Beautiful Woman*—and began publishing in 1979, thus providing a national vehicle for any marketers who were savvy enough to use it. But Shaw had started raising consciousness even earlier by marching into the offices of chain store buyers and saying: "I want you to meet a fat lady in person." .

The brightest of the startled buyers were all ears. They'd read a decisive demographic study (commissioned in 1978 by an international association of *female* clothes execs) that debunked many of the negative myths about Fat Chicks, but good. Two stats were especially eye-opening: Working women, even if they earned as little as $10,000, spent more on clothes than the non-salaried wives of men who earned four or five times as much; and fully 37 per cent of size-16-and-ups held jobs. The industry was also buzzing about the astounding success a Manhattan retailer named Nancye Radmin was having with a plus-size boutique she'd pointedly named "The Forgotten Woman." And it was beginning to dawn on the rag trade that many of the big-spending Baby Boomers were bound to "plump up" as they aged.

Before long, a whole gaggle of enthusiastic marketers were pursuing the very women they'd dumped nearly two decades earlier. But, observed Shaw, "it wasn't that they decided to love our big beautiful bodies. [It was that] they noticed we had that green stuff in our fat little fists."

In the vanguard among U.S. innovators were Liz Claiborne (who conferred her own first name—Elisabeth—on her large-size line), Bloomingdale's, Macy's, and The Limited, which bought Lane Bryant in 1982. And the result wasn't just burgeoning quantity, but also the quantum leap in quality that Fat Chicks had been pining for. Granted, bulletproof polyester *didn't* die a richly deserved death. But now elegant natural fibres, in an array of flattering styles and colours, were also becoming available. In 1980, *Ms.* magazine scooped its media colleagues with what it called "the garment business story of the year." When the others did catch on, their consensus matched the conclusion reached by the *Wall Street Journal* in 1985: "The large woman has arrived."

In Canada, good old monopolistic Pennington's began feeling something new on the back of its corporate neck in the late 1970s. It was the hot breath of competitors, most notably the venerable coast-to-coast Eaton's chain, which had decided to substantially expand and rev up its ho-hum plus-sizes. Other retailers also gradually took the plunge. But it wasn't long before they bumped up against some conundrums that stymied their predecessors so badly that they probably merit an apology from yours truly and all the other Fat Chicks who maligned them for what we interpreted as indifference.

For starters, the best designers flat-out refused to risk their reputations by what they considered slumming—which was laughable, considering that Oscar de la Renta and several other biggies had happily created clothes for the Barbie doll! Gloria Vanderbilt was one of the few exceptions who *didn't* think catering to we-know-who would hurt her image. But even enlightened designers were daunted by the challenge of adapting their creations for bodies that were roughly double what they were used to. It wasn't as simple as just "blowing up" regular-size patterns. Proportioning was a lot trickier than that because, while small women need comparatively straight up-and-down lines, heavier bodies tend to come in either "pear" or "apple" distributions. And someone whose bust isn't all that big may have very large upper arms—a combination that makes balancing shoulders and sleeves extremely difficult.

Even when retailers did find designers who were willing and able to tackle all this, getting garments made could be equally tough. Manufacturers prosper by cutting in high volume. So even major players like Pennington's and Lane Bryant were usually forced to place their orders far in advance, yet wait for delivery until all the more profitable regular-size orders were completed. Still another problem was that, while extra fabric was obviously required, plus-size customers felt they were being gouged if prices seemed significantly higher than those paid by smaller women.

Even in the face of these stumbling-blocks, however, start-up gambles soon started paying off on both sides of the border. And a whole lot of other ears began perking up when industry analysts reported that, far from being aberrant or inconsequential, the size 16-and-ups now represented at least one out of every three women in North America, and 14-and-ups typified a whopping 50 per cent of adult females. What really drove the point home was the fact that, while marketing myopia had kept the regular-size sector struggling, those who'd been perspicacious enough to serve Fat Chicks had shared in a market bonanza that leapt from $2 billion to $10 billion between 1982 and 1992.

Now even top designers, including Versace and Givenchy, saw the light and reached for their sketch pads. Meanwhile, up-scale retailers such as Bullock's and Saks Fifth Avenue, as well as down-market giants like Kmart, J.C. Penney, Wal-Mart, and Target rushed to get in on the action. And Sears, Spiegel, and other major catalogues followed suit.

All this activity created a niche for plus-size models to exhibit the nifty new clothing in fashion shows. Before long, specialty agencies started opening up—notably Montreal's lively and successful L'Agence de Mannequins Plus—and such influential traditionalists as Ford and Wilhelmina gradually began recruiting large models.

It took quite a while for their rotund images to start turning up in catalogues and advertisements, and there are still some surprisingly doltish hold-outs (see below). But, during the past year or so, plus-size bodies modelling a wide range of clothes began appearing regularly in retail flyers, newspaper ad layouts, and a few magazines. When a Kentucky department store chain called Bacon's took the virtually unprecedented step of choosing a plus-size model for a newspaper swimsuit ad in the summer of 1995, the response was so strong that several branches had to reorder the featured suit twice during the following two weeks. And I saw another first not long ago: half a dozen large-size models wearing Just My Size lingerie and hose in a TV commercial.

"They finally found out that we're not just housewives looking to buy a couple of blouses and a few pairs of polyester pants—we are doctors and lawyers and businesswomen," remarked Maryanne Bodolay, a coordinator for the National Association for the Advancement of Fat Acceptance, once the plus-size ball really got rolling. By 1992, even Carole Shaw was almost satisfied. "I can go shopping now and find just about everything I need," she told a *Los Angeles Times* fashion writer, "but not everything I want."

Revolution Struts on Stage

Nearly everything Shaw—or any other plus-sized fashion enthusiast—could possibly wish for actually turned up two years later on a modelling runway in Toronto. It was concocted by a genuine revolutionary who is, aptly enough, named Hope—Jackqueline, or "our hero, Jackie," as she came to be known to Fat Chicks all over the country within the span of a single decade.

The Rubenesque young Canadian had spent years dejectedly trudging from one store to another, searching for pretty clothes—but finding only indifference and hostility every step of the way. By the early 1980s, she'd become aware that the dismal situation was beginning to improve south of the border. But what was putting so many smiles on the faces of so many suddenly well-turned-out Fat Chicks were mostly top-down developments from industry veterans. Hope decided it was high time large women themselves started waging revolution from the grass roots up.

Their clout, as she envisioned it, would first manifest itself in looking and feeling attractive. But after reviving their own self-esteem, the long-term objective would be to set the world on a saner course—and eventually lead to restoration of the tolerance for size diversity destroyed by the "billion-dollar brainwash." Hope didn't know it then but, dotted all over North America, other big women were picking themselves up, dusting off the negativity that had descended upon them since the late 1960s, and setting out in pursuit of the same ideal. (Some of their accomplishments are described in Chapter 10.)

Hope started small, "just trying to prove I was a feeling, thinking, loving, intelligent human being," while modelling for the few local retailers who were taking a chance on plus-size fashion shows. She remembers "feeling very intimidated at first, like some kind of large object" that seemed to mystify audiences. Puzzled people often queried her after shows about how she could *possibly* have such nice-looking hair and make-up when she was so . . . uh, big. "They seemed to think there must be a different world somewhere for large people."

Stunned and stung by the assumption, Hope scraped up enough cash to rent a basement room, where she started conducting what she called "confidence seminars" for plus-size women. Even though she "didn't see anything outstanding" about herself except that she "knew how to pull it all together," she must have been doing something right. Her subterranean little business took off immediately. Word got out and she was soon invited to give motivational speeches.

Then, deciding that her solo mission to "stop any more women from shedding any more tears" would be more successful if she could also train others to be her "little soldiers," she opened a plus-size modelling agency in 1985. The name: Big Bold & Beautiful. Three years later, Hope and her husband added an imaginatively designed, exceptionally inviting clothing boutique, where shoppers are greeted by, not just friendly sales assistants whose girth resembles their own, but also by a pair of peach-faced love-birds whose cage sits beside a comfy couch, over which hangs a pleasing print by one of the few latter-day artists who appreciated and painted large ladies—Fernando Botero. And beside that is a TV set on which a video shows some of the shop's smashing plus-size clothes in action. On the cash counter are bright dishes filled with candies and nuts, and a stack of Big Bold & Beautiful's sophisticated catalogues.

Above Hope's boutique, which is located in Toronto's chic Yorkville area, is the bustling agency that includes a growing stable of queen-size models (including the daughter of veteran TV newscaster Harvey Kirck). They work constantly, in the United States as well as Canada. And many of them participated in that astonishing event at Toronto's Harbour Castle Hotel in the fall of 1994. It *sounds* like pure fantasy from some poor schnook who's gagged down one too many diet shakes. But trust me. It really happened.

In a glitzy hotel ballroom, music suddenly begins pulsating. The lights dim dramatically. A curvaceous figure appears, nude except for a fluffy twirl of chiffon, and a knock-'em-dead fashion show hits the ground strutting. Over the next ninety minutes, a stunning succession of sumptuous clothes are paraded by an array of lovely professional models.

Enticing evening wear. Authoritative office outfits. Sprightly sports togs. Alluring lingerie. And romantic, $7,000 bridal gowns that drift dreamily to the love theme from Phantom of the Opera.

The audience goes wild. The buyers' order books are scribbled to smithereens. And the collective jaw of the fashion press drops with an audible thud. Why?

All of the models and all of the garments they wore were sizes 14 to 22.

Big Bold & Beautiful's first major fashion show not only paid off on the promises implied in its name, but also generated the excitement it deserved. The hip VH1 channel sent a camera crew up from New York. BBW's new editor, Linda Arroz (who succeeded Shaw) flew in from

California and declared that she was "totally blown away." Even *FT—Fashion Television*'s globe-hopping Jeanne Beker covered the show.

No other plus-size marketer has so far even come close to Hope's calibre of creativity. It's the sort of special thing that seldom springs from those whose motivation is strictly monetary. It *had* to come from the heart and soul of a Fat Chick whose dedication was forged in a crucible of prejudice and exclusion.

But the best of the other marketers, from high-end *haute* to the egalitarian atmosphere at Wal-Mart, are catching on reasonably well. And the wisest among them understand why good clothes are so important, whatever one's size happens to be. As Roberta Pollack Seid defines this human imperative in *Never Too Thin: Why Women Are at War with Their Bodies*: "Dressing is . . . a process of self-creation, or self-portraiture. It reveals the way we see ourselves and the way we want others to see us. . . . We reveal our estimation of our attractiveness, of our qualities and personality traits. . . . Clothing is crucial to an individual's 'identity kit.'"

Just How Good Is It Getting?

Transformations I never expected to see, at least not until precisely one day before I checked out and headed for the Planet Rubens (my version of heaven), are turning up all over. Some of the highlights include:

• A growing number of designers who most definitely *don't* need to be dragged, kicking and screaming, into catering to Fat Chicks. Among the best is Toronto-based Linda Lundstrom. Another is Brian Bailey, who—against advice from colleagues—included plus-sizes in his collection from the get-go. Bailey, whose mostly upscale clients often fly in from Montreal and New York, insists that the models who wear his designs on the runway are never smaller than size 18. He told me his initial motivation came from being part of a "pretty hefty family, which included me." Today he says he likes nothing better than creating clothes that empower large women to say, "I really feel wonderful and there's nothing that's going to get in my way."

Bailey's enthusiasm puts the ambivalence of such other designers as Alfred Sung to shame. While Sung's once-thriving empire was toppling into near-bankruptcy recently, a spokeswoman told me that he refused to consider adding any size larger than 14 to his collections, yet quietly designed beautiful wedding gowns up to size 20. Why? Well, it probably has something to do with the fact that these nuptial nifties retail in the high four-figure range.

• Serious research is finally being done into the dimensions and proportions of a wide variety of body sizes. Spiegel, for example, started planning its excellent For You plus-size catalogue by meticulously measuring sixteen body points on a large number of big women, including hips, waists, busts, arms, and inseams. The University of Arizona also recently did what might be termed "one size *doesn't* fit all" studies on 7,000 women over age fifty-five to pinpoint what apparel alterations should be taken into consideration as women age (i.e., hips and rears often flatten, while backs may widen and chests may narrow). And a spokesperson for the American Society of Testing and Materials told *Glamour* magazine that the quest to figure out what *real* women really look like—aimed at coming up with the same kind of standard sizing that men enjoy—is being encouraged by a great many of the apparel industry's movers and shakers.

• It's finally sinking in with designers and manufacturers that being horizontally large doesn't necessarily mean a corresponding vertical dimension. Hence a plus-size "petite" category is being developed by a lot of marketers—which comes as very welcome news to those of us who usually drown in too-long tops and are forced to wreck the lines of other garments by lopping several inches off the pants and sleeves.

• Fashion consultants from marketers such as Liz Claiborne's Elisabeth line are starting to travel around the continent to host fashion shows in department stores that sell their products. Until this development, the opportunity to talk face-to-face with the people who control our shopping choices just didn't exist for large women. The personnel at the Elisabeth shows I've attended in the past year were eager to hear customers' opinions and relay them back to the design department. And the Elisabeth line also sends free quarterly newsletters regarding fashion trends and tailoring improvements to anyone who requests them.

• Some marketers—notably Spiegel and The Greater Woman—not only offer well-executed catalogues for home shopping, but also send fashion shows directly to customers via videos whose reasonable price (about $10) can be applied towards purchases.

• Victoria can just keep her secret because plus-size lingerie options are mushrooming. Cotton Ginny, for example, has opened a chain of shops, called Plus Intimates, that carry a full line of gorgeously romantic unmentionables.

• For the budget-minded, and/or those whose weight tends to cycle at significantly different levels, plus-size consignment shops such as Full Figure Fashions in Calgary, are beginning to appear.

• Just My Size and several other large-size accessories and clothing companies now have free 800 telephone numbers so potential customers can find out the nearest location of advertised items that interest them.

• A few—make that a *very* few—magazines are making a conscientious effort to put a stop to the anti-fat madness. Pats on the back go to (among others): *Glamour*, which recently reported that its art department occasionally uses computer magic to make photographed models look, not taller and thinner—as has been common for years at women's magazines—but larger "so that [they] don't look so anorexic"; and *First* magazine, which published a super layout called "Looking Great at Any Weight" last spring.

• Similarly, a handful of advertisers are finally getting a clue about how to pitch to women who can spot insincerity wherever it lurks. One of my favourites is for Lee jeans, which now come in "loose" and "relaxed" fits: "Isn't it time women's clothes were designed for women? . . . How could any sane woman . . . have possibly dreamed up the bustier? What about the girdle? (Named after the sound you make when you try to put one on.)"

• And speaking of girdles, I know everyone won't agree with me on this, because it may seem like I'm endorsing a return to mandatory foundation garments—which I certainly *don't* favour. But I do applaud the best of the "shape wear" that's now available in lightweight lycra and spandex briefs, slips, pantyhose, and swimsuits (with "butt-boosting" jeans on the horizon). If you want to feel and look firm, they're a heck of a lot better than punitive dieting or liposuction (but definitely shouldn't discourage exercising).

• While certainly not as good an idea as extending size ranges, the new "Fits Most Sizes" labels are an improvement over the fantasyland "One Size Fits All" that made so many of us feel like some kind of mutants for so long.

• The transformation of the choices available to Fat Chicks is by no means confined to North America. To name just a few other lucky locales: Many English plus-size shoppers love a London shop called "1647" whose name was chosen to emphasize the fact that 47 per cent of British women wear size 16 or bigger. Large Israeli ladies are served by a store in Jerusalem called Matim Li, which, in English, means "It Suits Me." And Australia has a wide variety of chains and shops, including the upscale My Size stores in Melbourne and many other locations. And, sporting what's arguably the most in-your-face name of all Down Under, there's Non-Petite, in the small town of Nelson.

And Now for the Bad News

Apparel choices available to Fat Chicks are still far from perfect. After all, how much can we expect from folks who, for decades, were too dim-witted to wake up and smell the billions of dollars they were missing out on—or notice the millions of potential customers who were right under their snooty noses? Just how clueless do you have to be to keep focusing on 5 per cent of your base market, while the other 95 per cent are clearly doing without your stock-in-trade?

But some fashion biggies apparently *are* getting an inkling that there are women in the world with more meat on their bones than a couple of waifs glued together. How do we know this? Because, beginning in about 1990, they started a quiet little boondoggle that involved playing around with the numbers on the size tags. Rather than venturing into the apparently scary terra incognita beyond size 14, they simply upsized their garments and left the skinny little numbers in place. Upshot: "What used to be a size 8 we now call a size 6, and an 8 is what we used to call a 10," a surprisingly candid designer named Randy Kemper recently told *Glamour* magazine. Another source said that many of the most frequently used size-10 dress forms have been inflated to, on average, 36-27-38, whereas they used to be 34½ - 24½ - 34½.

There are plenty of other deserving nominees for Dolt of the Century awards. I'm sure some of their names are occurring to you even as we speak. My own include:

• The Lane Bryant chain, which has been around longer than almost any other plus-size marketer on the planet, but still hasn't learned that "fat" isn't a synonym for "stupid." I am, of course, referring to the fact that even after fairly admirable efforts to get with the "Fat Chicks are valuable customers" program, Lane Bryant still refuses to use large models in its catalogues. If there's a reasonable explanation for this, I was unable to elicit it in several rounds of phone tag with spokespeople in New York and Columbus. So I have no choice but to stick with the obvious explanation: They think Fat Chicks are so deluded we believe that buying their clothes will make us look just like the size 8s and 10s in all their pretty pictures.

• Ironically, some of the most future-oriented designers of all are making the same classic mistake that cost their predecessors a fortune. Case in point: the new Levi jeans that are precisely fitted to a customer's dimensions by computer and assembled by robotic tailoring. But are these space-age britches available for the majority of female consumers? No. The size range stops where millions of women's waists begin: 35 inches.

• And, most important, because of their massive influence for good and ill, the scores of women's magazines which continue to stay in lock-step with the profiteers who perpetrate the "billion-dollar brainwash." Yes, of course, the major advertisers who keep them financially afloat *want* magazines—and movies and television and billboards—to be populated exclusively by slender, young women. But to never let a heavier, or older, woman anywhere within camera range means, by inference, telling the majority of their own readers they don't count.

Women have put up with that sort of disrespect for decades. Actually, centuries. But there are signs that the days of female passivity are coming to an end. So by completely knuckling under to the bullies with the money, women's magazines are becoming less and less relevant to their readers with every passing day. And that means taking a shortcut to Dinosaurland—where all the once-mighty, now-extinct fashion moguls who couldn't, or wouldn't, do simple math ended up.

Bottom Line

Even amidst the fury of thousands of women on both sides of the Atlantic, Christian Dior was certain that his retrogressive New Look of 1947 would soon be worn by everyone who aspired to be fashionable.

His confidence proved to be well-founded and, for decades afterward, women obediently continued doing whatever designers told them to. Marching orders were, of course, delivered mostly by women's magazines—which, in turn, obeyed the big-bucks marketers who manipulated them as if they were so many marionettes.

If Dior could somehow fast-forward himself to the mid-1990s, however, he'd be in for a big surprise. But it wouldn't sink in if he merely checked out what was strutting down the runways or being touted in magazines like *Vogue*, which recently printed a subhead the Parisian would doubtless consider flattering: "Take a deep breath. The corset and the 'waspie' waist—made popular by Christian Dior . . . in 1947—are receiving unanimous support again."

So far so good. But if Dior then strolled the streets of North America and took a good look at what real women are really wearing these days, he'd have a tough time spotting *Vogue*'s purported "unanimity" about corsets, or many of the other ludicrous irrelevancies designers have tried to foist on us recently. In time, the centime would doubtless drop and the maestro would realize that the jig is just about up. As the authors of *Megatrends for Women* express it: "The days when women followed fashion blindly are over. . . . Fashion will have to start following women."

As a delicious irony, (and practically the only positive aspect of the No Fat Chicks era) *we* have been the catalysts in the attitudinal revolution that's gradually overthrowing fashion tyrants and their handmaidens in the mass media. And the short-sighted, exclusionary dolts brought it on themselves when they deliberately prevented millions of women from wearing the latest duds.

We tried hard—so hard that it broke many of our hearts—to whittle ourselves down to what designers, marketers, and their assorted mouthpieces told us we *should* be. But it's only a matter of time before the edict that all women should, and could, look like the thinnest 5 per cent of the female population will be exposed for the coercive fantasy it always was. I believe the time is almost here. With millions of Baby Boomers hitting middle age, the majority of buying power is now in the hands of womanly sized women—most of whom are old enough and wise enough to refuse to be diminished to the size, shape, and powerlessness of waifs, baby dolls, sex kittens, or submissive 1940s-style ladies.

Yet, despite the optimism prompted by this logic, a distinct danger still remains. The cunning fashion industry, and the marketers who keep it afloat, may simply end up hijacking and co-opting our demands once again—catering to mature women *only*. Meanwhile, our daughters, and their daughters in turn, will be exempted stylistically and remain hypnotized by an indestructible *idée fixe*: The only way to be attractive is to be thin.

CHAPTER TEN

Fed-Up

Why hasn't every window in every diet clinic in the country been smashed? Why haven't tons of pills, potions, and supplements been shoved over Niagara Falls? Or dumpsters full of diet books, exercise videos, and fashion magazines been tossed off the highest Rocky Mountain? Why haven't the worst profiteers been sued, hanged in effigy, or force-fed some of their own noxious products? Why, in short, isn't the word "No" being screamed from coast to coast by fed-up Fat Chicks?

Because the hardest enemy to fight is the one with outposts in your head.

The memorable aphorism from feminism's pioneer days could have no better application than this. When you're part of the only group it's still okay to hate, when your every step is dogged by condemnation, your judgement clouded by shame and guilt, your body exhausted by starvation—and you're brainwashed to blame *yourself* for all this misery—how likely is it that you'll even think of rebelling? As Naomi Wolf wrote in *The Beauty Myth*, "A quietly mad population is a tractable one."

Granted, other stigmatized groups also have to wrestle with the inner demons of doubt and fear. But the injustices faced by racial minorities, homosexuals, and the disabled are obvious to anyone who's not a bigot, and the entire culture isn't insisting that their tribulations are caused by their own character flaws—or that the solution is merely exercising sufficient will-power. For women, on the other hand, liberation from what Betty Friedan called "the problem that has no name" had to be generated from inside each individual's mind. But once the famous epiphanic "clicks" rose to a cacophony, the true foes were sighted and the appropriate strongholds began to be stormed.

Not so with the obese. Our stumbling-block isn't that the problem has no name but that we—and everyone else—have been deliberately trained to call it by a crushing litany of *wrong* names: gluttony, sloth, greed, stupidity, weakness, lack of will-power, lack of self-respect, self-betrayal, antisocialism.

All of which makes it truly remarkable that, after decades of passively taking grief, a growing number of plus-size activists have finally begun dishing out some of their own. A single name for their efforts has yet to emerge so, for now, various groups characterize themselves as the size-acceptance movement, the anti-diet movement, fat pride, fat power, and fat liberation. They have also been developing their own booming sub-culture, as we will see later in this chapter.

What did it take to motivate and embolden these Fat Chicks? Probably more than any other single factor, the overwhelming and unprecedented success of two of their own: Oprah and Roseanne. After seeing women like themselves either portrayed as inconsequential buffoons or being invisible altogether, watching these two role models achieve mogul status, on their own terms, has been enormously empowering. (And subsequent weight losses by both women did nothing to diminish the effect.)

The go-button was also punched by the discovery of exonerating medical evidence that obesity is *not* caused or perpetuated by simply eating too much. Not only have "fat genes" been discovered, but the counter-productivity of dieting is now uncontestable. So when Fat Chicks insist that we're not gorging ourselves, that our metabolisms have been wrecked by dieting, and that it's impossible for 95–98 per cent of *all* dieters to sustain weight loss, we know we're telling truths that are finally beginning to be believed.

The breathtakingly cruel depths to which anti-fat profiteers have recently sunk has acted as a third motivator. When, for example, *Harper's Bazaar* magazine virtually *endorsed* the potentially lethal scourge of bulimia as a normal beauty imperative, hackles were raised all over the continent. And one of the worst flops in fashion history occurred when what might be termed "Operation Waif" (actually "Twiggy Revisited") tried to convince women that the new standard of beauty was epitomized by gawky teenage girls who looked as if they needed rescuing.

That the attitudinal tide is starting to turn—and not just among Fat

Chicks—was recently demonstrated by an unprecedented, evidently spontaneous, graffiti campaign that recently defaced dozens of Calvin Klein jeans ads featuring "superwaif" model Kate Moss. Across her concave bare stomach were scrawled variations on the theme of "Feed this woman." And beside her droopy mouth cartoon-type balloons appeared saying, "I'm so hungry!" Irate mothers of "waif wannabes" also protested this ad campaign by mailing jeans back to Calvin Klein with blistering comments about his irresponsible attitude.

Comes the Revolution

Radicalized by these events and similar factors, size-acceptance advocates are being galvanized into action by adding up the numbers and realizing their potential clout—economic, political, and, ultimately, social. When you figure in not only the truly overweight, but also the millions of women who are coerced into everlasting diets despite being average or even underweight, their numbers dwarf those of all other shortchanged groups combined. In Canada, including the 29 per cent who *are* overweight, the 78 per cent who *believe* they are too heavy, and the nearly 300,000 who suffer from eating disorders, we're talking about several million women. South of the border, at least a third of all women are 20 per cent or more overweight, while in excess of 95 million believe they are obese. And those with eating disorders have now topped the 11-million mark.

Tallying up these numbers reveals a horrifying total of well over 100 million women and girls in North America who are affected and afflicted by the "billion-dollar brainwash."

Small wonder, then, that those in the vanguard of the size-acceptance movement insist that their efforts represent the next cultural transformation. And that once the majority of Fat Chicks, and those who identify with us, finally comprehend the enormity of the disservice that's being done—not only to women of all sizes, but to yet another generation of girls—the revolution will be unstoppable.

Considering our collective purchasing power, plus the fact that our ranks include the estimated 80 per cent of big-spending Baby Boomers who become chunkier rather than scrawnier as they age—and therefore are more than likely to revamp injustices in this context, just as they've done in so many other arenas—simple logic suggests just one outcome: It's only a matter of time before Fat Chicks will stop being the only minority it's still socially acceptable to laugh at and discriminate against.

But no one thinks it's going to be easy. In Canada, the cadre of those who've wakened from the trance is still so small and scattered that, despite a handful of encouraging signs, the real battle for acceptance of size diversity has barely begun. In fact, Winnipeg's Moe Lerner, a 500-pound physician who is the country's best-known activist, told me he believes that "it may take someone getting shot or planting a bomb before anything improves."

In the United States, however, things are really starting to get interesting. Crusaders say they have the heady feeling that their struggle is approaching the stage where it can be legitimately compared with the early days of the civil-rights and women's liberation movements. The same general plot outline does indeed seem to be unfolding. The fight is proceeding amid identical derision from reactionary observers. The attitudinal first step has been taken, which is reclaiming the adjective that's used as the sharpest weapon of oppression. For African-Americans it was "black," and in this context, of course, it is "fat." And there were unmistakable echoes of earlier insurrections recently when the most prominent group of (primarily) Fat Chicks went on the offensive—by taking the battle out of their own heads and into the streets.

They chose the favourite tactic of all revolutionaries who want to symbolize their determination to overcome: a march on the capital. Near a spot in Washington, D.C., where Martin Luther King once appealed for racial equality, demonstrators from the National Association for the Advancement of Fat Acceptance (NAAFA) marked their twenty-fifth anniversary, on August 26, 1994, by declaring their own dream: "To be treated like human beings."

The poignancy of the plea reflected the sheer courage it had taken for most of the portly protesters just to show up. Like the women's liberationists, African-Americans, and homosexuals who preceded them down Pennsylvania Avenue years ago, these activists knew that their mere appearance would be inflammatory. But this time, it was bound to be worse. When you can't even step outside your door without attracting catcalls, you know that parading your despised body means deliberately venturing into harm's way.

The fear was well founded, and it didn't take long for the insults to come flying on that sweltering summer day. As undermining as it undoubtedly was for earlier protesters to hear racial and sexual epithets, or to see placards ordering women back to the kitchen, it was an infinitely more *personal* humiliation to have to stare down placards shrieking: "SAVE A WHALE—HARPOON A FAT CHICK!"

But the spunky demonstrators refused to be intimidated by the naked prejudice they endured during their march, or the demeaning media coverage by the few news organizations that paid attention. Typical was Gannett News Service's Carl Weiser, who facetiously estimated that the protesters "were burning off 300 calories an hour," and then dismissed the event by adding that "government has become a veritable food fight of special interests, leaving democracy paralyzed by a barrage of incoming vegetables."

While Weiser's unwieldy metaphor made little sense, the *Los Angeles Times*'s Scott Harris missed the point altogether. Sticking to the standard media approach of trying to sniff out dissension, he wound up his article about the size-acceptance movement with what he apparently thought was a humorous kicker. NAAFA executive director Sally E. Smith, Harris wrote, had "grumbled [that] the closest [she'd] come to killing a talk show guest" was when she shared a stage at the *Leeza* TV show with *Diary of a Fat Housewife* author Rosemary Green, who repeated her frequently expressed opinion that "big is not beautiful. It's ugly and disgusting."

The blatancy and prevalence of such insults explain why it took a quarter-century after the founding of NAAFA just to get this far. Despite increasingly overweight populations throughout North America, membership in what is, so far, the only viable fight-back organization on the continent stands at a meagre 4,500, with fewer than 100 in Canada. But then, as NAAFAns reassure one another, it took nearly fifty years after winning the vote in 1920 for women to raise enough consciousness to start rewriting the social contract—and about the same gap after its 1909 founding before the National Association for the Advancement of Colored People (NAACP) grew strong enough to begin righting racial wrongs.

Yet some commentators vehemently object to comparing the size-acceptance crusade to the civil-rights movement. "Ridiculous," said David Boaz, executive vice-president of the libertarian Cato Institute, when queried about a recent successful lawsuit launched by a 360-pound Tennessee woman named Deborah Birdwell against a Nashville cinema that refused to allow her to bring in her own folding chair, despite the fact that its seats could not accommodate her. "Trivializing," echoed Kansas City–based political movement authority Laird Wilcox, who provided an object lesson by opining in a syndicated article that NAAFA's efforts are merely "silly [because] people prefer to be around those who are attractive, not unattractive."

Even more inimical to the size-acceptance struggle for credibility, given that it appeared in one of the most influential of all magazines, was an uncharacteristically thoughtless *Time* essay by Margaret Carlson. After a breezy beginning—"Got a weight problem? . . . phone Uncle Sam . . . and you could get a wad of cash or that job you've been wanting"— the piece, titled "And Now, Obesity Rights," deplored the exemplary legal victories of two large women whose employment discrimination we discussed in Chapter 6. But, in the case of Bonnie Cook, the nursing aide who prevailed in court against a Rhode Island mental-retardation facility, Carlson (and many other journalists) left out some crucial information. The 320-pound Cook had already *performed* her duties satisfactorily at the same facility for three years before a daughter's illness forced her to resign. Yet when she reapplied for her old job, weighing exactly the same amount as before, she was turned down because of obesity.

Carlson concluded her short-sighted essay by warning that to include fat people in protective legislation would be "to fail . . . the truly vulnerable, the truly prejudged, the truly disadvantaged." But it's the firm conviction of size-acceptance proponents that they *do* belong in these negative categories that's fuelling the increasingly feisty efforts.

As the primary force in the size liberation movement, NAAFA has come a long way since its 1969 founding, when newsletters were sent out in plain brown envelopes to avoid embarrassing members. But the group's philosophy—that no one should have to be thin to enjoy the same rights and privileges due every other citizen—has never changed. Ongoing consciousness-raising activities by various NAAFA committees include lobbying lawmakers (see below), the medical community, advertisers, educators, housing authorities, airlines, film producers, and other industries. Media appearances by executive director Sally E. Smith and vigorous letter-writing campaigns by members have resulted in the sensitization of many (although obviously not enough) editors and news directors. One of Smith's personal bests to date, in terms of exposure for her cause, was convincing *USA Today* to publish her hard-hitting, advertiser-offending piece titled "The Great Diet Deception" in January 1995. Smith has also hit the lecture circuit, speaking to, among other crucial sectors, medical students and those who teach them. In addition, NAAFA's board of directors includes an impressive, influential, and exceptionally active group of health professionals.

Among other activist organizations and individuals currently working to undo the damage done by the "billion-dollar brainwash" are:

• A-HELP (Association for the Health Enrichment of Large People), which is an organization of professionals in the medical, mental-health, health-education, and scientific communities who share the belief that "fat" and "fit" are not mutually exclusive terms. In addition to sponsoring seminars and other consciousness-raising events, A-HELP members frequently publish articles such as a recent one in *Radiance* magazine by Joanne Ikeda, RD, titled "Confessions of a Radical Registered Dietician."

• Dedicated to furthering the anti-diet philosophy among clients and other health professionals, Hugs International is a Canadian company founded by Linda Omichinski, RD, of Portage La Prairie, Manitoba, that now has facilitators in four other countries. The author of a bestseller, *Calories Don't Count, You Do*, and co-author of a companion book, *Tailoring Your Tastes* (both published by Tamos Books, Winnipeg), Omichinski also publishes a newsletter and distributes video and audio cassettes "to help people move from dieting to focusing, instead, on health and energy."

• MediaWatch, a Toronto-based watchdog organization which, while not directly involved in the size-acceptance movement, monitors many media portrayals of women and opposes negative stereotypes at the highest possible levels of authority.

• In Santa Cruz, California, the Body Image Task Force has tackled the need for theatres to provide extra-wide seats and, at this writing, was negotiating with both the United Artists and Harris Group movie chains.

• In Halifax, a former nurse and bulimia survivor, Janet Beaton, helped establish Metro Eating Disorder Awareness Week in September 1994 and spends much of her time visiting schools to raise consciousness about anorexia and bulimia and to help those already afflicted. Beaton's activities, which are partially funded by Nova Scotia's Department of Health and Dartmouth College, also include distributing a video and brochure entitled *It's OK to Talk about It*, which chronicles her own struggle with an eating disorder.

• Similarly, in and around Toronto, Karin Davis, a recovering anorexic and bulimic, singlehandedly publishes *Body Pride—Redefining Beauty*, a thoughtful magazine to encourage the acceptance of a variety of body shapes and sizes. She also helps groups of youngsters battle eating disorders and appearance-based self-esteem problems.

• In Dallas, Texas, a group of women with a raucous sense of humour publishes a consciousness-raising magazine called *Rump Parliament*. They also confer annual Rumpie Awards on those who "perpetuate negative stereotypes about fat people." Columnist Ann Landers, for example, recently received a Rumpie in the category of "Broken Record" for, said the citation, her "insistence on using that tired phrase 'killing yourself with a knife and fork.'" Although Landers expressed ambivalence about the accusation, she good-naturedly gave the organization a quantum leap by featuring it in her column.

• In addition, a growing number of smaller self-help organizations are springing up all over the continent. These include Breaking Free workshops conducted by author Geneen Roth (whose valuable books I've gratefully borrowed from throughout *No Fat Chicks*); Great Shape fitness classes designed specifically for heavy women; and the Beyond Hunger and Overcoming Overeating groups, both of which teach their members how to stop dieting and relearn their natural appetites.

International No-Diet Day

Staged annually on May 5 for the past several years in various cities in England and Australia, International No-Diet Day was imported into North America about three years ago, largely through the efforts of *Rump Parliament* editor/publisher Lee Martindale. The object is to stage events to encourage fat people to publicly raise consciousness by picketing diet centres and weight-loss-surgery establishments, feeding the hungry, and enjoying guilt-free meals (such as mass picnics) themselves. Martindale's scheme got a big boost when Ann Richards, then the governor of Texas, proclaimed No-Diet Day in her state in 1994.

Regional wrinkles are being added by NAAFA members like Ron Karle, a computer programmer in Ann Arbor, Michigan, who mobilizes fitness walks for obese people "to show that we can exercise too, and that we have the right to use public parks without being ridiculed." Elsewhere, NAAFAns in Seattle and San Diego have held public smashings of bathroom scales and marched under such banner slogans as "Scales Are for Fish, Not Women."

New York City's National Center for Overcoming Overeating has sponsored a Diet Museum featuring outrageously useless and exploitive artifacts; while a huge picnic was held in Portland, Connecticut. And in Woodstock, New York, two activist groups—Substantial Women and the Fat Feminist Caucus of NAAFA—sponsored a recent exhibit called "Women Artists Celebrate Fat Women."

As one of the few major consumer magazines to get on the bandwagon so far, *Sassy* observes the annual event by offering its teenage subscribers free information kits from the International No-Diet Coalition. (The publication also refuses to print articles promoting dangerous dieting.)

For No-Diet Day 1995 in Toronto, NAAFA's Eastern Canada coordinator, Helena Spring, organized a discussion in the nurses' residence at Toronto Hospital that was co-sponsored by the National Eating Disorders Centre. Unfortunately, "because of general apathy," says Spring, only about twenty people turned out.

At this writing, there has been talk, but no action, regarding more radical ideas for celebrating International No-Diet Day. Example: "bombing" diet centres with exploding bags of ketchup to dramatize the fact that the H.J. Heinz food company, which owns Weight Watchers, nabs consumers coming *and* going—by first tempting us to gain weight with saturation-level advertising of its food products, and then signing us up for reducing classes, as well as selling us expensive items from its burgeoning repertoire of low- and no-fat products.

Consumer Boycotts

How about the ultimate fight-back tactic of any protest movement: the consumer boycott? NAAFA recently organized a boycott of Hallmark that succeeded in persuading the company to drop an offensive line of greeting cards, mugs, and other items that made fat people the butt of their dubious humour. (Sample: An elephant in a hammock above the quote: "I exercise as much as the next guy—provided the next guy is a fat, lazy slob!") In addition, NAAFA's threat of calling a boycott of the Denny's restaurant chain—because much of its seating is too small—succeeded in eliciting a pledge to correct the situation in all future restaurants.

In Boston in early 1994, a group called Boycott Anorexic Marketing (BAM) began targeting companies whose advertisements feature extremely thin models. Psychotherapist and eating disorders specialist Mary Baure says she helped facilitate the group's formation because "so many women [feel] powerless at the way our culture applauds anorexia. . . ." High on BAM's hit list are Calvin Klein, for those notorious Kate Moss jeans ads, and a Coca-Cola product called Diet Sprite because of its use of a skin-and-bones model, Kristin McMenamy, whom the print ad nicknamed "Skeleton." Although Coca-Cola officially denied any backlash from BAM's activities, the ad was cancelled. The group's power and visibility were enormously enhanced when the National Organization for Women endorsed its efforts in May 1994. Said NOW's Los Angeles chapter president, "Advertising has always been used to impact our society's way of thinking, and women have been paying the price for far too long."

Setting Watchdogs on the Profiteers

In Canada, I regret to report, no branch of federal, provincial, or city government has yet addressed exploitation by the "billion-dollar brainwash," although (as reported in Chapter 6) employment discrimination against the obese has been studied in two provinces.

In the United States, however, several victories for size-acceptance activists have occurred since 1990, when Representative Ron Wyden, a Democrat from Oregon, convened congressional hearings on the weight-loss industry. Before the final gavel pounded, several governmental bodies—the Food and Drug Administration (FDA), the Federal

Trade Commission (FTC), the Federal Communications Commission (FCC), and the Attorney General's Office—were officially blasted for letting things get so out of hand by failing to investigate abuses, or even to enforce existing regulations.

In a whirlwind of subsequent actions, the FTC commenced a three-year investigation that ended up charging five of the nation's largest commercial diet programs—including Weight Watchers, Jenny Craig, and Nutri-System—with deceptive advertising practices. By the end of 1994, when the dust had cleared, Weight Watchers' membership had plunged between 15 and 25 per cent (depending on which news report you believe). Nutri-System declared bankruptcy and closed its 283 centres (but metamorphosed eight months later into a wellness program called Live for Life). And Jenny Craig, which put up a fair bit of resistance, ended up with its stock at an all-time low, and a 19 per cent revenue drop, forcing it to close about thirty branches. Also, Jenny Craig paid out $10 million to settle a class-action suit on behalf of customers who accused the diet of leading to gall-bladder disease.

The FDA has investigated and banned 111 ingredients from over-the-counter pills, ruling them ineffective or potentially harmful, and cracked down on a wide range of products. At least six product-liability suits have been filed against Medifast (including charges that the program causes gallstones and gangrene).

Meanwhile, the FTC began hounding many of the worst profiteers regarding the safety and efficacy of their products and the grandiosity of their assertions. A ubiquitous pill, Fibre Trim, was put out of business altogether while, at this writing, a similar fate seemed to be facing such other snake-oil products as FormulaTrim 3000, Megaloss 1000, and MiracleTrim. But the most significant result of all was an edict that such disclosure statements as "For many dieters, weight loss is temporary" must be added to some product packaging, and to all broadcast ads of more than thirty seconds' duration.

After considering a report by a panel of experts it commissioned in 1994, the Washington-based Institute of Medicine issued a fairly well-publicized statement urging the weight-loss industry "to disclose the true effectiveness of its programs" and to consider establishing an accreditation process.

As for the future, NAAFA, which has done the lion's share of consumer lobbying, is now calling for the following steps: that the U.S. Centers for Disease Control track the incidence of deaths related to weight-loss efforts; that the ban that keeps tobacco advertising off radio and television be extended to include dangerous diet products; and that the Surgeon General begin requiring that *all* weight-loss products carry a warning about their probable ineffectiveness, similar to the cautionary messages now mandatory for all cigarette packaging.

Project Legislation 2000 is another American program that's under way, with *ad hoc* support from several activist groups. Its goal is to have the words "weight or size" added to existing anti-discrimination legislation by the turn of the century in all of the states where they are currently absent.

And, finally, spurred by the premise that, to change the future, it's essential to change the attitudes of the young people who will inherit it, the Human and Civil Rights Division of the (U.S.) National Education Association is currently investigating size discrimination in public schools.

A Rising Subculture

Civil-rights leader Malcolm X often spoke about how demoralizing it is to never see anyone who resembles you portrayed as a normal participant in popular culture. He meant African-Americans, of course, but large women have been marginalized in exactly the same way since the "billion-dollar brainwash" shifted into high gear in the late 1960s.

Not content to simply wait for readmission into the mainstream, the boldest and most entrepreneurial of the Fat Chicks are developing a burgeoning subculture all their own. Besides the proliferation of plus-size clothing and modelling agencies detailed in Chapter 9, there are social clubs with defiant names such as "Goddesses" and "More to Love," which range from supportive all-female get-togethers to dance parties which provide a comfortable atmosphere in which to meet men who appreciate fat women despite—or because of—their size.

There are religious groups, swimming parties, and even cruises and other vacation trips exclusively for overweight people. There are hairstylists, photographers, psychotherapists, cosmeticians, dieticians, exercise classes, fitness trainers, massage therapists, and even bankers who specialize in large-size clients.

There are also dozens of mail-order catalogues, with names like "Royal Resources," "Far and Wide," and "Amplestuff," that feature clothing, books, video and audio tapes, personal-care items (such as extra-size clothes hangers, tape measures, and hospital gowns), and posters like one that advertised a recent "vision-expanding" photographic exhibition called "The Belly Project." Among the most popular of the inspirational items aimed at size-acceptance proponents are replicas of the 30,000-year-old *Woman of Willendorf*, which is the oldest "Earth Mother" statue known to date. Her rotund image is being reproduced as jewellery, art objects, and even chocolates.

Fat Chicks have their own magazines, which not only feature flattering pictorial coverage of large women modelling attractive clothing, but also provide a forum for their stories, relevant news, pertinent articles, and resource indexes. The first of these publications was *Big Beautiful Woman*,* which began in 1979. Also popular are *Dimensions*, which includes a very active dating-service feature to introduce large women to men who admire them; and *Mirage*, which works the other way around by publishing photographs of male "fat admirers" who are interested in meeting heavy women. Two excellent sources of unbiased information about up-to-the-minute obesity research are the *Healthy Weight Journal* and NAAFA's newsletter.

The best of the bunch is *Radiance*, which has been published out of Oakland, California, for the past eleven years. A lively quarterly that's reminiscent of *Ms.* in its early days, the magazine occasionally engages in good-natured guerrilla tactics such as publishing a swimsuit edition that puts *Sports Illustrated*'s obnoxious equivalent to shame. *Radiance* also features unique and extremely useful articles (sample: "How to Cope with Anti-Fat Doctors"), plus an investigative column by NAAFA co-founder William J. Fabrey called "Big News," and a regular medical column by biomedical researcher Paul Ernsberger on vital topics such as the risks involved in weight-loss surgery.

The gutsy spirit of the size acceptance movement in general, and

---

*Some readers were offended recently when founder Carole Shaw sold *Big Beautiful Woman* to *Penthouse* publisher Larry Flynt.

Radiance in particular, was recently expressed in a punchy editorial by the magazine's founder and publisher, Alice Ansfield, who warned: "Watch out, thin people, we fatties are coming out. We're not going to stay safely in our homes anymore, so you'd better get used to it."

Media Coverage

Are the media catching on to the sensational story that's right under their noses? In most cases, the answer is no. And some of the pundits who are wising up to the size-acceptance revolution still resemble the proverbial blind folk trying to discern the outline of an elephant and misidentifying the parts they do manage to grasp.

Falling firmly in the former camp was a recent mean-spirited review in *Alberta Report* of a book by Charles Sykes titled *Nation of Victims.* Virginia Byfield began by making fun of NAAFA's campaign to increase the number of fat actresses cast as love interests on TV shows, and then went on to characterize all such protesters as a "squalling howl of grievance," "the horizontally challenged," and "afflicted beachball[s]." It's hard to imagine Byfield or any other writer getting away with applying such insulting terms to any other minority.

In the same sarcastic vein was a recent *Boston Globe* response to a letter from NAAFA's Sally Smith. Despite describing herself as a large woman, columnist Diane White trivialized complaints about an earlier column that, Smith claimed, had "reinforc[ed] myths and negative stereotypes about fat people." The tone of White's piece was an all-too-familiar winking at readers, as if to say, "We all know that fat people are fair game, so let's have at it."

There are, however, a growing number of writers and broadcasters who are beginning to sense something new in the wind. In Canada, the best print example of this to date was a comprehensive cover story in *Maclean's* magazine on May 2, 1994. In "Body Obsession," writer Mary Nemeth reported that a "quiet anti-dieting revolution [is making] the crash diet phenomenon . . . passe."

On television, CTV's *W5* tackled the topic of "Fat Power" on September 20, 1994. Because there is still so little organized protest activity in Canada, producers had to send a crew all the way to Washington to catch the NAAFA march. In addition to illustrating how the size-acceptance crusade is heating up in the United States, the show also gave much-needed exposure to the embryonic battle for inclusion of the obese in Canada's anti-discrimination labour laws.

South of the border, several of the most influential American publications have begun exploring the same theme. *People* magazine, using a phrase that has become almost extinct, urged "superwaif" model Kate Moss to "put some meat on her bones." In another issue, *People* put Moss on its cover beside the words: "Skin & Bones: . . . Is a dangerous message being sent to weight-obsessed teens?" The magazine also regularly features 155-pound Guess jeans model Anna Nicole Smith, and included a 180-pound plus-size model named Emme in its 1994 compilation of "The 50 Most Beautiful People." Certainly these items fall in the "fluff" category, but the routine inclusion of large women in just such popular coverage is a vital part of what's being strived for by size-acceptance advocates.

On a more serious note, *Ladies' Home Journal* editor Leslie Lampert took the dramatic step of having a realistic "fat suit" designed by theatrical costumers to let her pass for a woman of about 250 pounds as she pursued a week of normal activities in New York City. In an admirably eye-opening article titled "Fat Like Me," Lampert described not only the outward cruelty and discrimination she experienced while wearing her disguise, but also the inward depression such treatment fostered. "I feel ashamed of my culture," Lampert concluded, "[for the] pain we cause people who are less than our concept of ideal."

Three circulation giants, *Reader's Digest, Consumer Reports,* and *USA Weekend,* carried the very positive "don't diet—be happy" message of Martin E.P. Seligman's inspirational bestseller *What You Can Change and What You Can't* to millions of readers who might otherwise not have discovered the book. *USA Weekend* also published an excellent report on the anti-diet revolution by Jacqueline Shannon titled "New Research: Fat Isn't Voluntary"; and its "Fitness with Foreman & Flo-Jo" column also deserves commendation for a no-nonsense philosophy epitomized recently by Olympic athlete Florence Griffith Joyner in her answer to a reader's query: "You can't tell a person's fitness level by his appearance," she wrote. "It doesn't matter if you're 95 pounds or 300 pounds; what matters is being fit."

Among the most widely circulated women's magazines, a sort of schizophrenic identity crisis has recently been in evidence. Even while sprinkling their issues with "dump your diet" articles, they're still filling the remaining pages with photos of extremely thin women. The May 1995 *Vogue* was typical. Tucked into a waif-strewn issue that editor Anna Wintour inexplicably touted as "the first ever devoted to the body" was a top-notch investigative piece by Laura Fraser. Entitled "Dieting by Prescription," it cast a merciless eye on the recent resurgence of diet medications. Fraser, who candidly described herself as weighing "a robust 155 pounds," first wangled her way into a profit-making seminar at a convention of the American Society of Bariatric Physicians and later posed as a potential patient in the offices of a variety of pill-pushing doctors. Summing up, she said that she "became enraged thinking about all the people who trust their doctors to help them with a problem, pay them a lot of money, dutifully starve themselves, then blame themselves when they've gained the weight back."

Bottom Line

"The forfeited self" is an eloquent term Betty Friedan coined in *The Feminine Mystique* to characterize what women lost during the materialism-dominated decades immediately after the Second World War. But the label applies equally well to those of us who've been most damaged by the "billion-dollar brainwash." So does Friedan's formula for defeating oppression: "Refuse to be nameless, depersonalized, manipulated, and live [your] own lives again according to self-chosen purposes."

We certainly won't enter the twenty-first century entirely liberated from the No Fat Chicks commandment. But size acceptance and anti-diet activists are walking, talking, shouting, singing, scale-smashing demonstrations of what happens when the mental penny drops and Fat Chicks finally understand the enormity of what has been done to us— and what must be done to stop it.

The wisest of the protesters perceive the parallels with other oppressed groups and are borrowing vital strategic techniques from earlier revolutionaries. They believe that if their battle is fought on behalf of, and in solidarity with, every person of every size and circumstance who's ever been hurt by discriminatory commercial and cultural factions, they *will* overcome some day.

CHAPTER ELEVEN

Belly-Up?

Glaring evidence of the "billion-dollar brainwash" and its terrible toll surrounds us—yet it remains one of our culture's dirtiest little secrets. No one wants to tell the truth about it, or even admit it exists. There's just too much money to be made by telling the Big Lies that make us spend so obsessively.

But the reality is that the No Fat Chicks era is repeating the scenario Betty Friedan revealed thirty-three years ago in *The Feminine Mystique*. Her book detailed how what was won during the struggle for female suffrage was squandered and forgotten. But, women assured one another at the peak of modern feminist activity, such a profound loss *will never* happen again now that our eyes are open.

It *is* happening again. And this time the losses aren't the result of unavoidable historic calamities. This time, the dispossession is deliberate, and the technique of crushing our core self-respect has resulted in an undermining of the momentous social and economic gains women have made during the past three decades.

Yet the most brilliant technique of the anti-fat profiteers is hiding their puppet strings so well that women honestly believe we're thinking for ourselves and freely making our own choices about how we want to look and behave. Thus, some of the women I interviewed for this book responded with blank confusion. Others indignantly denied that they're being forced, or even duped, into denying their appetites, and driving themselves through busy days in a perpetual state of semi-starvation. Still others insisted that I'm overcomplicating the situation. Women have always wanted to look "nice," they said. That's all there is to it. And the fact that, at this particular time, "nice" happens to mean "thin," which happens to require prodigious expense and effort, just sort of . . . happened.

That the logical cause-and-effect continuum has escaped these people shouldn't be too surprising. It also seems to be as dead as a dodo in most other cultural contexts. When the occasional lonely voice does try to point out how the sky is falling upon us, the warnings simply waft in one collective ear and out the other. Amid dogged denial of even fundamentally inimical influences on our lives, it's obviously been a snap to smudge the connection between the high-pressure sales techniques of the "billion-dollar brainwash" and

• the epidemic of eating disorders that now affects 150 times as many women as are living with AIDS;
• the escalating incidence of clinical depression in the female population;
• the thousands of women who spend millions of dollars to have chunks of their own flesh lopped off, sucked out, or stapled shut;
• the millions more who "voluntarily" restrict their food intake to the point of courting malnutrition, exhaustion, and other medical calamities;
• and the many, many more who overexercise; smoke; abuse laxatives, diuretics, and amphetamines; and eschew birth-control pills for the sake of being slender.

Even when a woman actually drops dead at a weight-loss centre, we're so well indoctrinated that we ignore the glaring object lesson and chalk it up to simple vanity. Any fool knows the dead woman only had herself to blame for getting fat in the first place, we tell ourselves.

Any fool? Exactly. That's what the anti-fat profiteers have made of us in the three decades since implausible little Twiggy was catapulted into the beauty equation by the social and demographic elements *Vogue's* Diana Vreeland dubbed a "youthquake." She also remarked that "Twiggy couldn't have arrived at any other time. It's just as though this little old egg had been lying on the ground, and suddenly, on the right day, it hatched."

Vreeland's imagery is interesting viewed in retrospect. In fact, it's arguably less an egg than a modern equivalent of Pandora's box. For inside it was something that gradually metamorphosed from an emaciated teenager into an idea that was powerful enough to shift public opinion, perception, prejudice, and appetites through 180 degrees. The idea was, of course, that the strong, fertile, womanly sized women who've been favoured throughout history, by nature, men, and artists, would henceforth be deemed a caste of untouchables.

During the next three decades, a host of virtual incubators saw to it that every woman who didn't, couldn't, or (in increasingly rare instances) wouldn't knuckle under to the eleventh commandment—THOU SHALT NOT BE FAT—was punished and penalized so severely that she became a virtual teaching aid to reinforce the lesson among her slimmer sisters.

Fat Chicks—which is how every unslender woman was regarded by the time the profitable propaganda hit high gear—were not only stigmatized, stereotyped, and lied about in all the vehicles of popular culture, but hobbled by orchestrated intolerance at every turn. As described in this book, the process included being deprived of rewarding employment opportunities, denied the advantage of dressing appropriately, prevented from receiving decent health care, robbed of both romantic relationships and the children that might have resulted from them, lured into mortal danger, and generally laughed right out of our status as normal human beings.

All the while, Fat Chicks were taught to blame ourselves for our misery. Every message carried by every medium that inundated our lives reinforced this reprehensible "logic." In time, we internalized the blame so thoroughly that it paralysed both our common sense and our instinct for self-preservation. So we struggled to conform with what was expected of us, and spent every cent we could possibly spare. But nothing worked and we just grew fatter. That, of course, was also regarded as our fault.

Trying to explain that we actually ate less, not more, than many other women, or that science has now proven it's incessant dieting that keeps us fat, was pointless, as, in fact, was fighting back in any way. Nobody listened. So, we thought in our darkest moments, maybe we really were guilty of the horrendous crime everyone had convicted us of. And if that were true, then all the punishment made sense because we deserved it.

Thus did the despicable hoax I call the "billion-dollar brainwash" poison my life decade after wasted decade, just as it still threatens the health and compromises the happiness of millions of other women and girls who are deliberately taught to hate their bodies. Whatever our weight, we are flimflammed into forgetting that nature creates us in a rich variety of shapes and sizes—and believing instead that anyone who cannot permanently clone the physique of the thinnest 5 per cent of the female population is a contemptible, unlovable failure.

The futility and absurdity of trying to accomplish this senseless feat should have been obvious all along. In fact, we might just as easily have been told we all had to be seven feet tall, cut off one ear, and dye our hair pink. But if greedy marketers had tried something that extreme, we would surely have seen through their ludicrous ploy, laughed uproariously, and told them to take a hike.

Yet such is the power of what amounts to an implacable eleventh commandment for women that we've been coerced into everlasting pursuit of something equally unrealistic. And that means we're spending a fortune that's now fattening up assorted weight-loss profiteers throughout North America by more than $40 billion a year.

Luring us onward, like the ultimate carrot, is the fairy-tale "happily ever after," while, behind us, the whip of anti-fat prejudice cracks ever louder. Both carrot and whip are supplied in saturation quantities by the magazines, books, television shows, movies, and newspapers that relentlessly teach us to pursue happiness, love, and self-esteem by shopping. What are we taught to buy? Whatever the marketers who pay the media to brainwash us wish to sell.

Granted, this *modus operandi* also applies to innumerable other commodities and is actually a rudimentary blueprint for any market-driven economy. But there's a crucial difference between hoodwinking someone into hoping Brand X shampoo will make her the belle of the ball and browbeating her into believing that life isn't worth living unless she stays thin.

But the Orwellian No Fat Chicks propaganda is inescapable. And, like other evil campaigns which have swayed entire societies, it warps our perspective so severely that we use its message as a weapon against ourselves, each other, and every new generation. No female is safe from its corrosive influence—not a history-making prime minister, a popular princess,* a superstar entertainer, an obscure Canadian grandmother, or a bewildered schoolgirl.

Result: Millions of lives are being sacrificed psychologically, and the untold mortality rate may well number in the thousands. Like puppets

---

*Even after Princess Diana's poignant public admission to suffering severe bouts of bulimia, she was hounded about her appearance in a widely published Reuters "news" story that "reported" she had taken to wearing long coats to conceal cellulite on her thighs.

dangling helplessly on invisible strings, we think what the anti-fat prof-iteers want us to think. We do what they want us to do. And we buy what they want us to buy.

And Yet . . .

At the risk of contradicting my own conclusions, I must now declare my belief that the beginning of the end of the brutal No Fat Chicks era is gradually coming into view. Why? Chiefly because of the demographic clout of the Baby Boomers. The anti-fat propagandists were always right about one thing: Money talks. The whole phenomenon couldn't have happened if there hadn't been a lot of cash jingling in the jeans of the 80-million-plus North American teenagers whom they conned into assuming that all women could, and should, look like Twiggy in perpe-tuity. Those same Boomers are a lot older now. But they've still got "attitude" and they're still the sector with the most buying power.

A lot of marketers forgot that. Or, to be more precise, they forgot that people actually age as time goes by, and kept assuming that focusing on the youth market—which had paid off so magnificently in the past—would be a sure-fire formula forever. Reality check: Beginning this year, every 7.5 seconds someone in North America will turn fifty. The trend will continue for eighteen years and, all the while, about 80 per cent of the Boomers will "plump up" rather than "skinny down." And, as many authorities have pointed out, every time the Boomers say "gimme," sooner or later, they get what they want.

Small wonder, then, that there are scattered reports to the effect that the number of chronic North American dieters has dropped from a high of approximately 65 million to about 48 million during the past half-dozen years. A recent poll showed that the number of people who think "overweight" automatically means "unattractive" has dropped from 55 to 36 per cent. Another found that 65 per cent of female respondents said they'd rather win a Pulitzer Prize than be Miss America.* And several surveys have shown that, for the first time in more than a decade, both women and men are not automatically making dieting their number-one annual New Year's resolution.

---

*Mind you, Canadians are way ahead on this one, as evidenced by the fact that the Miss Canada, Miss Teen Canada, and Miss Toronto pageants all died natural deaths in the 1990s.

Also encouraging is the fact that fashion designer Calvin Klein—the leading purveyor of advertising celebrating waif-sized women, young-younger-youngest models, and nude-nuder-nudest photos—backed down for the first time in the summer of 1995 and withdrew a major campaign. Previously, he had only seemed flattered when his cheesy ads provoked outrage. But when a chorus of assorted complainants shouted that his latest sleazy photos had gone too far, Klein actually listened. Which means that, because he's the primary trend-setter, the concept of responsibility is being reintroduced into fashion and advertising.

Another hopeful sign is the fact that artists, who are always the first to catch the whiff of a new wind when it blows in, have begun discovering the rich variety of creatively exploitable themes inherent in the scam of the century. There's oppression to be revealed, mortal secrets to be uncovered, heroic physical and psychological battles, and villains galore. So far, only a few writers, actors, directors, photographers, and television producers have "got it." But what they're creating is powerful. Examples include:

• A Canadian documentary film called *Fat Chance: The Big Prejudice*, which was the sleeper hit of the 1994 Toronto Film Festival. Producer Jeff MacKay started with the premise that his star, a 370-pound Winnipeg social worker named Rick Zakowich, would attempt to lose half of his body weight, while cameras chronicled the odyssey. Both men believed their premise was not only doable but dramatically interesting, especially because they planned to include abundant evidence of prejudice (such as a woman whose hatred of obesity is so intense that she refuses even to walk in a fat person's footsteps in the snow). But the film's plot took an unexpected turn when dieting and exercising proved to be not only futile, but despair-inducing. As it turned out, it wasn't Zakowich's body, but his attitude that was transformed for the better. And it was spending time with a variety of fight-back activists in Virginia and New York City that accomplished the feat. The ending of *Fat Chance* shows Zakowich back in Winnipeg, at peace with himself at last, and crusading against damaging characterizations of obese people in the local media.

• In one of his trademark "pseudo-documentaries," entitled *Eating*, writer/producer/director Henry Jaglom effectively captured the anguished ambivalence of female friends who gather for a birthday party. As delectable food is passed from hand to hand, with almost no one partaking, each character reveals the lengths to which she has gone just to survive inside the strait-jacket of slenderness. (My favourite line: "I'm looking for a man who's as satisfying as a baked potato." I laughed out loud, and the fact that most of the women in the movie did not made the point even stronger.)

• Before actress and TV talk-show host Ricki Lake lost more than 100 pounds, she starred in *Babycakes*. A Hollywood remake of a romantic German film called *Sugar Baby*, it was probably the only movie in cinematic history in which the male protagonist falls in love with—and leaves his skinny wife for—an extremely large woman. (Shot mostly in Toronto, some of its sweetest scenes take place at Ryerson Polytechnic University's outdoor skating rink.)

• English actress Minnie Driver was put on a "reverse diet" to gain 20 pounds to star in a charming film called *Circle of Friends*. The ugly-duckling-becomes-a-swan (without losing an ounce) plot involves the heroine's unexpected romance with the local "catch" (played by Chris O'Donnell), whose screen father utters a line of dialogue that must surely be a first: "There's a lot to be said," he tells his son, "for these big, soft girls." Meanwhile, several other actresses were recently ordered to enhance their film characters' credibility by gaining weight. They include Meryl Streep, for *The Bridges of Madison County*; Toni Collette, who put on 42 pounds to star in *Muriel's Wedding*; and "super model" Elle McPherson, who gained 20 pounds for *Sirens*. Of course, this trend actually began twenty-five years ago, when Twiggy deliberately "porked up" so she could launch an acting career.

• Best of all, in terms of reaching mass audiences, acclaimed director Steven Spielberg (*Schindler's List*, *E.T.*) is currently producing a feature film tentatively called *Body Image*. Screenwriter Andrea King says it's about "a beautiful, smart, sexy, fat woman."

• In theatre, a new company called Weird Sisters Productions opened a lot of eyes, while tickling a lot of funny-bones, when it presented a satire called *Shapeless* at Toronto's Tarragon Theatre in the summer of 1994. Among the sketches were what a critic called "a wonderfully vile game show" titled *Name Those Flaws*, plus several others that blew the whistle on many grisly facets of anti-fat prejudice. In addition, 270-pound actress Camryn Manheim wrote, staged, and performed a one-woman show called *Wake Up, I'm Fat*, which was an Off-Broadway hit in 1993. Manheim also did a tastefully shot nude scene in a movie called *The Road to Wellville*, which *People* magazine said was so enthusiastically received that she was immediately cast in "not-fat roles" in two other films. *Blown Sideways through Life* is another innovative one-woman stage show, written and performed by amply proportioned Claudia Shear, which was recently filmed and broadcast by PBS. In it, Shear declares that "to be fat is to be branded not merely unerotic, but un-American, unattractive, unaesthetic, undisciplined."

• As for novels, no one has yet topped Margaret Atwood's *Lady Oracle*, in which a young girl combats her mother's domination by deliberately eating her way to obesity. To comfort herself, the heroine indulges in delightful fantasies such as being a fat but beloved opera singer, with permission to "stand up there in front of everyone and shriek as loud as you could, about hatred and love and rage and despair, scream at the top of your lungs and have it come out music." But best-selling author Pat Conroy makes an effectively caustic jest in his most recent novel, *Beach Music*, to the effect that society won't be satisfied until bulimia is included in bridal marriage vows. And *The Dieter*, by Chicago-based novelist Susan Sussman, is another affecting look at the complicated psychological factors involved in carrying what society considers to be too much weight.

• In music, a new generation of female composers, led by country stars such as Shania Twain, Mary Chapin Carpenter, and Pam Tillis, is boldly demanding a better deal for women in dozens of new songs epitomized by a current Michelle Wright hit, "New Kind of Love." Its central message, repeated many times throughout the song: That the world, and any man who wishes to befriend her, must accept her "just as I am."

• In a class by herself, and certainly the only person who can and does circulate subversive anti-brainwash messages on a daily basis, in hundreds of newspapers, is cartoonist Cathy Guisewite. It's a rare day when *Cathy* doesn't raise the consciousness of millions of readers with humorous jabs at a culture that's besotted with ludicrously unrealistic portrayals of skinny women.

Plus ça change . . .

But these heartening harbingers add up to little more than a glimmer of hope. Overall, it's still mostly business as usual, with the vast majority of people behaving as if an attitudinal about-face in this context is impossible. Even those who publicly deplore the pressure on women to be ultra-thin generally attribute it to inexplicable, intractable cultural forces. Nearly all commentators stop short of posing—let alone answering—the obvious question this book addresses: Why did losing weight become an international obsession?

Most vocal and deliberate among these obfuscators, of course, are those who stand to lose big time if millions of women snap out of the profitable trance, start living on their own terms, dreaming dreams of their own devising, and fulfilling them any way they see fit. But, both inside and outside the profiteering cartel, there's plenty of blame to spread around for perpetuating the No Fat Chicks era.

There are the celebrities, most notably Weight Watchers' Lynn Redgrave and Kathleen Sullivan, and Slim-Fast's Ann Jillian and Tommy Lasorda, who assure us, *ad nauseam*, that permanent weight loss is a sure thing, and that it's only a phone call and a few dollars away. This has the effect of making millions of us feel like failures when we cannot duplicate the feats of the celebrities, who have the advantage of professional help, plus lavish encouragement and monetary rewards.

Even worse are those who become stars by losing weight and then turn into virulent anti-obesity bigots. Rosemary Green, best-selling author of *Diary of a Fat Housewife*, calls herself "the last honest fat person in America" and regularly blabs on TV talk shows about the ugliness of obesity. Green actually wrote a letter to "Dear Abby," taking her to task for defending Fat Chicks ("Of course people are discriminated against because of their size! Do you want our next Miss America to weigh 237 pounds?"). And she littered her book with self-degrading, prejudice-reinforcing remarks such as: "Did I oink out? Do dogs have fleas? Does chocolate have calories? Yes, yes, yes, and yes! Disgusting, horrible, despicable."

In a category all her own is long-time *Cosmopolitan* editor Helen Gurley Brown. She was a hero in the early 1960s for almost single-handedly making women understand that the time we spent after growing up and before getting married needn't be an anxious, unrewarding race to get a ring on our fingers before too many people scornfully called us spin-sters. But in recent years, Brown, whose influence on the millions of women throughout the world who read *Cosmo* is vast, has become one of the worst "sizeist" bigots on the planet. Even in her autobiography, *The Late Show*, she makes such cracks as: "Anybody who sits around rationalizing that she can eat what she wants to . . . I'm afraid I think is an asshole . . ." and "I feel superior to fat people, drinkers, drug users and real dummies. . . ."

Then there are government and legislative leaders, especially those whose mandate is protecting human and civil rights, who turn a blind eye to discrimination against the obese. As Dr. Moe Lerner, Canada's best-known size-acceptance advocate, expresses this: "If you call a woman 'babe' or an African-American 'boy,' you're in trouble with the law. But it's still socially and legally acceptable to call someone a 'big fat dope.' That's just [considered] fun."

There are the airlines, which often refuse to accommodate very large people, or automatically charge them for two seats, and humiliate them in front of other passengers. Air Canada, for example, mistreated Lerner in this manner. To make amends, he says the airline invited him to con-duct sensitization seminars for their personnel. But then, without expla-nation, Air Canada ceased communicating with Lerner before he could do so. In the United States, a Los Angeles woman, Pam Hollowich, recently sued Southwest Airlines because of a "terribly traumatic, degrading" incident she says involved a ticket agent pulling her out of line at the boarding gate and loudly demanding that she buy a second ticket on the spot.

There are the cinemas and other theatres which no longer routinely sprinkle in a few of the double-wide "sweetheart" seats that were com-monplace thirty or forty years ago, yet refuse to allow large people to bring in their own chairs for use in the areas reserved for wheelchairs.

And there are the myriad publications that feature tobacco ads luring women and girls* into a potentially fatal trap by suggesting that smoking will keep them thin. Examples include ubiquitous full-page,

*Teenage girls are currently the fastest-growing cohort among smokers, and represent the majority of the estimated 1,000 American teenagers who start smoking every day of the year.

full-colour cigarette ads for Misty Lights, which repeat the operative term three times: "slim 'n sassy," "slim price, too," and "Slims" on the side of the pack. Similar tobacco advertisements (e.g., Capri's "the slimmest slim in town") are the life's blood of nearly all mass-circulation American magazines, and litter the landscape on blaring billboards.

In Canada, this atrocious situation was done away with several years ago, when the federal government wisely banned tobacco advertising in all mass media. But, as of this writing, the Supreme Court of Canada had just handed down a shocking decision outlawing the ban as an infringement on free speech. Needless to say, the impetus for the legal challenge came from the tobacco industry, which spends in excess of $6 billion per year to advertise products that are currently producing a devastating annual mortality rate that's estimated at 400,000 in the United States alone.

Also in my "most despicable" category are the producers of TV shows aimed at children, which get rich from saturation advertising of food products that guarantee kids will develop weight problems—thus manufacturing future customers for the "billion-dollar brainwash." A recent report from the U.S. National Center for Health Statistics showed that obesity has more than doubled in the six-to-seventeen age group since the 1960s.

And another troubling aspect of entertainment aimed at children is the hyper-sexy images of the female characters in animated movies such as Disney's *Beauty and the Beast*, *Aladdin*, and *Pocahontas*, and cartoons like *The Power Rangers*. Anyone who claims to be mystified as to where little girls get the idea they have to be thin (and have large breasts), and how little boys develop their notion of female attractiveness, needs look no farther than these examples.

Then there are the educators who allow fat youngsters to be attacked and excluded throughout their childhood. And, later on in their academic lives, according to several studies, fat teenage girls are at least 33 per cent less likely to be selected for top colleges than slimmer students with identical academic qualifications.

And last, but by no means least, in terms of cruelty to everyone who is noticeably fat, there is the general public, in far too substantial numbers. The legacy of anti-fat and anti-diversity attitudes they bestow on their children results in overweight youngsters being the first to be taunted and the last to be chosen for sports and other activities. It continues with "just happening" to forget to invite overweight teenagers to parties. It rolls onward every time someone tells an anti-obesity joke, or laughs at one. And it ends up preventing Fat Chicks from being seen for who we really are, punishing us for things we aren't, depriving us of many of our legal and human rights, and generally making our lives a living hell.

Bottom Line

Although *No Fat Chicks* was a horrifying story to write, living through the era inside a Lillian Russell–sized body was much worse. But when my research and analysis made me realize that the thinness edict was never really about weight at all, but simply about money, I made the joyful discovery that to see through the scam is to be liberated from its clutches.

The war with my body is finally over. I won.

And so can others, despite the overwhelming odds I'm attempting to expose. My fiercest wish is that this book will inspire women and girls, whatever their size, to repeat for themselves what simple knowledge empowered me to do: Awaken from the obsession, open the door of a psychological prison, and step out free forever. If they do so in massive numbers, the "billion-dollar brainwash" will—to use an apt colloquialism—go belly-up.

What can you do to guarantee that this happens? Plenty.

Start by really listening when little girls express their admiration for the grotesque body standard epitomized by the Barbie doll. Listen to older girls bemoaning their imaginary fatness. Listen to your own female friends complaining about those proverbially unbudgeable 10 pounds. Listen to yourself whenever a glance in the mirror elicits an automatic reproach. Then realize that we've all been obediently mouthing lines from a script written by robbers.

The next time you flip through a women's magazine, really see the towering, dead-eyed, flat-hipped, exclusively young women with the disproportionately large breasts plopped on their chests like bizarre merit badges. Check out the pathetically bony shoulders, stringy arms, and emaciated legs of supermodels such as Claudia Schiffer as they lope along the fashion runways. When you see an awards show on television, count the number of hollow cheeks, protruding clavicles, and jutting hip bones among the actresses who totter on stage. Then realize that these are all literally female impersonators, and that you have been duped into trying to join their ranks.

Whenever you're stuck in a check-out line, really look at the double-dealing magazine covers that hook us with headlines lecturing us about losing weight and photos of delectable food that lead us into temptation—and then back to dieting.

Realize that, like the slaves of yore, you have been sold to marketers by magazines and other popular media vehicles—and that you are paying for your complicity.

Watch for the next big "scientific" study bemoaning our "epidemic of obesity." And then figure out which giant conglomerate sponsored it just to soften up consumers for its next diet-product launch.

Connect the dots whenever you hear so-called experts, who are actually mouthpieces for these companies, loudly attacking every promising discovery of genetic causes, or possible cures, for obesity.

Ask yourself—or, better yet, the media who repeat these dubious stories—why we don't see equivalent headlines about the devastating fall-out from obsessive weight-loss efforts, including eating disorders that are now 150 times more prevalent than AIDS.

Recognize that the attitude that attacks large women is actually the precise kind of social discrimination that has finally become unacceptable in every other context.

Understand that, while many aspects of obesity are complicated, one thing is perfectly clear: Civil and human rights should not depend on size.

Think about how wonderful it would feel to know that you've dieted for the last time.

Do the simple math that'll convince you womanly sized women are not deviants; we are actually the norm. We are, in fact, the majority among the majority gender on this planet.

Now, get angry. Angry enough to snap your puppet strings by
• realizing that our society's obsession with extremely thin women, and our knee-jerk fear of fat, are as artificial as they are nonsensical, and did not "just happen";

• saying NO! to the ventriloquists' voices inside and outside your head that tell you the only way to be attractive, or even socially acceptable, is literally to belittle yourself;

• figuring out for yourself what your natural body weight seems to be, and what the most reasonable methods are for maintaining it;

• educating as many doctors as possible about the reality that "fat" and "fit" are not always mutually exclusive terms;

• refusing to accept appearance-based substandard treatment from anyone whose services you engage, be they physicians, hair stylists, haberdashers, or whatever;

• taking a similarly self-respecting stance with anyone who employs you;

• telling anyone who'll listen—and especially the audiences for phone-in talk shows—how the anti-fat profiteers manipulate us to accept the premise that it's normal for women to go hungry;

• lobbying legislators and public health officials for the introduction of appropriate regulatory measures that will—to borrow Susan Powter's vivid phrase—"stop the insanity";

• contacting magazine editors to demand a halt to the onslaught of "before and after" make-over articles that perpetuate the belief that women must always be "fixed";

• writing letters to editors of newspapers, and telephoning producers of television and radio shows, asking them to explain how items such as speculations about former prime minister Kim Campbell's weight, or Princess Diana's supposedly wearing long coats to conceal flabby thighs, can possibly be treated as genuine news;

• conversely, bombarding the media with positive reinforcement when they do get it right in reports such as a recent attention-grabber in the *Wall Street Journal* (reprinted in the *Toronto Star*), to the effect that women are indeed "dying to be thin" by smoking;

• stopping the entrenched habit of teaching young children that fat is a taboo by shushing their innocent observations about large people;

• developing a repertoire of snappy retorts for whenever someone criticizes your weight, or that of another woman. ("Why do you care? Are you planning to bounce us on your knee? Take us up in a hot-air balloon? Fed-X us to Finland?");

• refusing to participate in the never-ending attitudinal beauty pageant that pits woman against woman in a classic divide-and-conquer strategy, while simultaneously stalling our progress towards true social and economic equality;

• understanding that, for the sake of profit, our energy has been diverted, our dreams have been dislodged, and our quests for fulfilling lives have been diminished to a single, senseless pursuit;

• reviving the kind of consciousness-raising sessions feminists once used to, first, work through their own psychological conflicts and, then, to plot unified action to redress wrongs;

• above all, comprehending that, to quote Naomi Wolf's admonition in *The Beauty Myth*, "we do not need to change our bodies, we need to change the rules."

If you need *more* provocation to become sufficiently outraged to do these things, consider the sheer enormity of the situation. During the shockingly brief span of three decades, the anti-fat juggernaut has transformed its own self-serving agenda into a virtual religion that's sweeping the world. Its many moguls are counting on women to continue behaving as vain, gullible, fearful fools. This strategy has always paid off in the past and the high-rollers are now gambling more than $100 million a year, in advertising costs alone, that it will also do so in the future. In fact, the monolithic H.J. Heinz Company, which owns Weight Watchers, has already prepared for a turn-of-the-century splurge by reserving ad space on the gatefold covers of several major magazines scheduled for January 2000.

That fat-fighting will be an even bigger bonanza in the next millennium is such a strong corporate conviction that major conglomerates are globalizing at a furious pace. Nutri-System catapulted from the ashes of its 1993 bankruptcy by joining with some twenty-six other enterprises—including the mighty Johnson & Johnson health-care firm and a subsidiary of Japan's giant Fuji Bank—to develop an ambitious range of "wellness-oriented" products and services.

Weight Watchers is multiplying its international market lead in many countries, including France, where—against all odds—it's persuading thousands of formerly sensible *femmes* to swap their succulent cuisine for freeze-dried banalities. Elsewhere, WW is teaming up with a raft of insurers to inundate its millions of members with rebate offers on life insurance premiums. And its parent, Heinz, has bought up so many competitors that it recently leapt to command the number-three spot in the $3.3 billion American frozen-entrée industry.

Now, Heinz's double-dealing formula for capturing consumers coming and going, which was recently epitomized by yet another mega-deal—with Eskimo Pie ice cream—is attracting enthusiastic imitators. Among them is mammoth International Pizza, which encompasses Domino's franchises as far away as Poland. Its new venture: a coast-to-coast chain of weight-loss centres.

Making all of this even more threatening is the recent escalation of media mergers. There was precious little safety in numbers in the past. But, as more and more magazines, newspapers, broadcasters, and film-makers are swallowed up by fewer and fewer entities, the multiple voices we used to hear are being sucked into a mere handful of corporate megaphones. The incestuous result is bound to be, not just the perpetuation of diet-til-you-drop propaganda, but increased amplification of all the Big Lies that victimize women.

Case in point: At the urging of his wife—who was outraged by the anorexia-related death of a schoolmate—the British branch manager of the Omega watch company recently cancelled an ad campaign in *Vogue* and declared a future boycott of the magazine. His motivation for doing so, said Giles Rees, was the "extremely distasteful and irresponsible" use of ultra-thin models. He had also been shocked by estimates that eating disorders now affect more than 580,000 British women; and by news that two of London's major modelling agencies had tried to recruit an anorexic fifteen-year-old patient at an eating disorder clinic. Yet, even though his boycott was widely applauded, international behind-the-scenes negotiations to restore *Vogue*'s $50,000-plus ad campaign resulted in Rees overruled by higher-ups at Omega's Swiss headquarters.

Obviously, the pigheaded anti-fat profiteers are now confident that women will *never* awaken from the hypnosis they induced so they could pick our pockets. If their estimation of our idiocy is accurate, then our dream of achieving "ideal" bodies will continue to be the nightmare it became when the definition of attractiveness was set so thin it became a virtual impossibility.

Unless we wake up from this "billion-dollar brainwash" and begin thinking for ourselves, we will go on spending ourselves blind on false promises—and waging unwinnable wars within our own souls that undermine us psychologically, endanger us physically, and, ultimately, impoverish our entire society.

Acknowledgements

My abiding gratitude to my mother, Betty Postill, and my late grand-mother, Margaret Anhorn, for functioning as dedicated "language cops" throughout my childhood;

to my sisters, Bonnie Cox, Lynn Postill, and Louise Poirier; my friends, Gay Claitman and Kent Bowman; my uncle, Ray Anhorn; and my parents, Betty and Bill Postill, for vital practical support;

to my friend, Beth Kaplan, and my editors at Key Porter, for crucial creative support;

to Rona Maynard, for helping to shape an early version of my intro-duction, and for publishing it in *Chatelaine*;

to library personnel in Louisville and Toronto, for shepherding me through cyber labyrinths, as well as dusty historical avenues;

to many gallant women, for confiding painful memories, in person and via e- and snail-mail; and to numerous authorities, for providing insiders-only information;

to my agent, Helen Heller, for tracking me down and handing me an opportunity that rescued me from delusion and despair;

and to Betty Friedan, Gloria Steinem, Susan Faludi, Naomi Wolf, Susie Orbach, and many other feminist writers for guiding and inspiring me—long before, and while, I wrote *No Fat Chicks*.

Source Notes

INTRODUCTION: *Discovering a Billion-Dollar Brainwash*

9   Oprah wailed to her diary ... : Marjorie Rosen and Luchina Fisher, "Oprah Overcomes," *People*, January 10, 1994, p. 45

9   Ninety-eight per cent of dieters regain all the weight they lost: Renowned University of Pennsylvania study by Dr. Thomas Wadden, plus many other sources

10   "No one can make you feel inferior without your consent": Eleanor Roosevelt, *This Is My Story* (New York: Harper, 1937)

10   One-third of all North American women now 20 per cent overweight ... : National Center for Health Statistics, "Fatter and Fatter" (editorial), *New York Times*, May 21, 1994, p. A14; 78 per cent believe they're too heavy ... : Deborah Pike, "Mental Makeover," *Vogue*, May 1995, p. 291

13   Assigned a story on a women whose lifelong obsession ... : Terry Poulton, "A Death by Denial," *Toronto Life*, February 1982, p. 27

13   "begging in beauty's disguise" ... : Leonard Cohen, "The Singer Must Die"

13   Poulton's columns appeared in *Starweek* from 1983 to 1987

14   Profits of weight-loss industry estimated at $3 billion in Canada ... : Sharon Driedger and John DeMont, "Body Obsession," *Maclean's*, May 2, 1994, p. 44; $40 billion in the United States ... : "Is Fat Your Fate?" (editorial), *New York Times*, March 10, 1995, p. A28

14   Definition of "brainwashing": *The Random House Dictionary*, 1980 ed., p. 108

15   Poulton's classified ad published in *USA Today*: March 4, 1994, p. 5D

15   Lillian Russell weighed 200 pounds ... : Irving, Amy, and Sylvia Wallace and David Wallechinsky, *The Intimate Sex Lives of Famous People* (New York: Delacorte, 1981), p. 36

17   Average weight of models, actresses and beauty pageant contestants plunged ... : Roberta Pollack Seid, *Never Too Thin: Why Women Are at War with Their Bodies* (Englewood Cliffs, NJ: Prentice Hall, 1989), p. 261

17   Nearly 30,000 women stated ... : "Feeling Fat in a Thin Society" survey by Drs. Susan and Wayne Wooley, University of Cincinnati College of Medicine, *Glamour*, February 1984

17   Would rather be blind, deaf, or have a leg amputated ... : Natalie Angier and Gina Kolata, "Fat in America" series, *New York Times*, November 22–4, 1992, p. 1

17   More than 50,000 weight-loss surgeries performed annually ... : William Bennett, MD, and Joel Gurin, *The Dieter's Dilemma: Eating Less and Weighing More* (New York: Basic, 1982), p. 169

17   150 times more women in North America suffering from eating disorders as from AIDS/HIV ... : Literature of National Association of Anorexia Nervosa and Associated Disorders (U.S.), National Eating Disorder Information Centre (Canada), Centers for Disease Control (U.S.) Surveillance Report, as of December 31, 1995

21   Most Boomers are thickening as they age ... : Shelly Reese, "Boomers Have Affluence with an Attitude," *Cincinnati Enquirer*, May 22, 1994, p. A7

21   The almightiest dollars of all ... : Tracy Young, "Beauty and the Beat," *Allure*, February 1995, p. 109, and numerous other sources

20   Putting fat back in premium ice cream, etc ... : Jerry Adler, "The Joys of Living Large,"
      Newsweek, May 17, 1993, p. 55; also "'Eat, Drink and Be Merry' May Be the Next Trend,"
      New York Times, quoted in "Running on Empty?," *Hartford Courant*, January 25, 1994

CHAPTER 1: *Juliette*

24   The Juliette Christie story ... : Poulton, "A Death by Denial"

35   "Hush money" from plaintiffs keeps mortality rates secret ... : Frances M. Berg, "Sudden
      Death Syndrome Continues to Chill Treatment Centers," *Healthy Weight Journal*, May/June
      1994, p. 51

35   Most likely causes of death ... : Ibid.; also "Low-Calorie Diets Carry Some Risks, Physicians
      Warn," *Chicago Tribune*, January 5, 1990, and author interviews with various authorities

35   "One of the fundamental tenets of the weight-loss industry ... and be better off": Steven
      N. Blair, "Harvard Alums Risk Disease by 'Always' Dieting," *Healthy Weight Journal*,
      May/June 1994, p. 52

36   Liquid-protein diets have been blamed for at least fifty-eight deaths ... : U.S. Centers for
      Disease Control report, quoted by Bennett and Gurin, *The Dieter's Dilemma*, p. 238

36   Liposuction resulted in nine deaths in France and twenty in the United States in its early
      years ... : Susan Faludi, *Backlash: The Undeclared War Against American Women* (New York:
      Crown, 1991), p. 221

36   Epidemic of eating disorders compared with AIDS/HIV ... : Literature of National
      Association of Anorexia Nervosa and Associated Disorders (U.S.), National Eating
      Disorder Information Centre (Canada), Centers for Disease Control (U.S.) Surveillance
      Report, as of December 31, 1995

36   Death of Sheena Carpenter ... : Author interview with Sheena's Place spokesperson Jane
      Fenton

37   Jane Fonda forced herself to throw up twenty times a day ... : Marjorie Rosen, "Eating
      Disorders: A Hollywood History," *People*, February 17, 1992, p. 97

37   150 times more North American women suffer eating disorders as AIDS ... : Literature of
      National Association of Anorexia Nervosa and Associated Disorders (U.S.), National
      Eating Disorder Information Centre (Canada), Centre for Disease Control (U.S.)
      Surveillance Report, as of December 31, 1995

CHAPTER 2: *Better Dead Than Fed*

40   Twiggy's arrival in New York ... : Thomas Whiteside, *Twiggy & Justin* (New York: Farrar,
      Straus & Giroux, 1967), p. 4

40   Twiggy's weight and height ... : *Newsweek*, April 10, 1967, p. 62

41   "just like your next door neighbor if ... skinny 12-year-old boy" ... : *New York Times*,
      March 20, 1967

41   *Women's Wear Daily* denounced ... : *Newsweek*, April 10, 1967, p .63

41   Vreeland gushed ... : Whiteside, *Twiggy & Justin*, pp. 105–6

41   30 million teenage girls in North America ... : Ibid., p. 64

41   "Whether the Twiggy look will now sweep ... emaciating American teen-agers as it goes" ... :
      Newsweek, April 10, 1967, p. 62

42   "It was a nightmare trying to keep up," ... : Michael Gross, *Model: The Ugly Business of
      Beautiful Women* (New York: Morrow, 1995), p. 179

42   Wilhelmina's hummingbird diet ... : Ibid.

42   Jane Fonda admitted to a 20-year eating disorder ... : Seid, *Never Too Thin*, p. 247

42   Sally Field developed bulimia ... : Rosen, "Eating Disorders"

43   1968 Miss America pageant protest ... : Myra Marx Ferree and Beth B. Hess, *Controversy*

and Coalition: The New Feminist Movement across Three Decades of Change, rev. ed. (Oxford: Maxwell Macmillan International, 1994), p. 42

44   *Woman from Willendorf* (also called *Venus of Willendorf*) ... : *Encyclopedia Americana*, Vol. 22, p. 543

44   Venus de Milo's measurements ... : Terry Nicholetti Garrison, *Fed Up! A Woman's Guide to Freedom* (New York: Carroll & Graf, 1993), p. 21

45   Technological breakthroughs ... : J. Anderson Black and Madge Garland, *A History of Fashion* (New York: Morrow, 1980), pp. 194–5

45   Butterick Patterns invented ... : Norman King, *The Almanac of Fascinating Beginnings*, (New York: Carol Publishing Group, 1994), pp. 194–5

45   Charles Frederick Worth created salons ... :Black and Garland, *A History of Fashion*, p. 194

45   Employing live mannequins ... : Ibid, p. 191

45   Ready-to-wear clothing begin to be manufactured ... : Stuart Ewen, *All-Consuming Images: The Politics of Style in Contemporary Culture* (New York: Basic Books, 1988), p. 75

46   Secular bibles piloted by Sarah Josepha Hale ... : Gloria Steinem, "Sex, Lies & Advertising," *Moving Beyond Words*, (New York: Simon and Schuster, 1994), p. 153

46   "the American craze" ... : Seid, *Never Too Thin*, p. 61

46   "Our willowy girls are afraid of ... strikes us as a monster," ... : Harriet Beecher Stowe, quoted by Schroeder, *Fat Is Not a Four-Letter Word*, p. 49

46   Louise drank vinegar ... : Ibid.

46   Raison d'être of women's magazines ... : Steinem, *Moving Beyond Words*, p. 154

47   "Perfect feminine beauty no longer ... thinness was a necessary condition": Anne Hollander, *Seeing Through Clothes* (New York: Viking, 1975), p. 154

47   "[Women] found it necessary to remodel ... in favour of the prevailing silhouette ...": Caroline Routh, *In Style: 100 Years of Canadian Women's Fashion*, (Toronto: Stoddart, 1993), p. ix

47   Canadian women's journals ... : Ibid., p. 8

47   "For the first time ... a magazine had encourged them to want": Steinem, *Moving Beyond Words*, p. 154

47–8   Sarah Bernhardt caricatured ... : Bennett and Gurin, *The Dieter's Dilemma*, p. 199

48   "Does your form lack ... air form corset waist inflated to any desired size ... ": Schroeder, *Fat Is Not a Four-Letter Word*, p. 59

48   "The hoop-skirt ... all emblazoned in sartorial terms": Ibid., p. 53

49   "the rapidity with which the new, linear form ... [was] startling.": Hollander, *Seeing Through Clothes*, p. 154

49   "Women measure themselves ... gobbled them up,": Jeanine Basinger, *A Woman's View: How Hollywood Spoke to Women*, 1930–1960 (New York: Alfred A. Knopf, 1993), p. 212

49   "There is one crime ... than to be guilty of growing fat": *Vogue*, July 1, 1918, p. 78

49   "viewed with distrust, suspicion, and even aversion": Lulu Hunt Peters, *Diet and Health with a Key to the Calories* (Chicago: Chicago Publishing, 1918), p. i

49   "quasi-scientific diet programs ... special baths, pastes, and thinning salts ... ": Joan Jacobs Brumberg, *Fasting Girls: The Emergence of Anorexia Nervosa as a Modern Disease* (Cambridge, MA: Harvard University Press, 1988), p. 232

50   Adult Weight Conference ... : Ibid., p. 248

50   "To keep a slender figure ... Reach for a Lucky instead of a sweet": Patricia Fallon, Melanie Katzman and Susan Wooley, *Feminist Perspectives on Eating Disorders*, (London: Guilford Press, 1994), p. 413

50   A million scales sold ... : Ibid., p. 339

50   "We grew up founding our dreams on ... advertising,": Zelda Fitzgerald, quoted by Diane

Epstein and Kathleen Thompson, *Feeding on Dreams: Why America's Diet Industry Doesn't Work and What Will Work for You* (New York: Macmillan, 1994), p. 10

51   "It is very little to me ... in my absolute right": Lucy Stone, quoted by Andrea Dworkin, *Pornography: Men Possessing Women* (New York: Putnam, 1981), p. 11

51   Uneeda Biscuit ... : Earl Shorris, *A Nation of Salesmen: The Tyranny of the Market and the Subversion of Culture* (New York: W.W. Norton, 1994), p. 53

51   The canniest profiteers went right on developing ... : Paul Ernsberger and Paul Haskew, *Rethinking Obesity: An Alternative View of its Health Implications*, special monograph published in *The Journal of Obesity and Weight Regulation*, Summer 1987, p. 42

53   "mirrored the yearning ... that existed for women then": Betty Friedan, *The Feminine Mystique* (New York: W.W. Norton, 1963; Dell, 12th reprinting, 1975), p. 34

54   "crammed full of food ... the life of the mind and spirit.": Ibid., p. 31

54   Canadian magazines joined the coercive chorus ... : Routh, *In Style*, pp. 8, 51

55   "Nobody Loves a Fat Girl" ad ... : Brumberg, *Fasting Girls*, p. 252

55   "The Fattest Girl in the Class" ... : *Seventeen*, January 1948, pp. 21–2

56   Marketing had become a science ... : Shorris, *A Nation of Salesmen*, p. 191

56   Chronology of TV shows ... : Alex McNeil, *Total Television: A Comprehensive Guide to Programming from 1948 to 1980* (New York: Penguin, 1980)

56   Market research a $2.5 billion industry ... : Leslie Savan, *The Sponsored Life: Ads, TV, and American Culture* (Philadelphia: Temple University Press, 1994), p. 2

56   "Behavior essential for economic reasons ... transformed into a social virtue.": John Kenneth Galbraith, quoted by Michael H. Minton with Jean Libman Block, *What Is a Wife Worth?* (New York: McGraw-Hill, 1984), pp. 134–5

56   "Before television ... one of the forces that determined the world": Shorris, *A Nation of Salesmen*, pp. 89–91

57   "as in all wars ... determined to be thinner" ... : *Newsweek*, March 22, 1969, p. 140

57   "[B]y promising to to melt and float ... determined to be thinner": "Trapping the Obese," *Newsweek*, August 19, 1957, p. 60

57   "They Take Your Money, You Keep Your Weight," *Reader's Digest*, December 1959, p. 28

57   So many weight loss products belonged in snake-oil category ... : "Trapping the Obese"

58   Part of the first generation of females ... : Friedan, *The Feminine Mystique*, p. 47

58   "the feminine mystique began to spread ... stranglehold on the future": Ibid., p. 37

58   "You just can't write about ... like the price of coffee": Ibid., p. 31

59   "Reduce the Way the Models Do": *McCall's*, July 1960, pp. 80, 118

59   Sucaryl ad ... : Ibid., p. 146

60   Five publications had perished ... : Friedan, *The Feminine Mystique*, p. 58

60   *Ladies' Home Journal* taught a lesson ... : Steinem, Moving Beyond Words, p. 154

60   *McCall's* ads and complementary copy ... : Ibid., p. 157

60   "pulse to the ... patterns tend to fade away ... ": Savan, *The Sponsored Life*, p. 5

61   Weight Watchers had enrolled nearly 500,000 ... : "Changing Lost Pounds into Dollars," *Business Week*, March 4, 1967, p. 110

61   Weight Watchers techniques ... : quoted in ibid., March 4, 1967, p. 111

61   "creampuffs, there's no escape ... stay that way": "The Tuned-Up Body," *Mademoiselle*, May 1970, pp. 174–75

61    $500,000 spent on "Sweeta Stakes" ... : *Ladies' Home Journal*, July 1968, p. 11

61   "Inside I was Crying Until I Lost 150 Pounds": Ibid., September 1968, p. 64

61   Fleishmann's margarine ad ... : Ibid., p. 46

61   "How I Lost 80 Pounds by a Governor's Wife": Ibid., October 1969, cover

61    $200 million "waistline industry" ... : *Business Week*, March 22, 1969, p. 140

62   High school girls considered themselves too fat: Seid, *Never Too Thin*, p. 150

62   "Aren't you jealous ... tells me her secrets.": Fallon, Katzman, and Wooley, *Feminist Perspectives on Eating Disorders*, p. 408

62   Chubby dolls were ugly ... : Yale University study, quoted in NAAFA (National Association for the Advancement of Fat Acceptance) literature

62   Teen suicides quadrupled in past three decades ... : Mary Nemeth, "An Alarming Trend," *Maclean's*, October 31, 1994, p. 15

62   "I can't take it anymore ... ": "Student Kills Himself in Class in Cherokee," *Atlanta Constitution*, March 26, 1994, p. C4

62   An estimated 70% of American families using low-cal foods ... : Lois Anzelowitz, "You Call This Progress?," *Working Woman*, October 1992, p. 95

63   Physicians were by now prescribing some 10 billion amphetamines ... : Seid, *Never Too Thin*, p. 138

63   Weight Watchers had spread to 49 states ... : "Fortune from Fat," *Time*, February 21, 1972, p. 71

63   First generation of liquid-protein resulted in three deaths ... : Anzelowitz, "You Call This Progress?"

63   Jane Fonda creating a one-woman fitness empire ... : W. Wolf, "Principles & Profits," *New York*, December 14, 1981, p. 90

63    $285 million spent on exercise videos ... : *People*, January 10,1994, p. 36

63   Diet-food business was fastest-growing segment ... : "The Food Giants See the 'Light,'" *Business Week*, June 1, 1981, p. 112

63   Nestlé, Stouffer, and H.J. Heinz "mounting intensive ad campaigns" ... : Ibid., p. 113

64   Liposuction resulted in twenty deaths yet became the most popular cosmetic surgery in history ... : Faludi, *Backlash*, p. 221

64   Liposuction leapt from zero to 250,000 operations by 1989 ... : James Patterson and Peter Kim, The Day America Told the Truth (Englewood Cliffs, NJ: Prentice Hall, 1991), p. 54

64   First news stories about anorexia ... : Bill Dampier, "Dying to Be Thin," *Maclean's*, February 23, 1976, p. 89; and "Dieting Till Death," *Science Digest*, May 1970, p. 27

64   "It's a hold-up ... disrespect they have for women.": Sey Chessler, quoted by Gloria Steinem, "Sex, Lies & Advertising," *Ms.*, July/August 1990, p. 27

64–5 Pressures routinely exerted by marketers ... : Ibid., pp. 18–28

65   "revolution in marketing ... with spending money": Michael Hoyt, "When the Walls Come Tumbling Down," *Columbia Journalism Review*, March/April 1990, pp. 35–41

65   "with newspapers facing tough times ... criticizing advertisers in print": G. Pascal Zachary, *Wall Street Journal*, quoted by Jon Swan, "The Crumbling Wall," *Columbia Journalism Review*, May/June 1992, p. 23

65   "solicited advertisers first ... feature them in [a] program": Joanne Lipman, *Wall Street Journal*, quoted Ibid.

66   McDonald's gave the producers of Santa Claus—The Movie $1 million ... : Eric Clarke, *The Want Makers* (New York: Viking, 1988), p. 366

67   "The media may not directly ... on what the public thinks about": David Croteau and William Hoynes, *By Invitation Only: How the Media Limit Political Debate* (Monroe, ME: Common Courage, 1994), p. 51

67   "favor impact over information ... spread into a worldwide pandemic": Mort Rosenblum, *Who Stole the News?* (New York: Wiley, 1993), pp. 3, 9

67   Epidemic of eating disorders affects more than 11 million women and girls ... : National Association of Anorexia Nervosa and Associated Disorders (U.S.), National Eating Disorder Information Centre (Canada) literature

67   "vomiting bathrooms" ... : Kathryn J. Zerbe, M.D., The Body Betrayed: Women, *Eating Disorders and Treatment* (Washington, D.C.: American Psychiatric Press, 1993), p. x

67   "People were dieting long before ... as did the Egyptians" ... : Tina Gaudoin, "Body of Evidence," Harper's Bazaar, July 1993, p. 74

67   "Major advertisers ... essentially 'sell' the audience to advertisers": Croteau and Hoynes, *By Invitation Only*, p. 24

67   "Hey Coke, want 17 1/2 million very interested women ... lively articles about staying in shape": *Advertising Age*, quoted by Fallon, Katzman, and Wooley, *Feminist Perspectives on Eating Disorders*, pp. 399–401

68   "the more we are bombarded ... the more we are affected": Clarke, *The Want Makers*, p. 13

68   Just three years after Twiggy's Manhattan triumph ... : "Twiggy to Retire as Fashion Model," *New York Times*, March 11, 1970, p. A7

69   Jacqueline Kennedy went on a diet ... ": Susan Brownmiller, *Femininity* (New York: Simon and Schuster, 1984), p. 48

70   "The feminist entreaty ... quest for true self-determination": Faludi, *Backlash*, p. 71

70   "Ironically, as the role of women was redefined ... the pressure to be thin": Seid, *Never Too Thin*, p. 261

72   Sharp downturn in women's apparel sales and magazine subscriptions ... : Faludi, *Backlash*, p. 93

72   "Corporations saw ... gold in them thar thighs": Susan J. Douglas, *Where the Girls Are: Growing Up Female with the Mass Media* (New York: Times Books, 1994) , p. 260

72   Weight Watchers' "taste of freedom" bread commercial ... : Fallon, Katzman, and Wooley, *Feminist Perspectives on Eating Disorders*, p. 405

73   "much as an Arab prince ... considered the male prerogative ... ": quoted in "The Most Significant Social Change of the Past 20 Years Is ... ," Gary Michael Dault, *Toronto Life*, November 1986, p. 82

73   "a wailing wall for every scatterbrain ... pope in skirts": *Vancouver Sun*, quoted Ibid.

74   1,500 images flicker before our eyes every day ... : Savan, *The Sponsored Life*, p. 2

74   Coca-Cola bottle redesigned ... : Ewen, *All-Consuming Images*, pp. 179–180

74   Columbia Lady slimmed down ... : "Weight Watcher," *The New Yorker*, August 16, 1993, p. 25

74   Saks Fifth Avenue's Grace Kelly-sized mannequins replaced ... : "Rat Patrol," *Working Woman*, April 1995, p. 9

75   Weight of actresses, etc. plunged ... : Seid, *Never Too Thin*, p. 261

75   Average weight and height of North American women ... : Faludi, Backlash, p. 171

75   Kate Moss's weight and height ... : Gaudoin, "Little Miss Moss," *Harper's Bazaar*, December 1992, p. 34

75   Height of supermodels ... : Charlotte Raven, "Super Models Icons for Young Women," *The Guardian*, December 15, 1994, p. F4

75   "We now have cultural norms ... our biological heritage" ... : C. Wayne Callaway, MD, quoted by Lori Miller Kase, "Weight Game," *Harper's Bazaar*, April 1993, p. 291

75   "feminine esthetic at odds ... in its natural state" ... : Susan Brownmiller, *Femininity*, p. 48

76   Women now aspire "not to look like the great beauties ... and computer technique": Vicki Goldberg, "Advertisements for the Insecure, Unreal Self," *New York Times*, April 11, 1993

CHAPTER 3: *Misery Loves Companies*

78   "When you control a man's thinking ... and stay in it": Carter G. Woodson, quoted in the [Louisville, KY] *Courier-Journal*, June 24, 1995, p. A9

78   Majority of 33,000 female respondents declared ... : "Feeling Fat in a Thin Society" survey by Drs. Susan and Wayne Wooley, University of Cincinnati College of Medicine, *Glamour*, February 1984

78   Eleven per cent of respondents would opt to abort: Geoffrey Cowley, "Made to Order Babies," *Newsweek*, Winter/Spring 1990, p. 981

78   14 years after Twiggy's debut, weight-loss industry profits were $10 billion ... : G. Ferry, "Food and Behavior," *World Press Review*, December 1983, p. 30

78   Profits of North American weight-loss industry quadrupled to more than $40 billion ... : "Is Fat Your Fate?"

79   Most North Americans have gained weight in the past three decades ... : Patricia Chisholm, "The War on Fat," *Maclean's*, January 16, 1995, p. 46

79   "incredible Squee-Zer-Ciser ... like rubber bands" ... : Dave Barry column, syndicated in the *Toronto Star*, March 24, 1996, p. D16

79   Gadgets and gizmos ... : Donald Dale Jackson, "The Art of Wishful Shrinking Has Made a Lot of People Rich," *Smithsonian*, January 1986, pp. 150–6

80   Four million people tried liquid protein ... : reported in *Newsweek*, according to Bennett and Gurin, *The Dieter's Dilemma*, p. 238

80   U.S. Centers for Disease Control investigated fifty-eight deaths ... : Ibid.

80   "the full pink tint of a Beaujolais ... only you can fail": Robert Linn, MD, *The Last Chance Diet*, (New York: Lyle Stuart, 1976).

80   Dr. Herman Taller convicted of mail fraud ... : Bennett and Gurin, The Dieter's *Dilemma*, p. 234

81   Dr. Robert Atkins called to appear before a congressional committee ... : Ibid.

81   "The more time you spend ... the idea": Judy Mazel, *The Beverly Hills Diet* (New York: Macmillan, 1980)

81   "Any so-called hunger 'pangs' ... rather than true hunge.": Allan Cott, MD, *Fasting as a Way of Life* (New York: Bantam, 1977)

81    $321 million spent at fitness centres in Canada in 1992 ... : Driedger and DeMont, "Body Obsession"

82   Annual attrition rates of 35 to 40 percent ... : Judith Newman, "Why We Don't Exercise," *Allure*, August 1995, p. 124

82–3 Techniques of TOPS and other weight-loss clubs in early years ... : "Changing Lost Pounds into Dollars," *Business Week*, March 4, 1967, pp. 110-11; and Donald Dale Jackson, "The Art of Wishful Shrinking ... ," *Smithsonian*, January 1986, pp. 150–6

82   "So what did you give yourself ... pot of fat?": Jackson, "The Art of Wishful Shrinking"

83   The pig song ... : Hillel Schwartz, *Never Satisfied: A Cultural History of Diets, Fantasies and Fat* (New York: The Free Press, 1986), p. 207

83   Japanese-manufactured seaweed soap to lather fat away ... : *Wall Street Journal*, November 2, 1995, p. B1

83   Thigh creams to make unsightly cellulite vanish ... : Tufts University *Diet & Nutrition Letter*, February 1994, p. 3, and numerous other sources

84   "no work, no muss, no fuss ... smile on your face": Epstein and Thompson, *Feeding on Dreams*, p. 9

84    $50 million spent on January marketing spree alone ... : Kathy Tyrer, "The Big Weight Watch Is On," *Marketing*, January 31, 1994, p. 6

84   Counsellors fired if quote prices on telephone ... : Ibid, p. 10

84   Costs and practices at commercial diet centres ... : Ibid., pp. 14–21

85–6 TV reporter took hidden camera to Jenny Craig ... : Author interview with Karen McCairley

86   Weight Watchers sells more than 250 food products ... : *Frozen Food Digest*, October 1995, p. 20

86   Weight Watchers' fees and practices ... : Epstein and Thompson, *Feeding on Dreams*, pp. 13–19

86   Weights-and-measures inspectors raided English reducing centres ... : Jane Gordon, "You're Only as Fat as You Feel," *The Times*, April 5, 1996, p. 17

87     $77.6 million spent to launch Ultra Slim-Fast ... : "Nestle Targets Dieters with New Chocolate Fix," *Advertising Age*, August 24, 1992, p. 6

87   Weight Watchers spent $40 million on ads ... : Tyrer, "The Big Weight Watch Is On"

87   Jenny Craig spent $50 million on ads ... : Ibid.

87–8   Biological basis for "Cro-Magnon Catch-22" ... : Bennett and Gurin, *The Dieter's Dilemma*, and numerous other sources

88   Fewer calories than if we hadn't dieted ... : study by Dr. Rudolph Liebel, Rockefeller University, reported in *The New England Journal of Medicine*, March 9, 1995

88–9   Conscientious objectors' experiment ... : Bennett and Gurin, *The Dieter's Dilemma*, pp. 11–16

89   "At Treblinka, 900 calories were ... sustain human functioning": Wolf, *The Beauty Myth*, p. 195

90   Discovery of "ob" gene ... : Natalie Angier, "Researchers Link Obesity in Humans to Flaw in a Gene," *The New York Times*, December 1, 1994, p. A1

90   Fitness can result from thirty minutes of exercise per day ... : Panel of physiologists from the Centers for Disease Control and the American College of Sports Medicine; Stephen Brewer and Janis Jibrin, "Pound Foolery," *Modern Maturity*, May 1995; and numerous other sources

CHAPTER 4: *Prescription for Profit*

92   Authorities declared that obesity is not merely a moral failing ... : Jane R. Hirschmann and Carol H. Munter, *When Women Stop Hating Their Bodies: Freeing Yourself from Food and Weight Obsession* (New York: Fawcett Columbine, 1995), p. 97

92–3   "Fat people are waddling reminders ... blame the victim.": Schwartz, Never Satisfied, p. 207

93   Health care costs are estimated at a whopping $70 billion ... : Jennifer Warren, "Living Large," *Los Angeles Times*, December 27, 1994, p. E1

93   "fat people are blamed ... victims than its perpetrators.": Marcia Millman, *Such a Pretty Face: Being Fat in America* (New York: W.W. Norton, 1980)

93   Shape Up America is largely funded by Weight Watchers ... : William J. Fabrey, "Big News" column, *Radiance*, Summer 1995, p. 46

94     $250,000 Heinz Award given to C. Everett Koop ... : [Louisville, KY] *Courier-Journal* December 1, 1995, p. 2

94   *Rump Parliament* published a cartoon of Koop as a hand puppet of the weight-loss industry ... : Fabrey, "Big News"

94   Weight Watchers' membership is dropping ... : Janice Turner, "Are We Losing the War against Losing Weight?," *Toronto Star*, June 19, 1995, p. A1; and Ellen Neuborne, "Slimmer Revenue Has Weight-Loss Industry Going on a Crash Diet," Gannett News Service, July 31, 1994

94   "Fat" and "fit" are not mutually exclusive terms ... : Susan Carlton, "The Weight Debate," *Mirabella*, April 1994, p. 96, and many other sources

95   Female patients talked down to, etc ... .: Laurence and Weinhouse, *Outrageous Practices*, p. 3

95   Doctors refuse to treat until weight is lost ... : Angier and Kolata, "Fat in America"

96   Raped woman traumatized, etc ... .: William J. Fabrey, "The Discriminating Doctor," *Radiance*, Fall 1988, p. 53

96   "Lose 50 Pounds and Call Me in the Morning" syndrome ... : Ibid.

96   One-third of family practice doctors admit to feelings of discomfort ... : Ibid.

96   Doctors' negative attitudes toward fat patients ... : D. Klein, J. Najman, A.F. Kohrman, and C. Munro, *Journal of Family Practitioners* 14 (1982), pp. 881–8.

96   "Unlike most sick people ... why should I?'": William Bennett, MD, quoted in NAAFA literature

97   Restricting dietary carbohydrates so severely ... : Dr. Bryant Stamford, "The Body Shop,"
      [Louisville, KY] *Courier-Journal*, March 15, 1994, p. C3

97   Elevated blood pressure, high cholesterol, etc. caused, not by obesity ... : Janet Polivy and
      C. Peter Herman, *Breaking the Diet Habit: The Natural Weight Alternative* (New York: Basic
      Books, 1983)

98   Relatively benign effect of excess weight on "pear-shaped" women ... : Jean-Pierre Despres,
      MD, *Homemaker's*, March 1995, p. 131

98   Fat women eat less than thin women ... : *American Journal of Clinical Nutrition*, 1988,
      quoted by Ellen Hodgson Brown, *With the Grain* (New York: Carroll & Graf, 1990), p. 22

98   Study of identical twins at Quebec's Laval University ... : Mary Louise Bringle, *The God of
      Thinness* (Nashville: Abingdon Press, 1992), p. 122

98-9 Some degree of fatness is beneficial ... : Ernsberger, *Rethinking Obesity*

99   Complications and failure rates of weight-loss surgery ... : Ibid.

100   Intestinal bypasses leapt from 30,000 to 50,000 in 2 years ... : Wolf, *The Beauty Myth*, p. 261

100   Even women whose weight was as low as 154 pounds ... : Ibid.

100   Liposuction's popularity drooped after complications and deaths: Pike, "Mental Makeover"

100   Liposculpturing fees ... : Driedger and DeMont, "Body Obsession"

100   "27% OFF Large Volume Liposuction and Breast Enlargement" ... : [Louisville, KY]
      Courier-Journal, May 28, 1995, p. A13

101   Photographically bloated "before" picture of Michelangelo's David ... : Jewish Hospital
      Health Care Services Newsletter, Summer 1995, p. 16

101   Amphetamines prescribed by the billions ... : Seid, *Never Too Thin*, p. 138

101   Fenfluramine may have caused brain damage in monkeys ... : Jane E. Brody, "Diet Drug
      May Harm the Brain," *The New York Times*, May 11, 1994, p. C11

101   Dexaflenfluramine caused deaths and incurable lung disease in France ... : Sylvia Chase,
      Prime Time Live, ABC TV, May 8, 1996

101   Annual revenue of $8 billion is projected for Redux ... : Susan Powter, *Nightline*, ABC TV,
      May 7, 1996

101   Protein-sparing fasts cost $54.75 per pound ... : Rita Rubin, "The Cost of Weight Loss,"
      American Health, June 1994, p. 91

102   American physicians have conflicts of interest ... : Sally E. Smith, "The Great Diet
      Deception," *USA Today*, January 1995, pp. 76–8

102   North American Association for the Study of Obesity conference sponsored by ... : Ibid.

103   Nutritional studies financed by Wonder Bread and M&M/Mars ... : Cynthia Crossen,
      Tainted Truth: The Manipulation of Fact in America (New York: Simon and Schuster, 1994),
      p. 42

104   "a fundamental change in public thinking ... a problem of willful misconduct": Institute of
      Medicine report quoted by Marlene Cimons, "Public Is Urged to Treat Obesity as Chronic
      Disease," *Los Angeles Times*, December 6, 1994, p. A14

104   "there is no commitment to obesity as a public health problem ... on gluttony and sloth.":
      William Dietz, MD, "America the Bountiful," *New York Times*, July 19, 1994, p. A18

104   "There is an increasing number of ... confines of established medicine": Theodore Isaac
      Rubin, MD, *Alive and Fat and Thinning in America*, (New York: Coward, McCann and
      Geoghegan, 1978), pp. 27–9

CHAPTER 5: *Mind Warped*

105   Eleven per cent of respondents would opt to abort: Geoffrey Cowley, "Made to Order
      Babies," *Newsweek*, Winter/Spring 1990, p. 98

108   "The thought of anyone parading naked ... ": Suanne Kelman, "Fat in a Thin Society,"
      Chatelaine, September 1993, p. 57

108 "How dare they impose that body on the rest of us?" ... : Dr. Irvin Yalom, *Love's Executioner and Other Tales of Psychotherapy* (New York: Basic Books, 1989), pp. 87–8

109 "bombarded with non-stop images" ... : Douglas, *Where the Girls Are*, p. 11

109 "We turn our bodies into metaphors" ... : Hirschmann and Munter, *When Women Stop Hating Their Bodies*, p. 91

110 Average weight women believe they are too fat ... : Thomas Cash, *What Do You See When You Look in the Mirror?: Helping Yourself to a Positive Body Image* (New York: Bantam, 1995), quoted by Deborah Pike, "Mental Makeover," *Vogue*, May 1995, p. 291

111 Women suffer major depression at twice the rate of men ... : Laurence and Weinhouse, *Outrageous Practices*, pp. 264, 275–6

111 Women are prescribed 83 per cent of antidepressants, etc. ... : Ibid.

111 Chronic emotional distress doubles health risks ... : Daniel Goleman, *Emotional Intelligence* (New York: Bantam, 1995)

111–12 "want to go away and hide" ... : Judith Jordan, Ph.D., quoted by Natalie Tannen, "Heavy Soul," *Weight Watchers Magazine*, November 1994, p. 38

113 "I am invisible" ... : Ralph Ellison, *Invisible Man* (New York: Random House, 1947), p. 3

113 "When I'm Thin Fantasy" ... : Geneen Roth, *When Food Is Love: Exploring the Relationship between Eating and Intimacy*, (New York: Dutton, 1991)

114 Just ask Canada's only female prime minister ... : Sydney Sharpe, *The Gilded Ghetto: Women and Political Power in Canada* (Toronto: HarperCollins, 1994), p. 16

114 Monique Begin's weight sarcastically chalked up to pregnancy ... : Ibid., pp. 98–9

115 "shape is quite literally round" ... : Karen Schoemer, "Linda Ronstadt: The Reluctant Superstar," *Mirabella*, April 1994, p. 58

115 "For a good part of my life ... ": Patricia Foster, ed., *Minding the Body—Women Writers on Body and Soul*, as reproduced in *Toronto Life Fashion*, Fall 1994, p. 99

115 They'd rather be blind, deaf, or have a leg amputated ... : University of Florida study cited by Gina Kolata, "Fat in America," *The New York Times*, November 22, 1992, p. 1

116 "the obese must be put in their place" ... : Susan Bordo, *Unbearable Weight: Feminism, Western Culture and the Body* (Berkeley: University of California Press,1993)

118 "exhibiting weaknesses or flaws" ... : Jane Rachel Kaplan, *A Woman's Conflict: The Special Relationship between Women and Food* (Englewood Cliffs, NJ: Prentice-Hall, 1980), p. 7

118 "It is too bad that these women are begging to be left in their chains" ... : Elizabeth Cady Stanton, *Words of Women*, Anne Stibbs, ed. (Aylesbury, UK: Market House Books, 1992)

118 "I've been a lot less passive" ... : Hirschmann and Munter, *When Women Stop Hating Their Bodies*, p. 91

119–20 "I wake every morning hating myself" ... : Marjorie Rosen and Luchina Fisher, "Oprah Overcomes," *People*, January 10, 1994, p. 45

120 Oprah was reluctant to accept Emmy Award ... : Ibid.

120 "If shame could cure obesity" ... : Dr. Susan Wooley, quoted by Dr. Judith Rodin, *Body Traps: Breaking the Binds That Keep You from Feeling Good about Your Body* (New York: William Morrow, 1992), p. 89

121 "what was really starving" ... : Elizabeth Taylor, *Elizabeth Takes Off ...* (New York: Putnam, 1987)

121 "collective worship at the shrine of slimness" ... : Brumberg, *Fasting Girls*, p. 257

121 "profound humiliation that the body exists" ... : Kim Chernin, *The Obsession: Reflections on the Tyranny of Slenderness* (New York: Harper & Row, 1981), p. 50

121 "[Women] are vomiting our guts out" ... : Kim Chernin, *The Hungry Self: Women, Eating and Identity* (New York: Times Books, 1985), p.8

122 "Restrained eating" ... : Janet Polivy and C. Peter Herman, "Diagnosis and Treatment of Normal Eating," *Journal of Consulting and Clinical Psychology*, 1987

122 "Even 'normal' women have completely lost their perspectives" ... : Elizabeth Gleick "The Fat Mind," New York Woman, April 1990

122 "The only way to get rid of temptation" ... : Oscar Wilde, quoted in *Bartlett's Familiar Quotations*, 16th ed. (Boston: Little, Brown, 1992), p. 566:14

123 "the myth that we can force our bodies" ... : Louise Dickson, "It's Your Body, So Don't Abuse It," *Ottawa Citizen*, July 17, 1994, p. D6

123 Survivors of sexual abuse ... : Zerbe, *The Body Betrayed*, p. 201

123 An inability to handle anger appropriately ... : Jane E. Brody, "Personal Health" column, *New York Times*, November 24, 1993, p. B9

124 "afraid that if I didn't eat" ... : Chernin, *The Hungry Self*

124 "the one thing that will take care of me" ... : Millman, *Such a Pretty Face*, p. 109

124 "attempt to ward off depression" ... : Rubin, *Alive and Fat and Thinning*, pp. 105–6

124 "Eating functions as a form of self-medication" ... : Zerbe, *The Body Betrayed*, pp. 18, 30

125 "eating is the primary way of maintaining ... complex societies": Peter Farb and George Armelagos, *Consuming Passions: The Anthropology of Eating* (Boston: Houghton Mifflin, 1980)

125 one-third of all North American women now at least 20% overweight ... : National Institute of Nutrition for Canadians and National Institute of Health for Americans

126 Christina Applegate "doubled over and passing out" ... : Rosen, "Eating Disorders: A Hollywood History"

126 Fat teenage girls less likely to be selected for top colleges ... : Jean Mayer, *Overweight: Causes, Cost and Control* (Englewood Cliffs, NJ: Prentice-Hall, 1968), p. 91

126–7 stupidity, ugliness and mutilation preferable ... : "Growing Up Fat," *20/20*, ABC TV, July 28, 1995

CHAPTER 6: *Hungry for Work*

128 Sixty per cent of overweight women denied employment ... : Angier and Kolata, "Fat in America" series, *New York Times*, November 22–24, 1992, p. 1

128–9 One-third of overweight women are routinely passed over for promotions and raises ... : Ibid.

129 Seventy-eight per cent passed over for promotions and raises ... : Ibid.

129 Obesity results in $6,700 less per year ... : Doug Levy, "Obesity affects economic health," *USA Today*, September 30, 1993, p. D1

129 Overweight workers are penalized $1,000 for every "extra" pound ... : Angier and Kolata, "Fat in America"

129 NAAFA survey regarding employment discrimination ... : Ibid.

129 We're running out of people that we're allowed to hate ... ": Ibid.

130 "The disabled serve as constant, visible reminders ... a fearsome possibility": Robert F. Murphy, *The Body Silent*, (New York: Holt, 1990)

130 Attitudinal survey of 1,139 CEOs ... ; and "I don't like fat people ... opened his mouth": Judy Neuman, "Weighty Consequences of a Thin Argument," *San Jose Mercury News*, June 3, 1989, p. 1E

130–1 "Grossly overweight females are penalized more severely ... same problem": Laurie Baum, "Extra Pounds Can Weigh Down Your Career," *Business Week*, August 3, 1987, p. 96

131 "The American white relegates the black ... nothing but shining shoes": George Bernard Shaw, quoted by Sharlene A. McAvoy, "Fat Chance: Employment Discrimination Against the Overweight," *Labor Law Journal*, January 1992, pp. 3–14

131 "The profundity of the narrowmindedness ... is incredible": Martin Everett, "Fat Chance," *Sales & Marketing Management*, March 1990, pp. 66–70

131 "I've had employers say to me ... has a flat stomach?": Elizabeth Kuster, "'Lookism': The Workplace's Dirty Little Secret," *Glamour*, September 1993, p. 133

131 "Over the phone, they liked ... never even considered": Diane Wildowsky, quoted by Everett, "Fat Chance"

131 "Anyone who's supposed to ... a big-time problem": Ibid.

131–2 "Managers assume that ... lose them faster": Ibid.

132 "lazy, unkempt, jolly ... and insecure": Ibid.

132 "most sales executives won't ... field sales talent": Ibid.

132 "All fat people are 'outed' ... stay in my body": Jennifer A. Coleman, "Discrimination at Large ("My Turn" column), *Newsweek*, August 2, 1993, p. 9; and author interview

133 Business students hate being served by overweight people ... : Everett, "Fat Chance"

133 "If a business claimed that ... 'fix' herself": Lindsy Van Gelder, "When Our Looks Aren't Good Enough," *Allure*, September 1992, p.78

133 "Employers did not simply develop ... calls itself a meritocracy": Wolf, *The Beauty Myth*, p. 28

134–6 Blimpos Anonymous meeting ... : Author interviews in Cincinnati, Ohio

134 "always to be doing work ... my self, my soul ... ": Virginia Woolf, *A Room of One's Own* (London: Hogarth Press, 1949)

136–7 *Sandra Davison* case: Author interviews with Sandra Davison and Brian Graff

138 *Krein* v. *Marian Manor Nursing Home* case: McAvoy, "Fat Chance"

138 *Bonnie Cook* case: Tamar Lewin, "Workplace Bias Tied to Obesity Is Ruled Illegal," *New York Times*, November 24, 1993, p. 1; Stephanie B. Goldberg, "Obesity," *American Bar Association Journal*, February 1994, p. 95; and numerous other reports

139–40 *Toni Cassista* case: Maura Dolan, "Job Bias Ruling Gives the Obese Limited Rights," *Los Angeles Times*, September 3, 1993, p. A1; "I started small ... incorporated into the hiring process": *NAAFA Newsletter*, March/April 1993, p. 1

139 "a clear slap at the high court ... ": David G. Savage, "Court Makes Job-Bias Suits More Difficult," *Los Angeles Times*, reprinted in [Louisville, KY] *Courier-Journal*, June 26, 1993, p.1

140 Santa Cruz public form on appearance discrimination ... : *NAAFA Newsletter*, March/April 1993, p. 1

140 "I want an ordinance prohibiting ... during daylight hours": Rush Limbaugh, quoted ibid.

140 *Donoghue* v. *County of Orange* case: McAvoy, "Fat Chance"

141 "to make the tough decisions ... outcasts and unhappy people": Ibid.

141 *Nyleen Mullally* case: *NAAFA Newsletter*, March/April 1993, p. 1

141–2 *Sharon Russell* case: Andrea Sachs, "Excess Baggage Is Not a Firing Offense," *Time*, March 25, 1991, p. 50; and numerous other reports

142 Flight attendants' battle: Daniel Seligman, "Fat Chances," *Fortune*, May 20, 1991; and numerous other reports

143 Actress had to lose 35 pounds to play an "ugly bitch": Rob Salem, "The Truth About Janeane Garofalo," *Toronto Star*, April 26, 1996, p. D1

143–4 Catherine McDermott versus Xerox ... : Jane Cooper, "Overweight and Under-Employed?," *Weight Watchers Magazine*, September 1990, p. 68; and McAvoy, "Fat Chance"

144 "It is significant to note ... as a burden ... ": McAvoy, "Fat Chance"

144 "the first red flag ... claim-free labor force ... ": Ibid.

144 "all too often ... bad for the corporate image": Fabrey, "The Discriminating Doctor," p. 53

145 "The extent to which ... must be due to discrimination": Dr. Albert Stunkard, quoted by Sachs, "Excess Baggage Is Not a Firing Offense"

145 John Rossi awarded $1 million in damages ... : "Fired Obese Man Wins $1 million," [Louisville, KY] *Courier-Journal*, September 8, 1995, p. A5

145 Vriend ended up suing the provincial government ... : Celeste McGovern, "One Ruling Too Far," *Alberta Report*, May 2, 1994, p.6

145   "the IRPA is for everyone who faces ... cruelty of discrimination": Ibid.

146   U-Haul International "wellness" policies: McAvoy, "Fat Chance"

146   "barbaric ... unconscionable ... [and] outrageous.": ACLU quoted ibid.

146   "more than half ... implement such programs [as U-haul's]": Ibid.

146   Genetic pre-employment testing looming in future ... : Kathleen Zeitz, "Employer Genetic Testing: A Legitimate Screening Device or Another Method of Discrimination?", *Labor Law Journal*, April 1991, p. 230

146   A North American will turn fifty every 7.5 seconds ... : Reese, "Boomers Have Affluence with an Attitude"

147   Coors and Hershey's "wellness" policies: McAvoy, "Fat Chance"

147   Class-action suit against Stouffer Foods ... : Ibid.

148   "an employer shall not: fail or refuse ... weight or marital status": Michigan's Elliott-Larsen Civil Rights Act, quoted by Daniel Seligman, "Weightism," *Fortune*, May 25, 1987, p. 115

148   "one law too many" ... : Governor Mario Cuomo, quoted in *NAAFA Newsletter*, May 1993, p. 7

148   "For too many years ... must be ended": Assemblyman Daniel Feldman, quoted ibid.

148   "We are a society that prides itself ... regardless of body size": Sally E. Smith, quoted ibid.

149   "It is my conviction that obesity is ... ADA all about": Author interview with Coleman

149   "Protecting the obese ... legislative intent": McAvoy, "Fat Chance"

149   Poulton's first job ... : Great-West Life Assurance, Edmonton, Alberta, 1962

CHAPTER 7: *Life with Laugh-Track*

152   "I don't want her, you can have her ... ": "The Too-Fat Polka"

152–3 "Please don't feed the host" ... : Clip from *Late Show with David Letterman* shown on *Oprah*, February 7, 1994

153   "The psychic scars caused by beliving that you are ugly ... ": Joan Rivers, *Quotable Women* (Philadelphia: Running Press, 1989), p. 111

153   "like she devoured her previous husbands" ... : Rivers, quoted by Roz Warren, ed., *Revolutionary Laughter: The World of Women Comics* (Freedom, CA: The Crossing Press, 1995), p. 194

153   Fat jokes about Elizabeth Taylor ... : Rosemary Green, *Diary of a Fat Housewife* (New York: Warner Books, 1995)

153   "Save the Males—Shave the Whale" ... : *New York Times* News Service, August 13, 1995

153   "death-row inmate is too fat to be hanged" ... : Associated Press report, printed in the *Montreal Gazette*, September 20, 1994, p. F15

153   Forced a fat student to wear a "Wide Load" sign ... ": Reported in *USA Today*, April 28, 1994

154   "So, are you gonna take an ambulance ... ": Ted Heusel, quoted by Bill Laitner, "Heavy Mettle," *Detroit Free Press*, May 5, 1995, p. 3F

154   "never met a meal she didn't like" ... : Milton Berle, *Private Joke File*, (New York: Crown, 1989)

154–5 "Quarter Pounder in one hand" ... : Rachel Urquhart, "No-Sweat Exercise," *Vogue*, September 1994

155   "Where's the blubba, bubba?" ... : "Diet Winners & Sinners," *People*, January 10, 1994, cover

155   "nothing we humans like better ... ": Daniel Pinkwater, "Portly's Complaint," *Omni*, April 1995, p. 103

156   "fear that our body will betray us ... some can't": Author interview with Mark Breslin

156   "Women of substance led a shamefaced ... about her jeans size": *Revolutionary Laughter*, pp. 196–201

158   Comedians' habit of tacking on "ya fat pig" ... : Author interview with Breslin

160   Does Winfrey feel she's been punished ... : Clips from *In Living Color, Saturday Night Live, Seinfeld,* and *Late Show with David Letterman* shown on Oprah, February 7, 1994

161   "hips and thighs return to American couture" ... : Wendy Wasserstein, "Goodbye Waif, Hello Bulge," *Harper's Bazaar*, November 1993, p. 86

161   Nauseating lima bean shake ... : *The Tonight Show,* broadcast May 1, 1995

162   Los Angeles's mythical anti-fat laws ... : *Greg Kinnear Show*, broadcast August 8, 1995

162   "The reason men will never understand" ... : Mickey and Cathy Guisewite, *Dancing Through Life in a Pair of Broken High Heels* (New York: Bantam, 1993), pp. 21–2

162–3 *Adbusters*'s "Calvin Swine" bulimia ad: Author interview with *Adbusters*'s Kalle Lasn and Linda Gould

CHAPTER 8: *Starved for Affection*

164   Courtship of Lillian Russell by Diamond Jim Brady ... : Irving, Amy, and Sylvia Wallace, and David Wallechinsky, *The Intimate Sex Lives of Famous People* , pp. 36–8

164   "sonnets of motion ... ": Bennett and Gurin, *The Dieter's Dilemma*, p. 200

165   Just a sham to get the man a "green card" ... : *L.A. Law*, broadcast April 16, 1992

167   Fat Chicks ranked below cocaine users, etc ... : Warren, "Living Large"

167   Large women are least 20 per cent less likely to marry ... : Doug Levy, "Obesity Affects Economic Health," *USA Today*, September 30, 1993, p. D1, quoting a study reported in *The New England Journal of Medicine*

167   Forced into celibacy ... : Ann Landers, Creators Syndicate, March 21, 1995

167   Attempting to have his wife killed ... : *The Virginian-Pilot*, February 7, 1990, p. A5

167   "They Hate Me Just Because I'm Fat" ... : *Carnie*, Fox TV, September 6, 1995

168   "weight as the central issue of their lives" ... : Seid, *Never Too Thin*, p. 29

168   "to tell a woman she is ugly" ... : Wolf, *The Beauty Myth*, p. 361–8

168   "the next thing you know, you're a ghost" ... : Whitney Otto, *Now You See Her* (New York: Villard Books, 1994), p. 296

169   Doctor traded stomach stapling for sex ... : "Sex Abuse Costs Doctor His Licence," *Toronto Star*, April 26, 1996, p. A7

169   "I couldn't say no to my husband" ... : Hirschmann and Munter, *When Women Stop Hating Their Bodies*, p. 284

169–70 "the size of three ordinary thighs" ... : Margaret Atwood, *Lady Oracle* (New York: Simon and Schuster, 1976), p. 121

170   "I just shut down" ... : Leslie Lampert, "Can a Woman Be Fat and Happy?," *Ladies' Home Journal*, March 1995, p. 123

170   "spent more time in bed pulling our stomachs in" ... : Laura Fraser, "A Critic Looks at Pornography from the Inside," *Extra!*, July/August 1993, p. 19

170   How to pose in bed so you won't look fat: *Cosmopolitan* magazine article, quoted by Wolf, *The Beauty Myth*, p. 201

170   Fully 90 per cent of women feel bad about their bodies: Eating Disorders Centre literature

171   "The tyranny of the ideal image ... learn to hate ourselves: Fallon, Katzman, and Wooley, *Feminist Perspectives on Eating Disorders*, p. 396

172   "The need to be extraordinarily beautiful" ... : Millman, *Such a Pretty Face*, p. 220

172   "don't see things as they are" ... : Anaïs Nin, quoted in *Quotable Women* (Philadelphia: Running Press, 1989), p. 76

172   give up their husbands, boyfriends, careers and money ... : *Vogue*, 1989, quoted by Schroeder, *Fat Is Not a Four-Letter Word*, p. 201

173   "my hormones started bubbling" ... : Ibid., p. iv

173   Who could possibly be interested in marrying her ... : Rebecca Salner, "A Search for Size Acceptance: Big People Whittle Away at Social Indignities," *San Jose Mercury News*, August 8, 1988, p. 1A

173   Denounces "worship of the too-thin, childlike female body" ... : Ken Mayer, *Real Women Don't Diet: One Man's Praise of Large Women & His Outrage at the Society That Rejects Them* (Silver Spring, MD: Bartleby Press, 1993), p. 168; appearance on *Donahue* February 24, 1995

173   "I think I'm a throwback" ... : Mayer, quoted by Carla Wheeler, "Don't Diet," Gannett News Service, February 1, 1994

174   "Fat women are often harder to approach" ... : Dan Davis, *Radiance*, Summer/Fall 1986, p. 20

174-5   "we're missing the humanity in people" ... : Kathy Bates, quoted by Jeff Hayward, *Chicago Tribune*, May 14, 1995

175   "an enormous, life-altering mistake" ... : Roth, *When Food Is Love*, p. 97

CHAPTER 9: *On the Rack*

177   Any demographer could have told them ... : Average weight and height of North American women ... : Faludi, *Backlash*, p. 171

178   Spurning an estimated 50 million consumers, who had a combined buying power of $6 billion ... : Jolie Solomon, "Fashion Industry Courting Large Women," *Wall Street Journal*, September 27, 1985, p. 32

178   Princess Elizabeth and the Duchess of Windsor denounced the retrogression ... : Jeanne Perkins, "Dior," *Life*, March 1, 1948, p. 84

178   Rebellion against Christian Dior's "New Look" ... : Ibid., and "Counter Revolution," *Time*, September 15, 1947, p. 87

179   The lucrative New Look swept to supremacy ... : Ibid.

179   More North American women were working outside the home than staying in it ... : Grace Mirabella, *In and Out of Vogue* (New York: Doubleday, 1995), p. 182

180   "Well, they eat a lot ... so why not give them polyester?" ... : Terry Poulton, "Plump Profits," *Canadian Business*, June 1978, p. 54

180   "Added up to a big yech" ... : Una Abramson, *Chatelaine*, September 1970, p. 84

181   "Fashion came to be about nothing more than ... : Mirabella, *In and Out of Vogue*, p. 14

182   More than 80 percent of women were telling pollsters ... : Faludi, *Backlash*, p. 170

182   Women spent more on houses, cars, and restaurant meals ... : Ibid.

183   Might misportray the fashion world as "a nightmarish cartoon" ... : Martha Duffy, "Fashion's Fall," *Time*, April 25, 1994, p. 50

183   "We'd describe [Kate Moss] ... to describe Twiggy back in 1967": John Leland, "Back to Twiggy," *Newsweek*, February 1, 1993, p. 64

183–4   Waifs looked like "angelic little boys" ... : Elizabeth Tilberis, quoted by Amy M. Spindler, "How Fashion Killed the Unloved Waif," *New York Times*, September 17, 1994, p. B13

184   Foisted the bunkum and then wondered why subscriptions were sagging ... : Mirabella, *In and Out of Vogue*, p. 184

184   Scuttling together "like characters in an Agatha Christie novel" ... : Spindler, "How Fashion Killed the Unloved Waif"

184–5   Wintour "discovered" what she termed the switch to "Strong and Sexy" ... : (*Vogue*, May 1994), quoted ibid.

185   "A lot more people will be thanking us ... ": Elizabeth Tilberis, quoted ibid.

185   While regular-size sector was sinking, plus-size market was enjoying double-digit growth ... : U.S. Commerce Department report, quoted by Patricia Aburdene and John Naisbitt, *Megatrends for Women* (New York: Villard Books, 1992), p. 206

185–6 Shaw began raising consciousness by marching into buyers' offices ... : Mary Peacock, "The Fashion Industry Courts 'The Big Woman,'" *Ms.*, June 1980, p. 83

186 They'd read a decisive demographic study ... : Ibid.

186 "They noticed we had that green stuff in our fat little fists" ... : Solomon, "Fashion Industry Courting Large Women"

187 Oscar de la Renta and several other biggies designed for the Barbie doll ... : S. Shapiro, "My Mentor, Barbie," *New York Times*, November 6, 1994, p. 8

187 Far from being aberrant or inconsequential ... : National Institute for Health-Related Statistics report, quoted by Stephania H. Davis, "We're All Getting Bigger and So Are Our Fashions," *Hartford Courant*, July 31, 1994

187 Those who served Fat Chicks shared in a market bonanza ... : Jane Milstead, "Grandes Dames," *Los Angeles Times*, July 10, 1994, p. 26

188 Bacon's took the virtually unprecedented step ... : [Louisville, KY] *Courier-Journal*, June 18, 1995, p. A3; and author interview with Bacon's spokesperson

188 "They finally found out that we're not just ... doctors and lawyers and businesswomen": Lisa Respers, "Big Clothing Has Been a Bright Spot in the Struggling Industry," *Los Angeles Times*, October 25, 1994, p. D1

188 "I can go shopping now and find ... ": Gaile Robinson, "Big Gets Beautiful—Finally," *Los Angeles Times*, August 14, 1992, p. E1

188–91 Jackqueline Hope's "Big, Bold & Beautiful" story ... : Author interview with Jackqueline Hope

191 "Dressing is ... a process of self-creation ... ": Seid, *Never Too Thin*, p. 44

191 Today he says he likes nothing better than ... : Author interview with Brian Bailey

191–2 Alfred Sung refuses to add any size larger than 14, except for wedding gowns ... : Author interview with Mimran Group spokesperson Marina Gibson

192 Serious research is finally being done into the dimensions ... : Angela Bonavoglia, "What's *Ms.* Doing at the Fall Fashion Shows?," *Ms.*, September/October 1995, p. 53

192 Coming up with same kind of standard sizing men enjoy ... : Judith Egerton, "Custom-made clothing growing on consumers," [Louisville, KY] *Courier-Journal*, February 7, 1995, p. C1

193 Computer magic to make models look larger ... : Cara Wall, "FashionFax," *Glamour*, September 1993, p. 216

94 1647 shop named in honor of the 47 per cent of British whomen who wear size 16 ... : Karin Davies, "'Fashionably Fat' Briton Stums for the Plump," *Los Angeles Times*, June 19, 1994, p. A21

194 Simply upsized garments and left skinny little numbers in place ... : Wall, "FashionFax"

194 Standard size-10 dress forms have been inflated ... : Ibid.

196 Corsets receiving unanimous support again: "Waist Case," *Vogue*, September 1994, p. 244

196 "The days when women followed fashion blindly are over" ... : Aburdene and Naisbitt, *Megatrends for Women*, p. 205

CHAPTER 10: *Fed-Up*

198 "outposts in your head" ... : Sally Kempton, "Cutting Loose," *Esquire*, July 1970

198 "A quietly mad population is a tractable one" ... : Wolf, *The Beauty Myth*, p. 187

199 Virtually endorsed bulimia as normal beauty imperative ... : Gaudoin, "Body of Evidence"

200 Graffiti campaign defaced Calvin Klein jeans ads ... : Stuart Elliott, "Group Seeks Boycott of Calvin Klein," *New York Times*, May 4, 1994, p. D20

201 "It may take someone getting shot ... ": Author interview with Dr. Moe Lerner

201-2 NAAFA 25th anniversary march on Washington ... : Gannett wire service report, August 26, 1994

202   "government has become a veritable food fight ... ": Carl Weiser, Gannett News Service report, August 26, 1994

202   What he apparently thought was a humorous kicker ... : Scott Harris, "Fighting the Battle for Fat Liberation," *Los Angeles Times*, March 30, 1995, p. B3

203   Comparing size-acceptance crusade to civil rights movement ... : statements by David Boaz, and Laird Wilcox ... : Carl Weiser, Gannett News Service report, August 26, 1994

203   "Got a weight problem ... phone Uncle Sam ... ": Margaret Carlson, "And Now, Obesity Rights," *Time*, January 7, 1994

203   Bonnie Cook had already performed her duties satisfactorily ... : Lewin, "Workplace Bias Tied to Obesity Is Ruled Illegal"

204   One of Smith's personal bests ... : Smith, "The Great Diet Deception"

206   International No-Diet Day 1995 in Toronto ... : Author interview with Helena Spring

207   NAAFA threatened to boycott Denny's restaurants ... : Fabrey, "Big News," *Radiance*, Fall 1994, p. 60

207   Boycott Anorexic Marketing (BAM) began targeting ... : Stuart Elliott, "Group Seeks Boycott of Calvin Klein," *New York Times*, May 4, 1994, p. D20

207   National Organization for Women (Los Angeles chapter) endorsed BAM ... : Ibid.

207–8   Crackdowns resulted from Representative Ron Wyden's Congressional hearings ... : "Reins Tightened on Diet Aids," *Environmental Nutrition*, March 1994, p. 1, and Smith, "The Great Diet Deception"

208   Institute of Medicine issued a statement urging weight-loss industry "to disclose the true effectiveness of its programs" ... : Associated Press wire report, December 6, 1994

209   National Education Association currently investigating size discrimination in public schools ... : Joanne Ikeda, RD, "Confessions of a Radical Registered Dietician," *Radiance*, Spring 1995, p. 46

211   "Watch out, thin people ... ": Alice Ansfield, *Radiance*, Fall 1988, p. 2

211   "squalling howl of grievance" ... : Virginia Byfield, "How America Sank into Wimpdom," *Alberta Report*, May 10, 1993, p. 42

211   Trivialized complaints about her column ... : Diane White, "Fat Chance of Recruiting Yours Truly," *Boston Globe*, August 18, 1990, p. C7

212   "I feel ashamed of my culture ... ": Leslie Lampert, "Fat Like Me," *Ladies' Home Journal*, May 1993, p. 154

212   "You can't tell a person's fitness level by his appearance": Florence Griffith Joyner, "Fitness with Foreman & Flo-Jo," *USA Weekend*, September 8–10, 1995, p. 14

213   "Wangled her way into a profit-making seminar ... : Laura Fraser, "Dieting by Prescription," *Vogue*, May 1995, p. 182

213   "[R]efuse to be nameless, depersonalized, manipulated ... ": Friedan, *The Feminine Mystique*, p. 298

CHAPTER 11: *Belly-Up?*

215   "Twiggy couldn't have arrived at any other time" ... : Diana Vreeland, quoted by Whiteside, *Twiggy & Justin*, p. 117

217   Princess Diana hounded about cellulite on her thighs ... : Reuters wire service report published in the *Toronto Star*, April 10, 1996, p. A5

218   Someone will turn 50 every 7.5 seconds ... : Reese, "Boomers Have Affluence with an Attitude"

218   Number of chronic North American dieters dropped from 65 to 48 million ... : Calorie Control Council, quoted by Lori Miller Kase, "Weight Game," *Harper's Bazaar*, April 1995, p. 291

218   Drop in thinking "overweight" automatically means "unattractive" ... : Adler, "The Joys of Living Large"

218 Rather win a Pulitzer Prize than be Miss America ... : Anna Quindlen, "1990s Feminism: Babes or Sisters," *New York Times*, January 20, 1994

218 Not automatically making dieting number-one New Year's resolution ... : University of Pennsylvania study, reported in *Bottom Line* newsletter, February 15, 1994, p. 8

219 Calvin Klein withdrew a major ad campaign for the first time ... : Richard Martin, "The Ultimate Fashion Taboo," *Los Angeles Times*, September 3, 1995, p. M2

220 Steven Spielberg to produce *Body Language* ... : "Weight Watch," *Entertainment Weekly*, July 29, 1994, p. 13

222 Wrote to Dear Abby and littered her book with self-degrading remarks ... : Green, *Diary of a Fat Housewife*, pp. 25, 322

222–3 "superior to fat people" ... : Helen Gurley Brown, *The Late Show* (New York: Morrow, 1993), pp. 87, 155

223 "still socially and legally acceptable to call someone a 'big fat dope' ... ": Author interview with Dr. Moe Lerner

223 Air Canada mistreated Lerner ... : Ibid.

223 Pam Hollowich sued Southwest Airlines ... : Warren, "Living Large"

223–4 Ads linking smoking to slimness ... : *Working Woman*, August 1995, pp. 18, 21

224 Teenage girls are the fastest-growing segment of smokers ... : Lynda Dexheimer, "Puff Pieces: Magazines Increasingly Feature Smoking," Gannett News Service, May 7, 1995

224 Obesity has more than doubled in the six-to-seventeen age group ... : National Center for Health Statistics survey, quoted in the *Washington Post*, October 3, 1995

227 Women are "dying to be thin" ... : *Wall Street Journal*, reprinted in the *Toronto Star* as "Are Smokers Dying for Smaller Dress Size?," April 1, 1996, p. B3

228 Weight-loss industry is spending $100 million on advertising ... " Kate Fitzgerald, "Weight-Loss Biz May Get Crash Diet," *Advertising Age*, May 10, 1993, p. 3.

228 H.J. Heinz has reserved ad space for January 2000 ... : "Creative Media Plans Ahead," *Inside Media Online*, transmitted April 26, 1995

228 Nutri-System catapulted from bankruptcy and joined 26 other enterprises: Richard A. Melcher, "Care and Feeding at Nutri/System," *Business Week*, March 7, 1994; including a subsidiary of Fuji Bank ... : Bill Laitner, "Susan Powter Gets into Diet Business She Bashed," *Detroit Free Press*, May 18, 1995; and Johnson & Johnson ... : "Venture by Nutri-Systems," *New York Times*, March 5, 1994, p. 27

228 Weight Watchers' foods gaining success in France ... : "Weight Watchers veut peser plus lourd," *Tribune DesfossessOS*, March 7, 1995, p. 12

228–9 Weight Watchers teaming up with life insurers ... : Keith L. Alexander, "A Health Kick at Weight Watchers," *Business Week*, January 16, 1995

229 Heinz recently leapt to command the number-three spot ... : Ibid.

229 Weight Watchers' mega-deal ... : Chip Jones, "Richmond-Based Eskimo Pie to Make Treats for Weight Watchers," *Richmond Times-Dispatch*, January 24, 1995

229 International Pizza owns Domino's franchises as far away as Poland, and is venturing into operating weight-loss centres ... : *ABI Business NewsBank*, December 1, 1994

229 Media mergers are threatening ... : "Media Merger Mania," (editorial), *New York Times*, September 2, 1995; and numerous other sources

229 Omega watch company's ad campaign in *Vogue* ... : Deborah Sherwood, Jacqui Thornton and Nicola Davidson, "How Schoolgirl's Death Could Change the Face of Fashion," *Sunday Express*, June 2, 1996, pp.14–15

229 More than 580,000 U.K. women suffer from eating disorders ... : British Dietetic Association estimate, quoted ibid.

229 Top British modelling agencies tried to recruit anorexia patient ... : Ibid.

Select Bibliography

Aburdene, Patricia, and John Naisbitt. *Megatrends for Women.* New York: Villard Books, 1992

Atwood, Margaret. *Lady Oracle.* New York: Simon & Shuster, 1976

Basinger, Jeanine. *A Woman's View: How Hollywood Spoke to Women, 1930–1960.* New York: Alfred A. Knopf, 1993

Bennett, William, M.D. and Gurin, Joel. *The Dieter's Dilemma: Eating Less and Weighing More.* New York: Basic Books, 1982

Black, J. Anderson, and Madge Garland. *A History of Fashion.* New York: Morrow, 1980

Bordo, Susan. *Unbearable Weight: Feminism, Western Culture and the Body.* Berkeley: University of California Press, 1993

Brownmiller, Susan. *Femininity.* New York: Simon & Schuster, 1984

Brumberg, Joan Jacobs. *Fasting Girls: The Emergence of Anorexia Nervosa as a Modern Disease.* Cambridge, MA: Harvard University Press, 1988

Chernin, Kim. *The Hungry Self: Women, Eating and Identity.* New York: Times Books, 1985

———. *The Obsession: Reflections on the Tyranny of Slenderness.* New York: Harper & Row, 1981

Clarke, Eric. *The Want Makers.* New York: Viking, 1988

Cott, Allan, MD. *Fasting as a Way of Life.* New York: Bantam, 1977

Crossen, Cynthia. *Tainted Truth: The Manipulation of Fact in America.* New York: Simon & Schuster, 1994

Croteau, David, and William Hoynes. *By Invitation Only: How the Media Limit Political Debate.* Munroe, ME: Common Courage, 1994

Douglas, Susan J. *Where the Girls Are: Growing Up Female with the Mass Media.* New York: Times Books, 1994

Dworkin, Andrea. *Pornography: Men Possessing Women.* New York: Putnam, 1981

Ellison, Ralph. *Invisible Man.* New York: Random House, 1947

Epstein, Diane, and Kathleen Thompson. *Feeding on Dreams: Why America's Diet Industry Doesn't Work & What Will Work for You.* New York: Macmillan, 1994

Ewen, Stuart. *All Consuming Images: The Politics of Style in Contemporary Culture.* New York: Basic Books, 1988

Fallon, Patricia, Melanie A. Katzman, and Susan Wooley. *Feminist Perspectives on Eating Disorders.* London: Guilford Press, 1994

Faludi, Susan. *Backlash: The Undeclared War Against American Women.* New York: Crown, 1991

Ferree, Myra Marx, and Beth B. Hess. *Controversy and Coalition: The New Feminist Movement across Three Decades of Change.* Oxford: Maxwell Macmillan International, 1994

Foster, Patricia, ed. *Minding the Body—Women Writers on Body and Soul.* New York: Doubleday, 1994

Friedan, Betty. *The Feminine Mystique.* New York: W.W. Norton, 1963; Dell Publishing, 1975

Goleman, Daniel. *Emotional Intelligence.* New York: Bantam, 1995

Green, Rosemary. *Diary of a Fat Housewife.* New York: Warner, 1995

Gross, Michael. *Model: The Ugly Business of Beautiful Women.* New York: Morrow, 1995

Guisewite, Mickey, and Cathy Guisewite. *Dancing Through Life in a Pair of Broken High Heels.* New York: Bantam, 1993

Hirschmann, Jane R., and Carol H. Munter. *When Women Stop Hating Their Bodies: Freeing Yourself from Food and Weight Obsession.* New York: Fawcett Columbine, 1995

Kaplan, Jane Rachel. *A Woman's Conflict: The Special Relationship between Women and Food.* Englewood Cliffs, NJ: Prentice-Hall, 1980

King, Norman. *The Almanac of Fascinating Beginnings.* New York: Carol Publishing Group, 1994

Laurence, Leslie, and Beth Weinhouse. *Outrageous Practices: The Alarming Truth about How Medicine Mistreats Women.* New York: Fawcett Columbine, 1994

Millman, Marcia. *Such a Pretty Face: Being Fat in America.* New York: W.W. Norton, 1980

Mirabella, Grace. *In and Out of Vogue.* New York: Doubleday, 1995

Murphy, Robert F. *The Body Silent.* New York: Holt, 1990

Patterson, James, and Peter Kim. *The Day America Told the Truth.* Englewood Cliffs, NJ: Prentice-Hall, 1991

Peters, Lulu Hunt. *Diet and Health with a Key to the Calories* Chicago: Chicago Publishing, 1918

Polivy, Janet, and C. Peter Herman. *Breaking the Diet Habit: The Natural Weight Alternative.* New York: Basic Books, 1983

Roosevelt, Eleanor. *This Is My Story.* New York: Harper, 1937

Rosenblum, Mort. *Who Stole the News?* New York: Wiley, 1993

Roth, Geneen. *When Food Is Love: Exploring the Relationship Between Eating and Intimacy.* New York: Dutton, 1991

Rubin, Theodore Isaac, MD. *Alive and Fat and Thinning in America.* New York: Coward, McCann & Geoghegan, 1978

Savan, Leslie. *The Sponsored Life: Ads, TV, and American Culture.* Philadelphia: Temple University Press, 1994

Schroeder, Charles Roy. *Fat Is Not a Four-Letter Word.* Minnetonka, MN: Chronimed Publishing, 1992

Schwartz, Hillel. *Never Satisfied: A Cultural History of Diets, Fantasies and Fat.* New York: The Free Press, 1986

Seid, Roberta Pollack. *Never Too Thin: Why Women Are at War with Their Bodies.* Englewood Cliffs, NJ: Prentice-Hall, 1989

Sharpe, Sydney. *The Gilded Ghetto: Women and Political Power in Canada.* Toronto: HarperCollins, 1994

Shorris, Earl. *A Nation of Salesmen: The Tyranny of the Market and the Subversion of Culture.* New York: W.W. Norton, 1994

Stacey, Michelle. *Consumed: Why Americans Love, Hate, and Fear Food.* New York: Simon & Schuster, 1994

Steinem, Gloria. *Moving Beyond Words.* New York: Simon & Schuster, 1994

Taylor, Elizabeth. *Elizabeth Takes Off: On Weight Gain, Weight Loss, Self-Image & Self-Esteem.* New York: Berkeley, 1987

Warren, Roz, ed. *Revolutionary Laughter: The World of Women Comics.* Freedom, CA: The Crossing Press, 1995

Whiteside, Thomas. *Twiggy & Justin.* New York: Farrar, Straus & Giroux, 1967

Naomi Wolf. *The Beauty Myth.* Random House, 1990

Zerbe, Kathryn J, MD. *The Body Betrayed: Women, Eating Disorders and Treatment.* Washington, D.C.: American Psychiatric Press, 1993

Index